THE God Who Responds

THE God Who Responds

H.D. McDONALD

BETHANY HOUSE PUBLISHERS
MINNEAPOLIS, MINNESOTA 55438
A Division of Bethany Fellowship, Inc.

Published by Bethany House Publishers
A Division of Bethany Fellowship, Inc.
6820 Auto Club Road, Minneapolis, Minnesota 55438

Printed in the United States of America

Library of Congress Cataloging in Publication Data

McDonald, H. D. (Hugh Dermot)
God who responds.

1. Philosophical theology. I. Title.
BT40.M4 1986 230 85-28620
ISBN 0-87123-840-3

H. D. McDONALD was born in England and received formal theological training at the University of London (B.A., B.D., Ph.D., D.D.). Until his retirement he was the vice-principal of the London Bible College and visiting professor at Northern Baptist Theological Seminary, Trinity Evangelical School and Regent College. He and his wife make their home in London, England.

Other works by Dr. H. D. McDonald

Ideas of Revelation, 1700–1860
Theories of Revelation, 1860–1960
I and He
Jesus—Human and Divine
Living Doctrines of the New Testament
Freedom in Faith: A Commentary on Galatians
The Church and Its Glory: A Commentary on Ephesians
Commentary on Paul's Epistle to the Colossians
What the Bible Teaches About the Bible
The Christian View of Man
Forgiveness and Atonement
The Atonement of the Death of Christ.
Salvation

Contributor to:

The Scottish Journal of Theology
Faith and Thought
Spectrum
Harvard Theological Review
Christianity Today
Zondervan's Pictorial Dictionary of the Bible
Baker's Dictionary of Ethics
The New International Dictionary of the Church
Lion Handbook History of Christianity
Evangelical Dictionary of Theology
The Illustrated Bible Dictionary

Preface

The following chapters deal with some of the great issues of Christian faith by viewing them historically and then discussing them within the context of modern philosophical thought. Each generation must reconsider the perennial problems of the faith, then give relevant reasons for the hope that faith brings to the believer. The Christian apologist or preacher cannot merely repeat phrases which carry the mystique of tradition and the mustiness of age, for present difficulties for faith will not be removed by the recital of ancient formulae. The church must always present the Gospel in terms that its contemporaries find understandable and meaningful. T. S. Eliot rightly reminds us:

> For last year's words belong to last year's language
> And next year's words await another voice.

It is also healthy and necessary for the Church to study the past efforts of those who professed its faith and answered the questions raised by faith's own affirmations, and to note the way objections to that faith were answered in earlier times.

God's relationship to the world is the sole focus of the *Bible*. In the light of God's character revealed there as "Holy-Love," we must consider how this divine character controls His relationship to His creation. In this book we are concerned with some of the special problems that arise from this relationship.

Contents

Chapter 1

God as Person

All religions have had a god with a unique name. The Greeks had Zeus; the Muslims have Allah; and every other religion has had its own god. Each of these gods can be called "god," but the use of each proper name is limited to the individual religion. Christianity also speaks of God. But the name of the Christian God transcends limited use. Any name used of Him neither limits the fullness of His Godhead nor restricts His boundless being.

When the Christian talks of God in personal terms, he is not limiting God. The concept of personality does not make God a mere circumscribed something or someone. The idea of God as a Personal Being has always been essential and authentic truth in historical biblical faith. In much modern theology, however, talk about the God with personality has become confusing and embarrassing. It is now considered "old-fashioned, if not entirely out of date."[1] Those who deny the idea of a personal God as meaningful for modern man believe this concept inevitably robs Him of the spiritual sense of mystery and uniqueness which is appropriate for Ultimate Being. Some say that clothing Ultimate Being with intimate and personal qualities makes Him little more than a magnified man. The demand is then made to redefine the term "God," using such non-limiting terms as the *Ground of Being*, the *Cohesive Force of Society*, the *Law of Progress*, the *Principle of Concretion* or *Ultimate Concern*.

Such concepts are said to be more congenial to the modern mind, giving a nobler view of that nondescript Reality encountered in the depths of man's being and in the infinite breadth of human history. "God" is the nameless mystery which surrounds us, the

"Being" of all that is. But, they say, conceiving of God as personal is to surrender the Life-giving Force of nature and history for the impossible notion of a limited and localized Superman.

The Christian cannot accept this conclusion. He cannot remove God from nature and history, because he regards the Ultimate as a Personal Being who graciously confronts men. The Christian believes that he gains rather than loses by insisting that God is personal. He does not deny that God's presence permeates every part of life, of nature, and of history. But he insists that the real question of God only begins at the point where this claim breaks off. To find the ultimate unity of life, the ultimate force of nature, and the ultimate significance of history is not the final issue about God. The basic questions concern life's obligations and duties, its claims and destiny, and the final reason for its meaning and comfort. God is indeed the Coherent Principle, and the Ultimate Unity of the universe, but to speak of Him in these terms alone is to be content, as Luther says, with His mask, and to miss His countenance. It is to see His hand, but not to feel His heart. To know the biblical God is to find a personal, commanding, and loving "Thou." It is to know Him as the God who acts for me.

This does not mean that knowing God must drive a wedge between the belief in a divine purpose for the universe and a personal God confronting man with demands and daily bread. The God we must know and have is the complete God. Those who are satisfied with the idea of God as the Cause and Unifier of all things need to be reminded that they do not know God as God if they strip Him of the majesty of His personal being. On the other hand, those who view God as naively human must be corrected by emphasizing that they do not know God as God if they remove the mystery of His divine ways. Neither view has half of God; neither really has God at all. Thus, to truly believe in God is to believe in Him as an *active personal Being;* the extent of His activity is not limited by His personality. Nor is the reality of His personality eroded by His boundless activity.

Difficulties and doubts are aired today over the issue of His personality. The time has come for the problem of a personal God to be revisited. The question is of primary importance for faith. In fact, as Albert Einstein contends, the main source of the present conflict between science and religion lies in this concept of a personal God.[2]

The Idea of a Personal God

Although both the Old and New Testaments present God as a person, neither Testament uses "person" as a designation for Him.

However, the Hebrew scriptures do present the personal nature of God. But the significant point is that its anthropomorphic language does not leave us with the picture of God as a mere, magnified human. Throughout the Old Testament the Godness of God is never compromised. Even its most anthropomorphic statements never lose sight of the extraordinary nature and aweful majesty of God. God is God, not man; this is the central note. God is portrayed in stark human terms, but we are not given the impression that the God-who-acts is an extra-energetic man. We are aware that it is God who acts in personal ways. Although the Old Testament "could conceive of God only as person, differing in many ways from human persons, but still a person," it would be wrong to conclude that believers of the period were unaware of His essential uniqueness.[3]

The situation is not very different when we turn to the New Testament. God is presented there as "person." The Father-Son relationship Jesus claimed with God is understood only in terms of God's personality. Jesus Christ, as the final revelation of God, confirms the idea of God as Ultimate Personal Reality.

Both Testaments convey the unmistakable impression that we best comprehend God's personal character through His acts, but His acts flow from His perfect personality rather than produce it. The biblical concept is that of a "Thou," not of an "It." There is no feeling that the Old Testament seers, prophets, and psalmists were creating God in their own image, while in the New Testament Christ, who is described as the "image," the true replica of the invisible God, declares that God is personal.

Early Hesitancy Over the Term "Person"

C.C.J. Webb has pointed out that although God's personal being has been taken for granted in recent times as a principle doctrine of Christianity, the term never found a place in the historical creeds and confessions of the Church.[4] In fact, it was the unorthodox who first insisted that God is a person, excluding by definition the Trinitarian doctrine of the "three persons" in the Godhead. But we must not hastily conclude from this evidence that the early Church, by affirming the separate "persons" of the Godhead, had no interest in maintaining its conviction concerning the personal nature of God as Triune Being. O. R. Jones says, "Since the orthodox have persistently emphasized the unity of the three Persons in the Godhead, the ascription of personality to the three individuals cannot be construed as a denial that God himself is personal."[5]

William Paley is credited with first emphasizing the concept of God as a person by devoting a chapter in his *Natural Theology* to the subject. It was a natural conclusion to his teleological argument for the existence of God because purpose is an essential aspect of personality. The reaction from those who believed in the impersonal Absolute of Hegel and the growing stress on a personal God strengthened the belief that a personal Being was the ultimate reality of the universe. Meanwhile, the "theology of experience" derived from Schleiermacher also acted to force the concept of a personal God into the foreground.

Few have done more recently to emphasize God's personal nature than H. H. Farmer. He states on the first page of the introduction to his *The World and God*, "The conviction that God is personal, and deals personally with men and women, lies at the heart of Christian thought and experience." He then establishes an understanding of God as personal as the central fact in God's dealings with men in revelation, in providence, in miracles, and in grace. Christian experience is based on the living awareness of a personal God. It is essentially as John Oman says, a "gracious relationship." Farmer contends that "to uncover what is central in the awareness of God as personal is to uncover what is the essence of living religion all down the ages." He also emphasizes his contention that "the essence of religion in all its forms is a response to the ultimate as personal."[6]

The arguments for the existence of God have been commonly criticized for never getting beyond the idea of a higher sort of *Ultimate Somewhat.* But this criticism hardly does credit to the arguments. If there is any conclusion at all to be drawn from the so-called "proofs," it is that they point to an ultimate active Agent behind creation. They prove the existence of a personal Being, because a "person" is, as Stuart Hampshire says, essentially an "agent" who acts with purpose.[7]

The question asking whether God exists at all is, as John Macmurray observed, whether "the Ultimate Reality of the universe is such that can satisfy religious demands."[8] That is to say, if God exists, He exists as personal. An impersonal God is a contradiction in terms. It is within the response of faith to God that His personal nature comes into sharpest focus. H. P. Owen, although saying that personal response is not the basis of belief in the existence of God, is right in his contention that "no one can expect to be convinced of God's reality without personal response."[9] It seems, as William

Hordern contends, that "the language game that points with the least obscurity to God is that of personal language. This is rooted in the fact that God offers to man a personal relationship with Himself."[10]

Justification of the Idea of God as Personal

The belief in God as Personal Being is justified on religious and philosophical grounds. Divine acts such as revelation and grace, and human religious activities such as faith and prayer, are meaningful only if God is personal.

If a good case can be made for divine revelation (and we are sure that it can), then a case equally strong is being made for the idea of a personal Divine Being. Revelation at its highest form is God disclosing Himself as Divine Person. All God's self-manifestations operate within the area of the personal. No matter how God chose to reveal Himself through Israel's history, whether by means of lot, dream, theophany, or prophecy, the one fact remains constant: the personal God has most clearly unveiled Himself.

When the religious man talks of divine grace, he is asserting the personal activity of God. God's grace is His radiant adequacy extended to men. Grace is the personal presence of God in saving action. The tendency to conceive of grace as either some sort of fluid or force has, in Christian circles, generated unnecessary riddles and divisions. Whenever grace is thought of as a "sub-personal something given by God to work on its own as a doctor may give a patient a bottle of medicine to be taken three times a day after meals," the personal aspect of God's helpfulness is lost.[11] Such a "tertium quid [strange, indescribable substance] theory of grace," as Lindsay Dewar speaks of it, introduces a kind of third entity between God and the soul.[12] This becomes the reason for all those learned discourses and discussions of sacramental theology with their idea of an infusion taking place in the subconscious level. To think of grace as some sort of materialistically imparted fluid leads at once to the notion of the sacraments working *ex opere operato* (under their own power).

On the other hand, to conceive of grace as a force mechanically impressed upon the soul gives rise to such meaningless questions as, "Is God's grace irresistible?" In attempting to answer this question, the mind conjures the false idea of a cause-effect sequence in God's relation to man after the analogy of events within the physical world. Viewed as either a fluid or a force there is danger of obscuring the essential personal factor in the Divine-human relationship. To understand correctly the concept of grace is to understand that its central aspect is God's loving activity.

Ninian Smart argues that, "the dread experience of the holy," the spiritual awe in the presence of the ultimately mysterious, "implies encounter with a person." One recognizes the tremendous mystery, before which one can barely stand, and yet which inspires the conviction that only in His presence does one dare to stand. It is in the midst of the "holy," with the burdening sense of shame and guilt, which the presence of the holy itself creates, where the awakened soul arrives at the daring belief that human unholiness can only be dealt with by divine mercy. Thus, not consumed, but assured of a pardon which relieves the strain of tension and the stain of shame, the worshiper is convinced that a Holy Object deals with him in personal ways in love, forgiveness, and grace.[13]

Perhaps prayer best demonstrates belief in the personal nature of God. "It is no exaggeration to say," declares H. R. Mackintosh, "that with the vanishing of belief in the personality of God there must vanish the whole round of spiritual life of which faith, love and prayer are functions, except in some verbal sense which would be obviously far fetched and unnatural."[14] Prayer is, he contends, the major evidence of the believer's conviction of the Divine Personality. It is possible to speculate on the Divine or even to swoon into the Divine, without ever asking if God is personal or even when believing He is not. But we cannot pray unless we regard the Divine as a living Spirit.

This belief is indeed the "depth-grammar" of prayer. Prayer-language carries the belief in God as personal Being as its central conviction. However limited the analogy between talking to God and talking to another human may be, it brings out the fact that, "in both cases it makes a difference whether one says one thing or another."[15] Prayer is distinctive in that its talk is determined by the nature of the Object prayed to. Prayer is not addressed to just anything, but to God, who is known personally. Unless God is thought of as truly personal, prayer is little more than talking to oneself.[16] The emphasis of prayer is trust. To trust in God as the hearer of prayer is to act in the faith that there is a personal "Thou" who can answer the soul's need. Without that conviction, faith would be void, and prayer would be empty.

Apart from the religious convictions in a personal God, there are logical and philosophical reasons which account for the same understanding of what the Ultimate is. All conceptions which fall short of declaring the Final Reality of the universe to be a person seem to fail to reach the Ultimate. The meaning of the concept, "God," needs no stretching to cover some vague abstraction or impersonal idea. Those who talk of "God" in this way may even, as Freud says, "pride themselves on having attained a higher and purer idea of God, although their God is nothing but a substantial shadow and no longer the mighty personality of religious doctrine."[17]

Professor Bertocci, using what he calls, "the wider teleological argument," contends that, "the inter-connectedness of physical nature, life and human experience makes a personal God an inescapable necessity.[18] Ninian Smart, viewing a more restricted area, sees the radical contingency of things as demanding a Creator with the power of choice. This world is not the only possible world God could have created. He might not have created any world at all. But what He made is evidently what He *chose* to do. This power of rational choice is essentially a property of personality.

All evidences of law, order, and purpose in the world verify a personal God. We recognize physical forces only when they act to produce conscious experience. This means that the presence of physical forces takes for granted the action of a Personal Agent. To speak as did Herbert Spencer of an eternally existing force is meaningless; blind force without purpose and will cannot give a rational explanation for the existence of human personality. Only within the context of purpose and will can human personality exist and find its significance.

If all the actual data available are conscious experiences, everything inferred from these data must be consistent with and explanatory of conscious experiences. An explanation must be adequate for the facts of the case. Thus, blind unconscious force cannot be taken as the adequate explanation for the existence of self-conscious personalities. The facts require a Presence behind phenomena, an intelligent and ethical will. If the First Cause and the Ultimate Fact of the universe is required and proved by its manifestations to be both Rational Intelligence and Ethical Will, then we cannot but speak of this Cause and this Fact in terms of personality.

The concept of personality is, therefore, a rational alternative to the belief that God is either wholly unknown or that there is really no God at all. But the reality of revelation proves that God has made Himself known; on the other hand, all naturalistic theories which do not admit to a personal God are crippled by their own inherent logic. There is a fundamental absurdity in believing in a God, or in calling what is inferior to man "God." If God is anything less than the center of consciousness, then man the creature is superior to His Creator in that which is ultimate and sacred.

Awareness of God as personal is expressed in all aspects of religious worship and is required by philosophical thinking about religious experience. Anyone who honestly examines religious worship and experience cannot ignore this proof of the personal nature of Ultimate Being. If they teach anything at all it is this: at the core of religious experience and worship is the assurance that the Object of belief is worthy of worship as Ethical Personality. An intimate relation exists between the notion of the personal and the ethical. God, as a self-conscious and self-determining Being, has what is fundamental to the concept of personality. On the other hand, a self-conscious Being whose attributes are not ethical is not personal in the fullest sense.

The Meaning of Divine "Person"

What does it mean to speak of God as personal? It is clearly not quite the same as calling the Ultimate Factor of the universe "a person," because this suggests location and limitation. That would demean the glory of God by comparing Him to finite man. O. R. Jones offers as a better alternative the "clumsy word personhood," but he immediately drops it, because it is "so cacophanous."[19] Clumsy as the word may be, it prevents some of the difficulties which the concept "person" creates. The term "person" implies that God is a Superman located somewhere in a celestial realm. It is easy for the opponent to ridicule such an idea. There are simple believers naive enough to think of God like this. All we need to say in their defense is that it is better that they believe as they do rather than speak lightly under the illusion that they are speaking learnedly about the Ground of Being. Nevertheless, serious believers do try to have a worthy conception of God as "personal." They try to maintain both God's divinity and personality. Thus, they speak of Him as "Divine Personality." In declaring that God is personal, a qualifier is used to state that God is not an ordinary person. This is expressed in various ways by different thinkers. To some He is "Perfect Personality"; to others, "Complete Personality"; but to all who allow meaning to grace and prayer, He is "Divine Personality."

The essential feature of personality cannot be simply specified.

It is easy to recognize its presence, but not so easy to define its nature. Reason and will seem to be necessary elements of personality. To be personal is to act consistently and responsibly. To be personal is to admit another person into a relationship which recognizes that person to be capable of response. The traditional thinker in calling God "a person" was trying to capture the fact that His being has an inner conscious unity, that He knew what He was doing, and that He cared for certain ideals.[20] God is personal because, as F. W. Robinson says, he possesses "self-conscious will and character." Because God and man can enter into personal relationships, in worship, trust and love, the conviction of the divine personality is sharpened. C.C.J. Webb introduced the term "reciprocation" to describe the awareness of this personal relationship. He argues that the whole question of the personality of God centers upon whether "God is real as a person is real, with whom we may enjoy a reciprocal personal relationship."[21] Ian Ramsey seeks to give fuller meaning to this "relation of reciprocity." Its essential note, he suggests, is that of an "answering," out of which love, trust and caring for the other rise. There may be, he acknowledges, a response to a condition in which the personal element is missing. But he contends that a personal reciprocity relates to a frank and open relationship characterized by and rising out of a mutually varying pattern. The relationship means active involvement with another person whose behavior is mediated by that varying pattern, in a situation by which I, as a person living in self-disclosure, am not trapped.[22]

Ramsey warns, however, that "personal" can only be applied to God with certain restrictions. The concept is originally a reading of our own experience, and to apply it to God without qualifications would lead to anthropomorphism. By definition, God's acts are not the same as ours; nor is His reason on our human level. Our relationship with God is consequently a different kind from that which we enjoy with our friends, but not a wholly different kind, lest the idea of a personal "I-Thou" relationship between God and man be emptied of meaning. Throughout man's relationship with God the sense of the personal remains, the sense that we are being admitted into a relationship.

W. G. Maclagan sees the issue as a clear-cut choice between an outright anthropomorphism and a non-personal view of God. He opts for the latter, because he believes that the principle of analogy, by which belief in a personal God is entertained, rules out such a view. Starting with the human, there is no way of going beyond the human. We are not speaking of God, as Karl Barth says, when we say, "Man!" in a loud voice. Maclagan allows, however, that all but the "most simple-minded" can think of God as "a sort of working conflation of the ideas of the personal and the impersonal."[23] But when the concept of a personal God is questioned, then however "pragmaticly justified" it may be in the context of religious faith, it is theoretically indefensible. Maclagan will not allow any prefixes or qualifiers. To suggest with Bradley that God may be "personal and more" is, he thinks, to make Him less than personal. To say that God is "supra-personal" is just a polite way of saying that He is non-personal. "The 'supra' in 'supra-personal' does not indicate a 'more'; it indicates a 'more' such that the 'more' transforms the meaning of the term 'personal' itself."[24]

As Ian Ramsey observes, "Around the concept of the personality of God arises tensions between a theology which finds it difficult to incorporate the concept, and the Christian life and devotion which seem to demand it."[25]

Objections to the Idea of God as Personal

Objections have been raised against the concept of a personal God from religious, psychological and philosophical angles. Modern pantheists might be credited with developing a reasoned denial of God's personality. Pantheism is congenial to the modern mind and is instantly appealing to religious people outside Christianity. It is easy to sell the gospel of pantheism to those who think there is nothing standing between man and God that man himself cannot overcome. It appeals to the emotions because it joins God and man, and to the mind because it unifies the world. Its all-inclusive synthesis seems to give meaning to life by its impression of being complete and simple. This hunger for unification is a deep and real instinct, and pantheism assures man that his life is not detached and estranged. His dwelling and destiny are within the divine whole. Pantheism thus calls out a religious fervor and devotion by teaching that there is an ultimate unity which all human toil and trouble enrich in color and harmony. The man who desires a religious ingredient in his life easily adopts pantheism.

By denying personality to God, pantheism forfeits what it needs most to explain and enrich human personality. When we depersonalize God, we consequently depersonalize man. Individuals become bits of the ultimate stuff in pantheism, replaceable parts in a vast unintelligent and amoral machine. Lost are faith, prayer and worship, which make man's relationship to God meaningful and which give life moral integrity and social responsibility. Satisfying the hunger for unification fails to satisfy the hunger for personality.

Some argue that personality, as a human category, cannot refer to God. Personality is something which grows and develops and requires a social context. It is within the realm of relationships that a personality matures. It emerges in the give-and-take with other people who are different from oneself. Each person has to learn the use of "I" and "me," and must discover that he is different from the things he touches. For this reason Tillich denies the idea of a personal God. He argues that selfhood implies that one is separate and different from everything else.[26] Personality is a selfhood which sets itself apart and excludes everything else. On the other hand, God is by definition outside such contrasts. He is the Unlimited and the All-comprehensive, which excludes nothing except that exclusiveness which is part of Tillich's idea of personality. The argument is this: to be a person is to be finite, to be a selfhood is to believe oneself to be totally different from all others. The question then is asked, "How then can God really be said to be personal? Are we not transferring to Him a concept which has meaning only within a social context?" Are we not, as J.A.T. Robinson contends, making God finite "by encompassing Him in our categories of our own selfhood?"[27]

The strength of this objection to the idea of a personal God depends upon its presupposition that personality is self-contained and exclusive. But this is certainly not the case. The paradox of personality is this: it has a center all its own, which others cannot penetrate; yet because we are persons we can somehow overcome our isolation. The more unique a person is as an individual, the more completely he goes beyond the limits of himself. This is what the believer says of God. He has that in perfection, the essence of Godhood. To say that personality develops in a social context is not the same as saying that it is produced by it. The error in the argument is to confuse a fact about personhood with the way in which it is expressed. It may be true that human beings discover their personality by collision with others; but it is also true that there is selfhood which becomes aware of others, an "I" which takes notice. Thus, while we discover our personality through contact with others, it does not follow, as Dalgairns argues, that personality is created by the shock which comes by knocking our own self against another self.

To assert that man has personality and, therefore, God cannot have it is to beg the question. Might it not be, as Lotze has pointed out, that God is personality in its completest form? We are certainly persons, but second-rate persons. Man is personhood in ruins; he is incomplete personality. "Perfect personality," Lotze declares, "is in God only; to all finite minds there is allotted a pale copy thereof: the finiteness of the finite is not the producing condition of this personality, but a limit and a hindrance to its fulfilment."[28] Maybe then, as Barth says, the question is not "Is God a person?" but rather, "Are we?"[29]

Divine Personality as a Reflection of the Human

Tillich has strongly argued that the concept of a personal God imposes a limit on "God" as the "Ground of Being." He thinks it is bad theology to believe that God is "a heavenly, completely perfect person who resides above the world and mankind." Tillich considers the atheist's protest justified against such a conception of God as "higher person."[30] Tillich contends that God cannot be viewed as an Entity among entities, not even as *primus inter pares* (first among equals). God is not *a* Being, but very Being itself. Tillich will, however, allow us to speak of God in personal ways since He "is the ground of everything personal so that he carries within himself the ontological power of personality." In fact, he is ready to assert that, "man cannot be ultimately concerned about something which is less than he is, something impersonal."[31]

But this is a strange way to construe the idea of God as personal. The first and most obvious move in response to Tillich is to urge that he is making God in his own image. Tillich appears to be saying that we worship God as personal, not because He is personal, but because we are. Such a view makes God little more than a psychological fulfillment of man's need. Tillich can say that God is Ultimate Concern for Man, but he is unable to state anything precise about the Being about which he is so sure. The trouble is that Tillich, who repudiates the concept of a personal God so firmly, finds himself unable to speak coherently of the Ground of Being, except in terms emphatically personal. "He is not a person, but is not less than personal," he declares.[32] And as the Ground of everything personal, He is the ontological power of personality. But can the essential source of personality be other than, or less than, personality? Speaking about human selfhood, Tillich says that a man "is an individual person who participates universally."[33] He "is a dynamic self-transcendent agent." But is this not just what we wish to contend is especially and fully true of God? He is a personal Being who "participates universally." He is a "dynamic self-transcendent agent," that is to say, He is the living and personal God. As a religious naturalist, Tillich cannot avoid a contradiction between his refusal to regard God as being personal and his idea of faith as *ultimate concern*. Trueblood declares, "God is not the object of ultimate concern if He lacks the simple majesty of the freedom which man undoubtedly has."[34] Therefore, it is important to observe that Tillich himself asserts that there is in all religions, "a struggle for a personal God," a struggle which resists all philosophical attacks.[35]

Dr. Robinson thinks there is little to be said in favor of the "traditional case for belief in a personal God."[36] He regards the concept as out-moded, just as is the notion of a personal devil.[37] He believes the idea of a Superhuman Person was the projection of an immature generation; the idea was "an indispensable focus for the imagination." But for us, the mature, with an "up there" and an "out there" discarded, God cannot be thought of as an individual Being, a Divine Person. God is rather the dynamic depth of the world, where, according to Gerard Manley Hopkins, "there lives the dearest freshness deep down things."

Robinson views the personality of man as a pair of spectacles for seeing God in a personal way.[38] We speak of God "as though" He were Person, and in so doing we easily slip into the belief that He actually is. We conceive of God as "An Other over-against" us and we fall into thinking of our relationship with Being "in the subject-object schema." This personification of the God-reality may be a legitimate projection as long as we remind ourselves that it is "as if" and not actually what God is. God-language does not describe God as Person-in-Himself.[39] Therefore, we must get beyond traditional monotheism, beyond the subject-relationship which it assumes. The idea of "a Person behind phenomena" is a "picture" and an "image." This was, maybe, a necessary way of picturing God in the past. But "one of the insights of our century," is that the ultimate is itself "trans-personal."

Tillich and Robinson allow us to speak of God as personal as long as the concept has religious value. The criterion is not, Robinson insists, whether the statement about God is true or false, but whether it is helpful or unhelpful to the believer. But for those who want a religion which is true as well as useful, this pragmatic criterion will hardly work. This presentation of a personal God as merely the expression of the soul's own self-discovery has an almost naive inability to distinguish what is part of the religious awareness from the process itself. This is not evidence of a mature theology, but a return to adolescence. The difficulty of getting beyond ourselves and taking seriously what we find there is a teenage problem. The person engrossed with himself and concerned with his own self-expression, self-discovery, and self-fulfillment has not reached maturity. This obsession with the subjective accounts for the tendency in the new theology to equate statements about God with statements about ourselves. It needs to be asserted that self-understanding does not yield an understanding of God; nor is self-encounter an encounter with God.

Robinson is justified in asserting that God is not "a great big Man in the skies." Nevertheless, such a conception may be closer to the truth than thinking of God as a "great Big Thing," even if it is inadequate and dangerous. Norman Pittenger says, God as a great Big Man, "is not the total *contradiction* of everything which is most real to me as a Christian, as I find the 'big Thing' image to be."[40] Certainly the analogy between God and man made in His image is appropriate, but that between God and inanimate things is not.

Ian Ramsey presents a more acceptable view of God's personal nature. Dr. Ramsey attributes personality to God, because there "occur whether deliberately generated or not, cosmic situations of a deliberate kind, whose patterns are similar to disclosures of personal reciprocity."[41] He regards the idea of personality as a *model* expressing what God means. At the same time, he insists that impersonal models also represent God, although neither the personal nor the non-personal models will ever adequately replace "God" in a sentence.[42] When, however, he seeks "a sort of supermodel" to integrate the two, he finds that the personal model assumes priority and the non-personal becomes a qualifier.

Ramsey renounces the criticism that he ends up in "personalistic atheism." He argues, "When the Universe comes alive in a cosmic disclosure whose structure is modeled by a personal reciprocity, it declares itself to us as a person does; and as a characterization of the activity which we then know, 'person' is the most natural model of any to use."[43] Ramsey sees the mutual "coming alive" in the moment of "cosmic disclosure" as a guarantee of the existence and personality of God. He says, "It is the objectivity of what declares itself to us—challenges us in a way that persons may do. It is in this sense that God declares his objectivity, and some would say that in a similar sense Duty also declares its objectivity."[44]

Ramsey's argument has left too many problems unnoticed and unexplained. What, for example, is the relationship between the model and the reality? Ramsey, unlike Tillich, who at least maintains that the "symbol participates" in what it symbolizes, does not specify any connection. We want to know if the model characterizes the Ultimate as it is, or merely the way we feel the impact of the "cosmic disclosure"? Our interests are centered around the model. But that is poor fare for our spiritual need. We do not want models; we want God. We want the living and personal God.

Clarifying religious language in terms of models does not tell us whether it is true or false. By admitting that "models of God can be and always are being taken away, criticized, graded, and ordered," we are, "committed in this way to an endless explication of what cosmic disclosure reveals."[45] But if God is really personal, can such models ever be taken away? Ramsey says that we can believe in God, but we can question the view of God as personal of historic Christian theology. But to suggest that we can believe in and question the concept of God as personal is a different matter. To know God at all is to know Him as personal. It may be that, "it is within the context of religious language that the conception of God's reality has its place." But this does not mean that God is at the mercy of what anyone cares to say. If that were so, God would be no reality at all. The fact is, "What is real and what is unreal shows itself in the sense that language has."[46]

Ramsey says that religious language is "never descriptive." However, it is not very clear what he means by this, because it seems that he intends the very opposite. He suggests that we describe in personal terms what "comes alive" in the form of a "cosmic disclosure." Would he then have us understand by saying that religious language is "never descriptive," that it is "never indicative" of what God is?

The difference between the descriptive and indicative use of religious language is one that runs throughout history. William of Occam argued that the foundation of biblical hermeneutics was to think oneself into the role of those who wrote Scripture. By a sort of empathy, we have to feel their inner state of soul and read the Scriptures as expressions of their inner feelings. Taking his cue from Occam, Erasmus gave this doctrine of "intention" his own ethical and psychological twist. His principle of interpretation was to clarify Scriptures in terms of the writer's moral inwardness. This led to the view that religious statements are to be regarded as "descriptive" of the moral and religious attitude of the writer's soul.

Hilary of Poitiers suggested another alternative: he insists that God is not reducible to human statements about Him. Yet language does "indicate" something of what He is. He is this and not that, one thing and not another. Calvin, following Hilary, maintained that theological language refers beyond itself to God as God is in His transcendent reality. Thus, to speak of God as personal is not to describe God in His relationship with men, but to indicate God as He is in His fundamental being.

If Ramsey, in declaring that talk about God is "never descriptive," means to say that God is personal and not just a description of our experience of the universe expressed in a personal way, we agree. But we do not think that this is what he means. He intends to say that the "model" of the "personal" does not indicate what God is in His essential being. We cannot accept this. We must insist that if God discloses Himself as a Divine Person, then that is what He *is*; He is indeed more than that but not in essence other than that.

To speak of God is to speak of the Divine Personality. By using the designation *personal*, we do not put God in the same category as other beings. God is the Self-Existent and the Infinite in contrast with all else which is dependent and finite. He is certainly the Ground of Being; but the *personal* Ground of everything. He is personal, not as mere symbol and model, but as ultimate fact.

While we may hesitate to say that God is *a* Person, there does not seem to be anything inconsistent in saying that God is personal. Christians believe that this world is God's. He is the Creator of everything and everyone. The world is built for His love. God is the Great Cosmic Lover who holds all things together in His divine embrace. He is Ultimate Agape, whose personal nature is revealed in the most personal way—He loves and wants to be loved by us.

Man is personal in man's way; God is personal in God's way. This does not mean that no kinship exists between the two. We declare that man is made in the image of God, but that the divine image is marred and distorted, limiting the potential of man's personality. Therefore, difference and similarity do coexist between the personalities of God and of man. There is something unbroken, and something broken in the relationship between God's personality and man's. God's personality is unique because it is unmarred and undistorted by sin, and it is personal, therefore, in a way in which man is not personal because of his stained and broken personality. God is personal, but in divinest measure, in a way that man cannot be. God, being personal, cares, loves, and upholds. He seeks in grace to mend and remake soiled and spoiled human personalities. He meets the personal needs of man by revealing His own personality in the historic reality of Christ.

Chapter 2

Creation in Historical Perspective

Most normal people believe the world about them really exists. It is really "out there" and the fact that it really is there demands some explanation. There are basically two answers to the question of the world's existence.[1] It has either always been here or it was at some point in time created by an outside force in the fulfillment of some purpose.

Nontheistic existentialists are content to say that the world is "just there." We have to accept that fact without asking for a reason why. There is no reason for anything anywhere. The existence of the world and man according to Sartre is "quite idiotic." We have nothing to believe in but our determination to believe in nothing. The nontheistic existentialist does not even have the exciting mystery of contingency as the Christian existentialist does. No reason is offered for the world "being there." It just is; that is all there is to it.

The humanist has only a slightly different position. His creed is simply, "This life is all and enough."[2] Things are the way they are, and they must be accepted that way. The reason things are this way is merely because they happen this way. Matter is self-existing, self-creating, self-developing, and self-enduring. *Why* questions are forbidden: Why should there have been a universe in the first place? Why is it as it is? Why should things be as they are and not otherwise? Such questions presuppose the forbidden concept of purpose and the humanist does not admit the thought of purpose. The humanist would have us believe that all life, and eventually man himself, has risen out of the "remarkable stuff" called matter. It has always existed without the need for any power to create it or sustain it.[3]

But an unexciting doctrine such as this cannot smother curiosity and inquiry. The humanist fails to see that there is no support for the ladder by which man ascends. Ladders without some cosmic foundation in a meaningful Reality come crashing down to earth again. The ultimate question of the meaning of life is not answered.[4] But, as Dostoevsky wrote, "Where there is an ultimate question there is also an ultimate answer. How else could there be a question concerning it? It is only in the question that man can get hold of this answer, however, because there is an *ultimate* answer. God would certainly not be God if He were not really the solution. And, therefore, the problematical does not remain the final word of true knowledge of life. Behind it an absolutely final word can be received."[5]

God is the Creator. The Christian theist discovers the meaning of all things in this fact. He views the world as the expression of God's creative voice. Man lives in a world created and controlled by the living and personal God. Scripture starts with this affirmation. The Genesis account of creation is not merely an introduction which can be quickly passed over to get on to more important issues. The fundamental fact is that God is a Creator. This is the keystone in the arch of the biblical message. If it is dislodged, everything else collapses. Understanding the biblical view of God as Creator is to understand the whole Bible.[6]

Genesis focuses on God Himself, as Creator. This fact gives authority to the biblical record, not so much in its statement of the details of the method of creation as in directing our attention to God as the ultimate source and cause of all things. God is referred to thirty-two times in the thirty-one verses of Genesis one. Calvin believed that the order of the creative events heralded the fact of the unity of the Creator, manifesting the reality of God's fatherly goodness toward mankind. The bare essence of God's eternal wisdom and spiritual nature is established in order that we might not dream of any other God than the One who wishes to be known in this way.[7]

In this chapter, we want to trace the historical concepts of creation in Christian thought. Contemporary ideas will be discussed in the next chapter.

Creatio ex Nihilo

The idea that creation was an act of bringing into existence what was previously not, *creatio ex nihilo*, as the phrase goes, is a distinctively biblical concept. Even though the phrase is not biblical, Christian writers used it to express the idea of creation common to biblical authors.[8] Even Greek philosophy at its highest did not arrive at the concept of a Creator who produced the world by His word without the use of preexisting material. Plato came the nearest of pre-Christian philosophers in his Timaeus where he speaks of the Creator who "made this world of generation" to be a reflection of Himself.[9] This phrase has been translated several different ways, and some commentators have said that it expresses a concept virtually equivalent to the doctrine of *creatio ex nihilo*. But it is easy to read too much into Plato's words. His view was that the world was shaped from existing chaos.

Augustinian Creatio ex Nihilo

The phrase *creatio ex nihilo* was formulated to refute the view that God used eternally existing matter to make the world. Therefore, Irenaeus reproached the Gnostics for not believing that a God rich and powerful in resources could not create matter. He said, "While man indeed cannot make anything, God is in this point preeminently superior to man, that He has called into being the substance of His creation, when previously it had no existence."[10]

Augustine may be said to have given an orthodox connotation to the expression *creatio ex nihilo* by renouncing his allegiance to Manachaean dualism. He said that by declaring that the world was made from nothing, we do not give "nothing" personality, but rather distinguish the nature of God from the nature of the creation.[11] Augustine regarded creation as a unique event. To say that God created out of "nothing" is to distinguish the nature of God from the nature of things made and puts matter on a lower level than Himself. He interprets the Genesis account in a spiritual and mystical way, but he stresses that creation was an act of God. Therefore, God's desire to create comes from His own decision; there is no reason for His will apart from Himself.[12] All of the created order is solely from God's goodness. Augustine states, "In that it is said, 'God saw that it was good,' there is a sufficient indication that God made what was made, not by any necessity nor by any need for something useful, but solely out of His goodness, that is to say, because it is good."[13] He contrasts the Word which God begot from Himself, with what God created from nothing, including man's nature with its potential to accomplish evil.[14]

Augustine quotes Ecclesiasticus 18:1 as proof that creation was an instantaneous act of God.[15] God's creative act was accomplished "at once." The elements of every future thing were created then. The "roots" of which Empedokeles spoke and the "seeds" of Anaxagoras, which were both eternal and irreducible, were considered by Augustine to be the result of a single, unique creation.

In spite of Augustine's authoritative exposition, the phrase *ex nihilo* was later given different interpretations which either sharply distinguished the world from God or closely related it to Him. When the emphasis was put upon the idea of created matter of a nature other than the Creator, the tendency was to sever the universe from God and move toward deism. The problem with this view is understanding why there is anything other than God and how He relates to it today.

The other interpretation saw the absence of preexisting matter as proof that God created the world from the same "stuff" of His own Deity. He produced successive emanations of His being. This view understood the world and God to be intimately related, and it denied the independent role and status of matter. The more closely the world and God are thus associated, the greater the tendency toward pantheism. The meaning of God as a distinct and personal being became a problem.

Creation as Emanation

The influence of neo-Platonism gave this latter view, the emanationist, stronger immediate appeal. Even some mainstream orthodox Christians embraced this view. The pseudonymous fourth-century writer, Denys the Areopagite, although acknowledging his indebtedness to Plotinus and Proculus, sought to give a Christian stamp to this account of God's relation to the world. Denys so intimately united the natural world with God that he spoke of it as a "theophany." Creation has, for him, therefore, the character of a revelation of the divine Being. There is a "hierarchy," or scale of being, of emanations from Pure Being, the nature of each defined by its distance from Pure Being. The highest emanation is pure intelligence; the lowest is matter. The divine "illumination" emanates each member of this universal hierarchy after its kind. The Ultimate Being bestows the gift of light, its nature as Being, on the highest rank of being. This highest being transmits the light, in turn, to the next lower being. Yet the lowest rank finds its own cause and reason in Ultimate Being Itself. Thus, the wheel comes full circle: what is *of* Being, exists *through* Being, and returns *to* Being.

This view of the existing world emanating from God-Being and flowing back to God-Being became a root concept for numerous successive writers. Some accepted Deny's doctrine *in toto*, fascinated by his teaching that God, not wholly other and different, can thus be approached through His creatures. Others sought to modify his view in order to make it congenial to Latin minds. Thus, although Denys' doctrine required much modification, even reinterpretation of its underlying principle, it also provided subsequent thinkers with a framework for popularizing their own understanding of the world's existence.

Evidence of this heavy indebtedness to the pseudo-Areopagite surfaces in the work of the mid-ninth century writer, John Scotus Erigena. In his *De Divisione Naturae*, and his *Commentary on the Celestial Hierarchy of Denys*, John seeks to combine an emanationist with a creationist view. The source and goal of all things, he declares, comes from the Divine Nature. While he adopts Denys' idea of the cycle of being, he uses *creatio ex nihilo* more ambiguously than even Denys dared. For Erigena conceives of the "nothing" from which created beings originated, not as a substance alien from God, but as the very nature of Pure Being itself. To say that God created the world "out of nothing," he thus argues, is to say that He created it out of Himself.

Erigena clarifies his teaching by using the category "theophany." The Divine essence, which is beyond classification, and is, therefore, properly designated "Nothing," enters a spacial-temporal condition by means of theophanies. Creation and revelation are thus coordinated. Creation is precisely the self-manifestation of God, the expression of His unity through created pluralties. Creation is an "apparition of God." And since with God to create is to reveal, it follows that to say God reveals Himself is but another way of saying that God creates Himself. Creation is a procession from God, first of ideas, and on down through the hierarchy of genera, sub-genera, and species, to individual substances. But since the ideas are immediately related to God, they have their being in unbegun Godhead and are thus without temporal beginning. Yet since ideas are generated from the Divine Being they are created. So, too, is it with the world: as an archetype in the Eternal Mind it is without beginning, but by having a beginning "in time," a coming to be "out of nothing," it wears the appearance of a creation.

Nicholas of Cusa, in the fifteenth century, followed the scheme of Denys and Erigena. From 1438–1439 Nicholas scrutinized the works of pseudo-Dionysius and grounded *De Doctae Ignoratiae* of 1440 on these earlier writings.[16] But he more centralized Christ's person in his interpretation than had either Denys or Erigena. Thus he earned the title, Doctor Christianus. Nicholas saw the world as the visible appearance of the invisible God. God gathers into Himself the fullness of the world, and in Him all opposites have their coincidence. He is the Being of all beings; the Nature of all natures; the Essence of all essences. For Nicholas, to "see" is to "create." He thus declares, that a thing exists in the measure wherein God beholds it; for God's sight is God's essence.[17] God is, therefore, "Absolute Sight"; it is by His seeing that all things are and continue to be.[18] But since God can see only Himself, He can therefore create nothing which is not Himself.

Nicholas of Cusa pays homage to the conventional doctrine by insisting that God acted by His free will in creation. But in spite of his long expositions, he fails to clarify how creation as a necessary emanation of the divine Being can be reconciled with creation as a free act of God.

An emanationism with such pantheistic leanings was bound to lead some to a pronounced form of monism. Thus, David of Dinant in the thirteenth century taught what Thierry has called a *panthéisme matérialiste*, which more than superficially resembles Spinoza's view. The little that we know of David's view shows it to be a "reckless development of Erigena's doctrine."[19] He appears to make God and matter synonymous by making God the substance of all bodies and souls, and the soul a material entity like the body. A more extreme form of monistic absolutism was presented by Amuary of Bene, a senior contemporary of David. His condemnation in 1210 did not prevent the diffusion of his teaching through Amuarius and his followers, who continued to emphasize that God is identical with all things. Aquinas poured scorn on their ideas, referring to the "insania" and "absurdity" of David.[20]

Aquinas on Creation

But what does Aquinas say regarding creation? It is a merit with him that he took seriously the twin truths: that this is a God-originated universe, and that the idea of creation belongs to the realm of faith rather than to that of empirical facts. By starting with the world as a divine creation it became truth with him, that the cosmos as God's work is a sure evidence of His existence. Yet

Aquinas allows that the question whether the world has a temporal beginning is a matter of faith and is not demonstrable or knowable.[21]

Aquinas was, however, especially concerned to give concreteness and autonomy to created existences. In this way he struck a new and needed note of stark realism. The prevailing teaching leaned toward spiritualistic and symbolistic unworldliness. So denaturalized had the natural order become that it appeared unreal; most of Aquinas' contemporaries reckoned him the most truly religious, who treated nature the most unnaturally. Aquinas combatted the old Augustinian-Cluniac view, which regarded the natural world with something akin to a morbid contempt.

In this regard he had certainly caught something of the Hohenstaufen spirit of hearty and healthy worldliness, which emanated from the court of the emperors of Palermo. Under the influence of Aristotle's rediscovered works, his keenest teachers refused to write off the realm of nature as unreal and unworthy. Aquinas learned from Aristotle that the *libri naturales* (books about nature) were not forbidden books, but were open to all who would take the time and trouble to master their language and message. As a University of Naples student, Aquinas was spellbound by the eloquent Peter of Hibernia, who taught a radical non-theological Aristotelianism. Aquinas guarded himself from the secular spirit which pervaded that university and came to understand the world as an actual world of created entities, and not as an array of spiritualistic symbols.

Yet while Aquinas rejected an exclusively theological world view, his understanding of nature was nonetheless profoundly theological. He defends with all his might and skill the right of natural things; but he does not as a result, restrict the area of God's rights. He illustrates the conception of nature generally accepted in his day: fire, for example, was not conceived as fire, *a se ipso* (as a result of its very self), but only in so far as it referred to God and exhibited His divine sovereignty.[22] Aquinas sets himself the task of defending the right of everything to be itself. He was concerned with the real world, and he did not regard the presence of other existences as in any way robbing God of His glory. He sought to show that because natural things were *creatura*, they were real, and real moreover because created. Natural things possess self-contained intrinsic being because each is the result of God's creative will, whose will is by its very nature "being-giving." For Aquinas, "to create" is "to communicate being," to give actuality to independent, real existences. "The first fruit of God's activity in things," he declares, "is existence itself: all other effects presuppose it, existence."[23]

In contrast with Augustine, to whom to create is to give existence, Aquinas regards creation as the communication of being. Augustine's idea of creation as the act by which God makes things to be what they are, resulted, as Gilson observes, in a complete de-existentialization of the notion of creation. Aquinas argued that things are not "in existence" because of what they are, but as a consequence of the communication to them of the *actus essendi* (dynamic of being). That is, he contends, the true idea of creation: "Because God by virtue of His essence is existence itself, therefore the existence of what He has created is necessarily a producing particular of His essence; just as flaming up is the effect peculiar to the essence of fire." For this reason Jacques Maritain refers to Aquinas not just as one existentialist among others, but as *le plus existentiel des philosophes.*

For Aquinas, therefore, everything is good in its own order, because of its very createdness—because, that is, its distinctive and real "being" is communicated to it by God. In fact, for Aquinas, not only is everything that is, good—but it is good just because it is: "*Idem est unicuique rei essi et bonum esse*" (for everything to be and to be good, is the same).[24] Aquinas consequently sees the world of itself, and in its own right, as the proper subject of study. He has no need to dehumanize man or to denaturalize nature. Aquinas' concern, however, is not to defend natural and visible things so he may read the book of nature without theological glasses. Despite his efforts to justify the actuality of individual existences, Aquinas would not have us regard the world without God. Rather, he argues, since everything that is, is flamed up out of the *actus purus* (Pure Actuality), all things bring us face to face with this Reality, with God as Pure Ultimate Being.

At the same time Aquinas' realism, in which he sees man as bodily existent, leads him to give utmost stress to the Incarnation doctrine. In a commentary on St. John's Gospel, he underscores the phrase, the Word was "made flesh." He emphasizes that flesh is meant in its fullest and clearest meaning and measure. Not only does the expression exclude any Manachaean notion that the body, as such, is evil, but also it forbids the conclusion that the material world itself is not good. Thus, while he does follow Augustine in making nature real, Aquinas does not divorce the world from God. He will not give us nature without God. On the other hand, while he rejects the spiritualistic-symbolistic view of nature, he does not divorce God from nature.

In the eleventh century, Anselm took *creatio ex nihilo* (creation out of nothing) to mean that God is the sole cause of all that exists. It prohibits, he contends, the idea that God is the very matter of the world He has brought into being. In his *Monologion*, Anselm states emphatically that in creation God had no need of any preexisting material. What now exists, did not once exist: it came to be through the action of God's power in accordance with His wisdom and will. Anselm does, however, confess to difficulty about the word "nothing." He investigates several ideas the word can suggest and rejects them. And he dislikes his opponents' argument that what is said to have been created "from nothing" was created *de nihilo ipso* (from nothing itself), from what does not exist at all, as if this "nothing" were some existing "something" from which things were made. There was, Anselm insists, no "anything" before there was "something." When, then, it is said that God created, it must mean that "something" (then) was brought to be, and that when created it came to be a "something."[25]

In spite of the authority of Aquinas and Anselm, however, the spiritualistic and monistic tendency of emanationism continued. Absolute idealism followed medieval mysticism in expounding the idea of creation as the coming to be of temporary manifestations within the Absolute. Approaching the Ultimate-All through the feelings, the mystics came to a position of religious absolutism; approaching the All-inclusive Reality through the reason, the idealists arrived at a position of philosophical monism. Both were consequently driven to see creation as a mere appearance, which is as true for Eckhart as for Hegel.

Creation: God Communicating

Absolute idealism, however, despite the popularity given to it in England by Stirling and Bradley, did not survive long. Protest soon rose against its submerging of the individual in an all-devouring whole. The pluralistic and theistic idealists set themselves to rescue the world from being mere bubbles on the sea of being. They sought to give status and security to real entities. In so doing they again raised the problem of the relation of these entities to the Ultimate One. But by stressing their connectedness with, rather than their distinction from, Ultimate Reality, they found themselves reviving some form of emanationist theory.

Thus Pringle-Pattison, for example, argued that creation is a divine act of manifestation. It is not, he protests, the making of something "out of nothing" in the Augustinian sense. Creation is not to make concrete some previously non-concrete existence. It is, rather, the revelation in and to finite spirits of the infinite riches of the divine life. He rejects, therefore, what he considers the idea of a preexisting Deity not yet crowned with the highest attributes of goodness and self-revealing love. And he is at odds with Augustine, for whom, he says, creation was conceived of as a unique event not grounded in the nature of God.[26] Spirits are not to be viewed as "things made," detached like products from their maker. They are more aptly described, he asserts, in the biblical sense as partakers of the divine nature.[27]

Many advocated this idealist principle. They pictured creation as God translating His internal thought process into objects; thus, creation to the idealist is God communicating with Himself. But it is, as Leonard Hodgson observes, a question whether it is really a doctrine of creation at all. For to say that this universe is the mode in which the Eternal is expressing Himself to Himself, in what appears to us as space and time, is not the same as saying that the universe owes its separate existence to the will of God, and that God has created it for His own reason, and has given it reality which that reason requires.[28]

Even after the eclipse of idealism, theologians continued their fascination with the idea of the world as somehow the necessary other-side of God. They felt bound to relate God closely to the world to eliminate all deistic conclusions which would view God as far-off and unconcerned. They were eager to assert God's intimate relation with the cosmos, but in so doing they hardly escaped pantheism. Thus Martensen, for example, argues that without the world God is not God.[29] Love, not power, is the reason for its existence. Since love is the ground of creation we cannot think God made the world for His own glorification. Such an idea would, he contends, give us a picture of Him as a Being of "egoistic power, rather than, eternal love." Creation is really the love-act of God, in which "He glorifies His love to Himself through love to the world."[30] Martensen, to be sure, still uses *creatio ex nihilo*, but in the sense that, "The nothing out of which God creates the world are the eternal possibilities of His will, which are the sources of all actualities of the world."[31]

More recently, Nicholas Berdyaev has restated the same general idea. He states that God *with* the world is somehow more complete than God *without* it. For this reason, he contends, the very concept of creation needs revision and deepening.[32] The world is not alien to God. The "old doctrine," he declares, "according to which God created man and the world, having in no respect any need of them ought to be abandoned as a servile doctrine which deprives the life of men and the world of all meaning."[33] The world is not totally other than God. God is the very Ground and Core of its being.

Tillich's Concept of Divine Creativity

Paul Tillich believes the divine life is creative, actualizing itself in inexhaustible abundance.[34] Thus, he makes the divine life and the creative activity of God one and the same reality. God may then be said to be eternally creating Himself. It is meaningless, therefore, by Tillich's concept of God and creative action, to ask whether creation is necessary (something God must do) or contingent (something God could choose to do). It is not *necessary* because God cannot be compelled to do anything. Nor is it *contingent* because it does not *happen* to God. (For Tillich, God's divine life is His creative activity; God cannot alter the fact that He is the creative process.) Creation is consequently to be understood as the basic description of the relation of God to the world. It is not the story of an event which took place "once upon a time." Tillich agrees that the category, *creatio ex nihilo*, is distinctive to classical Christian doctrine, a protest against any type of dualism.[35] The phrase, therefore, renounces dualism. But Tillich is not satisfied with this prohibitive use of the expression. It must imply more than a mere rejection of dualism. The word *ex* seems to refer to the origin of the creature. "Nothing" is what *or where* it comes from. "Nothing" can mean two things for Tillich. It may mean the absolute negation of being (*ouk on*), or it can mean the relative negation of being (*me on*). If *ex nihilo* means the latter, it would be a restatement of the Greek doctrine of matter and form against which it is directed. If *ex nihilo* means the absolute negation of being, it could not be the origin of the creature. Nevertheless, the term *ex nihilo* says something fundamentally important about the creatures: Tillich says *ex nihilo* must replace what might be called "the heritage of non-being."[36]

For Tillich the world and man are simultaneously inside and outside the circle of divine life. Both are characterized by "creatureliness," and as such partake of the heritage of non-being. It is by participation in the creative power of Being that existence acquires the sense of "courage"—the courage to be. But by including in itself the heritage of non-being, the creature is subject to "anxiety."

It is not clear what Tillich really intends by his discussion of *creatio ex nihilo*. He asserts firmly enough that the "divine life is essentially creative." And he regards the three modes of time, past, present and future, as required to "symbolize" God's creative activity. God *has* created the world, He is creative in the *present* moment, and He will creatively fulfill His *telos*. Tillich specifies more particularly God's *originating* creativity to mean that all things derive their power of being from the creative Ground of divine life. The creation is *ex nihilo* in the sense that there is nothing "given" to God, "which influences him in his creativity or which resists his creative *telos*."

But his statement that creatures assume "the heritage of non-being" seems to suggest that he gives some measure of existence to "Non-being," and thus returns to the dualism which he admits that the phrase was designed to rule out. "What Tillich has done is to make *nothing* out of which we come to something with fatal power."[37] Tillich readily admits, of course, that his doctrine is out of harmony with the historic understanding of the phrase *creatio ex nihilo*. But in the end, that historic meaning which presents God in His fundamental being as other than the things He has made, and yet as the sole Cause and Reason for all that exists, is more in accord with the needs of faith than Tillich's blurred reinterpretation.

Creation and Dogmatic Theology

Although the emanationist doctrine made the stronger appeal throughout the medieval period, the Augustinian emphasis was carried through into constructive Christian dogmatics to become the standard statement of theological textbooks. Thus, A. H. Strong, for example, defines creation as, "that free act of the triune God by which in the beginning for His glory he made, without the use of pre-existing material, the whole visible and invisible universe."[38]

A compromise on the clean-cut option between the two extremes of creation as an event in the past, and of creation as a continuous process, was suggested by certain Lutheran theologians of the seventeenth century. Gerhard and Quenstedt set the fashion by initiating a distinction between *creatio prima seu immediata* (the first creation, with no intermediary) and *creatio secunda seu mediata* (the second creation, with an intermediary). The first phrase signified that originating act of God in which, by His own free volition, He created the primary substance and elementary essence of all things. The second phrase refers to the subsequent act of God in creating different species and forms of things out of these already created substances and essences.

Despite differences in details, the Christian faith in divine creation agrees that God is the sole explanation of the existence of the world and is directly responsible for it. Everything depends upon Him, although the world, as such, is not identical with Him. Central, therefore, in the dogmatic statements of the Christian faith is the affirmation that the world of matter is of a different *stuff* from the nature of Deity.

On the position of man, however, there is not quite the same accord. The Genesis account of man presents him both "of God" and "of the ground." It has been no easy matter to give theological and philosophical exactness to this duality. Yet Christians agree that man is a created being, bearing within himself a Godward and an earthward reference. Apart from a few speculative theologians, Origen, for example, in the fourth century, and Julius Müller in the nineteenth, the Church has consistently rejected the Platonic idea of the preexistence of souls. It has, instead, viewed man's origin as the unity of the natural, which God created, with the spiritual, which God communicated. Thus man, too, no less than his world, is a creation of God; he is a creature, whose sole cause of existence is the free, creative act of God. On the creation hypothesis, then, as W. R. Matthews says, we face the consequence of our faith: all things depend upon God, and He is responsible for the world because He willed it.[39]

Creation and Time

But the Christian assertion that the world came into being by the uttered command of God has prompted the question of God's apparent inactivity before His willed relation to His creation. According to Origen, that was the one subject objectors to Christian doctrine "generally raise." They ask, "If the world has a beginning in time, what was God doing before the world began? For it is at once impious and absurd to say that the nature of God is inactive and immoveable, or to suppose that goodness at one time did no good, and omnipotence at one time did not exercise its power."[40] Augustine, too, tells us he constantly faced the same objection. Some, "full of the old leaven," asked "What was God doing before He made the heaven and earth? For if (they say) He was unemployed and wrought not, why does He not also henceforth, and for ever, as He did heretofore?"[41]

Origen did not answer his critics in the same way as the later Augustine. Origen replied simply that this is not the first of God's created worlds. In this manner he thought he was giving "a logical answer in accordance with the standards of religion, when we say that not for the first time did God begin to work when He made the visible world; but as, after its destruction, there will be another world, so also we believe that others existed before the present one came into being."[42]

Augustine refused to treat the subject with the frivolity that some apparently did. When asked, "What did God do before He made the heaven and earth?" some evaded the pressure of the problem with the jest that He was making hell for those who ask silly questions.[43] Augustine answered that time has no reality for God. In fact, time came into existence with creation, for "without creation," there would be no "time." Augustine may have found the clue to his thesis in a passage in Plato's Timeaus, with which he was specifically familiar.[44] Plato relates time to the perpetual world of becoming, in distinction from eternity, which he relates to the intelligible world of being.[45] For Plato, time is regarded as the moving image of eternity. It had no existence before "the father and creator . . . set the heaven in order." There were, he asserts, "no days and nights and months and years before the heaven was created, but when he constructed the heaven he devised them also. They are all parts of time, and *was* and *will be* are created species of time which we in ourselves mistakenly apply to eternal being. For we say that it *was*, *is*, *will be*; but in truth *is* applies to it, while *was* and *will be* are properly said of becoming in time."[46]

Such was the solution Augustine offered. "But if before heaven and earth," he writes, "there was no time, why is it demanded, 'What didst Thou then?' For there was no 'then' when there was no time." At no "time" did God make anything; because time itself was made by Him; time came into existence with His creation. Thus, Augustine contends, the whole notion of a creation at a definite point of time is false. Time is not a sort of substance into which the world was placed. For time-form did not precede creation. Creation is not, *in tempore*, but *cum tempore* (not in time, but with time).

Augustine's explanation seems to have silenced objections and to have satisfied most thinkers since then. Leibniz, for example, accepted it. In more recent times, it has received respectable scientific justification. Thus, Professor A.C.B. Lovell declares that, if "the primeval atom" was created, space and time had their origin with it. "Time in the sense of being measured by any clock did not exist before that moment, and space in the sense of being measured by a yardstick was contained entirely within the primeval atom."[47]

Eternal Creation

Pringle-Pattison, however, allows Augustine only a "technical victory" over his critics. Augustine regarded creation as a distinct past event in which God brought into existence that which had no prior reality in any sense. He thus fails, according to Pringle-Pattison, to relate creation in any actual sense to the nature of God. Pringle-Pattison argues that God did not first exist as God, and then as Creator of the world. He did not, therefore, become a Creator, but is from eternity the Creator-God. Thus, the world, though not eternal in itself, yet exists from eternity as an act of the eternal Creator-God.[48]

Martensen, too, asserts that from one viewpoint creation may be described as eternal. He explains: "So far as a cosmogony (a theory of the origin of the universe), and with the cosmogony the 'birth of time,' has its ground in a creative will, which is independent of all conditions of time, the creation may be described as eternal. But as far as the activity of the creating will is conditioned by the successive growth of the creature, the world may be said to have originated in time."[49]

Although such views have merit in emphasizing the utter dependence of the world upon God, they do not deal convincingly with the "time" problem. Augustine is charged with acosmism (denying the existence of the physical world) by making the "time concept" an unreality for God.[50] But Pringle-Pattison's and Martensen's idea of an eternal creation makes it an illusion. If in their statement of eternal creation they merely mean that creation is potential to God from eternity, then there is nothing very original in the declaration. But they apparently wish to say more than this, to assert that the creation was somehow eternally real. But if this were so, then it cannot be distinguished from God; yet to admit such a distinction is to introduce an eternal dualism and thus to compromise the Godness of God. And it is precisely any such idea that the phrase *creatio ex nihilo* was designed to exclude.

The World's Beginning

The time issue opens up the allied question of whether the world had a temporal beginning. Those who argue for creation as having some eternal actuality naturally express skepticism, or, at least, uneasiness, about the idea of a beginning of the world. James Ward, approaching the subject of creation from the two sides, its relation to the world and its relation to God, rejects the view that there was a "beginning" in finite time past. Looked at from the former angle, he contends that if the existing world is in fact a special production of God's creative act, then, it would exhibit the most direct and tangible evidence of His existence. We would, indeed, be virtually compelled to acknowledge the fact. But, he claims, experience does not give any such support to this reading of the universe.

On the other hand, if we approach the subject of creation from God's side, the world must be viewed as something deeply involved in the divine nature. To speak of God as Creator is simply to express the dependence of the world upon God. And this is equivalent to saying that God and the world are in some essential relation to each other. God is the Ground of the world's being, its *ratio essendi* (reason and basis for being).[51]

W. R. Matthews maintains that an absolute beginning of the world *in tempore*, or even *cum tempore* (in time or even with time), is irrelevant to the religious understanding of the idea of creation.[52] According to E. L. Mascall, the concept of creation is an abstraction, although it does, he stresses, stand for a fundamental truth. Mascall regards as altogether irrelevant to the idea of creation, the fact, if it is fact, that creatures have a beginning "in time." If a creature exists, it is created, he asserts, whether begun in time or not.[53]

Yet others strongly contend for a "beginning of the world" and seek to justify it on scientific grounds. The entropological argument based on the Second Law of Thermodynamics (which states that the amount of useful energy in the universe is decreasing) has been taken by some as proof that the world must have had a beginning in finite time past. Both George Gamow and William Pollard, as scientists and Christian theists, argue that the world must have had a *terminus ad quo* (point of beginning).[54,55] Sir Edmund Whittaker, from the side of astronomy, asserts, "this is only one of the ways in which recent researches have led to the conclusion that the universe cannot have existed from an infinite time in the past, at any rate under the operation of the laws of nature as we know them: there must have been a beginning of the present cosmic order, a creation as we call it, and we are even in a position to calculate approximately when it happened."[56] Whittaker maintains that this beginning may properly be called a "creation." And he can refer to it as a unique event, although he insists that as such it must lie completely outside the scope of scientific investigation.[57] For this last assertion M. K. Kuntz attacked him for perpetuating a "methodological error in indulging in an *ignorabimus* (intentional oversight) which is nothing short of dogma."[58] In spite of this castigation, however, undisputable scientific evidence indicates the world began as a created entity.

Something seems perverse in the current situation. At a time when there was no scientific evidence for a beginning of the world, theologians were asserting it as a sure fact. But now with some scientific indications, theologians apparently seek to deny to the world any temporal commencement. E. L. Mascall regards it as ironical "that, in the days when a man of science was sure to be a deist if he had any religion at all, there was no scientific evidence for the fundamental hypothesis of deism, the hypothesis that the world has not always existed; for in recent years a number of diverse arguments deriving from very divers considerations, have converged upon the conclusion that something which it is at any rate possible to interpret as the 'beginning of the world' took place at an epoch which can be given approximated date."[59]

The so-called "steady-state" theory of an expanding universe, which enjoyed some recent vogue, has been unable to sustain support. To say, as did Bondi, Gold, and Hoyle, that the material of the universe "simply appeared" did not prove enlightening. And it was more comical to maintain that, like Topsey, "it just grow'd"; even when assured by Hoyle, that the idea, while seeming "very strange," is no "queerer" than the view of creation as coming about as the result of one "big bang."[60] Hoyle later said that he no longer subscribed to the "steady-state" theory which he taught for twenty years. He proclaimed his belief in an "oscillating universe theory," the view that the universe is in a state of flux, alternatively expanding and contracting in cycles of billions of years. The debunking of the "steady-state" theory by one of its chief advocates alarmed many, who feared he was about to open the way for the reintroduction of God into cosmology. But Hoyle had no such idea: for the "big bang" view of the world's beginning is as much an anathema to him as ever.

But even though the "big bang" theory may be more congenial to a creationist doctrine, it does not for that reason necessarily demand the action of God. There is no reason, therefore, for the friends of religion to become excited when they hear that certain notable scientists give their name to a "big bang" understanding of the beginning of things. Nor is there any reason either for them to be impressed to learn that "matter" has become less crude. Some have expressed rather naive delight on hearing that the totality of matter is being whittled away by modern physics, as though materialism would be any less dangerous or any more acceptable if only matter were made decently thin. It does not make the slightest difference whether matter be conceived to be hard as diamond, as stiff as suet, as volatile as gas, as agile as electricity, or as naked as a mathematical formula. The only relevant question is whether it is preexistent or created by God. And in the end this is a question upon which natural science has no final word.

The idea that matter came into existence as a result of a "big bang" due to an explosion, or, as a series of "little pops," as a consequence of the self-creating nature of matter itself, gives no sufficient answer for the existence of the universe. The Christian theist does not admit as adequate the deistic account of the world's relation to God, whether as the result of a single unique action or an infinite number of actions. God is not just the God of the "big bang" or of the "little pops." The "big bang" and the "little pops" theories could be as consistent with atheism as with theism. The Christian asserts that the whole universe in the concreteness of its being, and the actuality of its existence, depends upon God and upon God alone.

Chapter 3

Creation in Contemporary Thought

Last chapter we saw that no matter how important the scientific indications for the world's beginning, many contemporary thinkers believe the question is religiously irrelevant.[1] They view *creatio ex nihilo* not as expressing an absolute temporal beginning of the world, but the world's "dependence-for-existence" upon God. A deistic view of God's relationship to the universe, which views Him as an absent Creator, fails to do justice to the whole structure of biblical theology. The Bible shows an intimate connection between the creation and God's revelatory and redemptive acts in human history. Therefore, it seems that the doctrine of creation is not just an insignificant part of the Hebrew religion. Gästa Lindeskog has observed that the personal experience of the Holy One fused with the faith that God is the Creator and Ruler of all. It is precisely this fusion of personal and ethical faith in the Holy One and the idea of a Creator-God which made Hebrew religion so revolutionary in the Near East.[2]

The Created World as the Theater of Divine Redemption

Modern theology emphasizes the close connection between God as Creator and the world as the sphere of His redemptive acts. Barth sees creation as "the first in the series of works of the Triune God."[3] He does admit that the world had a beginning, and that there was a time when nothing but God and His purposes existed.

Commenting on the first article of the *Apostles' Creed*, he declares, "When we come to the word 'Creator' in the credal statement the main point to be made is that it encloses an event, a completed act. The 'Creator' does not just 'exist.' He has done something: *creavit* (create); He has accomplished the *creatio* (creation)."[4] But Barth is not content to interpret the creation story as merely indicating that God's relationship with the universe is over. The first article, "is not some kind of 'outer court' theology or world-view."[5] It is bound up with God's purposes of redemption: the creation provided God with the platform for the operation of His grace. "Creation sets the stage for the story of the covenant of grace."[6] Only this view of creation, Barth maintains, gives it "credibility and practical import."[7]

Consistent with his overall thesis, Barth believes that any attempt to get scientific understanding of the beginning of the world is religiously harmful. He says that the doctrine of creation is not a "part of a *general science* that has got to be crowned and completed by Christian knowledge."[8] To seek a "ground" for faith is to destroy faith. The origin of the world as *creatio ex nihilo* is an "insight" of faith.[9]

Creation and Man

The idea of a creation of the world *ex nihilo* sometime in the past is less important for Bultmann. He wishes to keep God outside all such activity. Bultmann does not want to have God meddling over much in the world's affairs. After the fashion of Kierkegaard, he thus separates God from the world by an "infinite gap." He also adopts Kant's famous distinction between the objective and subjective realms to indicate his view of God's relation to the world in terms which deny God the position of First Cause. The world, he argues, is a continuum of cause-effect relationships; as such it cannot be conceived as having been "caused" by God. God stands outside the natural order;[10] to speak of Him as "creating," "acting," or "making" is to use the language of myth.[11] God, according to Bultmann, is not involved in natural and historical events.

Believing Heidegger has correctly analyzed human existence, Bultmann transposes statements about God "acting" to refer to man's determination to take charge of his own becoming in the light of God in the "here and now." Consequently, while the biblical doctrine witnesses to the divine transcendence, it mainly concerns man. It expresses man's utter dependence, his sense of creatureliness. "In the last analysis," says Bultmann, "the Old Testament doctrine of creation expresses a sense of the present situation of man. He is hedged in by the incomprehensible power of Almighty God. The real purpose of creation is to inculcate what God is doing all the time."[12] For Bultmann, "Belief in creation, therefore, expresses our faith in the radical qualitative difference between God and the objective world—but it is precisely this difference that makes possible our decision for faith, since faith is recognition that we too, in our inmost selfhood, can be free of the objective forces of the past and freely open up the future."[13]

John MacQuarrie is obviously indebted to Bultmann, as well as to Heidegger's philosophical construction, for providing him a framework within which he reinterprets the biblical faith. He regards the idea of God as an "undifferentiated self-contained Being" to be sub-Christian. *Being* is the *fons et origo* (source and origin) of all beings.[14] This means the Christian doctrine of creation is not to be considered an act of God "in the beginning." It may be legitimate to trace one being as creator of another being, or set of beings, when dealing with earthly beings. But it is false to refer the world as a whole to some cause outside itself.[15]

Since, then, according to MacQuarrie, God is *Being Itself* and not just *a* Being, the question of creation must be recast. No longer should one ask: How did the world begin? or Who made it? but rather, What does it mean to be a creature? and How does it affect our understanding of ourselves and the world to believe that we, and it, are creatures of God? MacQuarrie approaches the problem of creation, therefore, from the standpoint of man as a creaturely existent. He regards the phrase *ex nihilo* as expressing the utter difference between an act of creation, which gives rise to the world, and the familiar act of producing one thing from another within the world.[16]

Yet he believes both "models," that of "making" and that of "emanation," must be retained for a correct understanding of creation. While the first model does not quite express the notion of *creatio ex nihilo*, it does emphasize the *transcendence* of God. The emanationist model unites the world and God, giving the idea of *immanence*: the two insights must be combined. By his concept of Being, MacQuarrie contends that he is able to combine "its transcendence as the mysterious act of letting-be. But, unless it is suitably modified, it may entirely miss the idea of immanent presence. The image of emanation insists on the one hand that God does really put himself into the creation, so that the risk of creation really matters to him, and he is already involved in it and concerned with it."[17]

However, MacQuarrie generally seems to put greater stress on the emanationist model. For, is not "letting-be-ness" God's essential nature? It is indeed precisely because God the Father is primordial Being, the Ultimate "Letting-be," that the creeds designate Him the maker of heaven and earth. Yet the creation has its being through the Son as "Expressive Being": and the whole creation rises toward God through the Spirit as "unitive Being," who brings beings into a reconciling unity with Being, yet without destroying their diversity. This is a higher and fuller unity than would have been possible had Being remained in isolation, not risking creation.[18]

The Category of *Creatio Continua*

Donald Evans, while apparently submitting to Barth's judgment that God's creation is regarded in the Bible as, "the historical enactment of the covenant of grace," yet argues that this does not of itself prove a world-beginning. He believes that "most of the biblical history" could be retained if it were shown that the world was not created as the theater for the historical enactments of the covenant of grace. He concludes, "It would be unwise to claim that a scientific discovery of a world-beginning would be totally irrelevant to someone who has a biblical view of history; the idea of a cosmos which is bound up with mankind in a common history. Nevertheless, the idea of a world-beginning does not seem to be indispensable for a biblical view of history. World-creation need not be the first event in world history."[19] Yet Evans does allow the relation between world-beginning and world history to be "obviously important." He even uses Scripture passages to prove that "Biblical writers repeatedly describe Creation as an event which happened 'in the beginning' "; world history began with the decisive act of Creation.[20]

Evan's argument interweaves the idea of continuous creation which he has already contended does not mean a continuous change from nothing to something.[21] It is at this point that Karl Heim starts his reinterpretation of *creatio ex nihilo* in terms of *creatio continua* (continuous creation). Heim considers the idea of creation "out of nothing" as a continuous, literal and universal action. He says, "We may say with justice that the universe, as it now appears, is created each instance out of nothing, just as the first day of creation."[22] Planting himself on the concept of the divine omnipotence, of the type defended by Peter Damian and Duns Scotus, Heim asserts that we cannot be sure that anything now existing will be existing the next minute. Everything that is remains as mere possibility, totally dependent on God's will for its continued actuality. The future is "pure possibility," of the nothingness of pure possibility. Creation is, then, conceived of as a moment-by-moment *creatio ex nihilo*.[23]

Heim claims that his view harmonizes well with the theology of the Reformers. Long before Schleiermacher made the phrase *creatio continua* popular, both the Reformed and Lutheran theologians had spoken of God's continuous creation. These theologians, however, generally equated *creatio continua* with providence. "Thus," observes Berkouwer, "though Reformed theologians use the term continuous creation in order to emphasize the greatness and divinity of the work of sustaining, they, nevertheless, reject the idea in the sense of renewed acts of creation out of nothing."[24] In fact, the Reformed theologians used the phrase to make the strongest statement of God's all-persuasive power in maintaining the world's continuity. Their statements harmonized with the drift of the Heidleberg Catechism, which speaks of creation as an act of the "eternal Father of our Lord Jesus Christ, who out of nothing created heaven and earth with all that is in them, who also upholds and governs them by His eternal counsel and providence." While providence itself is defined as, "The almighty and ever-present power of God whereby He still upholds, as it were by His own hand, heaven and earth, together with all creatures."[25]

Creation and Process Theology

Today's "process theologians" have tried again to define creation as a continuous and necessary activity of God. Drawing heavily on the philosophy of A. N. Whitehead, as distilled by Charles Hartshorne, they see paradox in the idea of God existing alone before the world in self-sufficient and changeless perfection, and yet bringing a world into existence by an act of His own free will as the center of His concern, as though He needed it. They argue that these two ideas cannot be held together; in fact, they oppose each other.

One of Whitehead's main points was that creation is not an act of a divine will. To suppose it were, he argues would be to credit the Ultimate Being with free choice. Arbitrariness, he insists, can have no place in the divine creativity.[26] Thus Whitehead rejects the idea of a world-beginning; there was no creation *ex nihilo*.[27] In Whitehead's thought the category of "creativity" is fundamental. This "creativity" is the nature if what "is." Although Whitehead does not make clear the relationship between "creativity" and the theistic concept of God as Creator, his general idea seems to be "that creativity in his system is what prime matter is to Aristotle, namely, the material cause . . . the role of the Creator is to provide form for the reality given to Him. The Creator does not create reality as such."[28] However, it would be inaccurate to say that "creativity" *exists*. It is itself the ultimate form of all things. The nature of reality is "process," everlasting "creativity." All is spontaneous, undetermined and self-creative. Echoing Bergson, Whitehead declares that all is "becoming," all is "invention"; it is that or it is nothing.[29]

Hartshorne believes this view of creation retains the truth of the classical doctrine. "Our doctrine," he asserts, "brings down the exalted theological idea of 'creating' and makes it a universal feature of reality as such. There can be no reality which is simply 'made' to be what it is by some power other than itself."[30]

A definition of the "process" view is given by Teilhard de Chardin. He weds Whitehead's basic evolutionism and creativity with a biblical theism. Teilhard quietly sets aside the idea of a special creation and sees it as a "process," with the ultimate perfection of all things assured by the Atonement. The orthodox theologian, Paul Evdokimov, while expressing his own view, gives a fairly accurate statement of Teilhard's thesis. He writes, "Creation in the biblical sense is like a grain of wheat which brings forth a hundredfold and never stops developing: 'My Father works until now, and I work also.' Creation is the Alpha moving towards the Omega, and indeed the Omega is already contained within it."[31]

In this context of *Le Milieu Divin*, we are faced with the question of ultimate reality. Teilhard then sets forth what he regards as the final logic of the meaning of existence. "At the heart of our universe, each exists for God, in our Lord. But all reality, even material reality, around each one of us exists for our souls. Hence, all sensible reality, around each one of us, exists, through our souls, for God, in our Lord."[32] It is not ultimately the rigid order of matter nor its large numbers, but the subtle combination of the spirit that gives the universe its consistency. Therefore, to be occupied with the world is not to lose God; it is, in a profound sense, to find Him. To be preoccupied with the world as the ultimate value is another matter. It is to miss God. It is "by virtue of the Creation, and still more, of the Incarnation, *nothing* here below is *profane* for those who know how to see."[33] The Christian believes reality will not dissolve into dreams. It will retain its concrete actuality, as firm and fixed as before; but it will be seen in its relation to God, just as God will be seen in relation to it. God is the Heart and Hub of the universe. While the message of Christianity is that God visited His universe, its background is the mystery that God can be seen in His universe. The Divine which comes to earth we know in Epiphany, the Divine which we see in the earth we call Diaphany. In this convincing activity of Divine Creativity, Teilhard contends that we find "the divinization of our activities."

These references to what today's thinkers claim about God's creative relationship to the world help us formulate at least three biblical facts about the world's existence. The first is that God is the decisive "cause" of all things. The second is that the beginning of all things was a creative act of God. The third is that Christ is the central factor and focus of all creation.

God: the Decisive Cause of All That Is

By declaring that creation is *ex nihilo*, the Church has disowned both ultimate monism and dualism. The world was neither made out of "something" nor is it part of God. "When we say that God created the world out of nothing, we are not asserting a process which we can comprehend or imagine, but declaring that God is the Source and Ground of all that is."[34] Everything depends on Him for its coming to be, and its continuing to be. "All that is not God depends for its existence upon God—this is the fundamental thought in the doctrine of creation."[35]

When the Old Testament writers spoke of creation and the Creator, they did not mean a mechanical "making" of the world. God was not perceived as a watchmaker who constructed a watch from existing materials. His creative power was not defined in terms of causality but in terms of sovereignty. He stood as master over the whole created order. "God, according to the Old Testament, not only made the world out of nothing, but remains personally the force that constitutes it and is the sovereign over it. His relationship to everything in it is one of direct and immediate mastery; everything is wholly dependent on Him."[36]

Ironically, however, some have sought to interpret the "nothing" in the declaration *creatio ex nihilo* as a sort of substance out of which the world was "made" by God. "Nothing" has been viewed as possessing a reality of its own, almost like the prime substance of Aristotle. From "nothing" God created the things which are; from "non-being" came forth "being." It is, of course, difficult for us not to think of a static non-being as the material of creation.[37] Gilson remarks, "Nothing is easier than to repeat that God has created things and created them *ex nihilo* but how can we prevent ourselves imagining, even while we deny it, that this 'nothing' is a kind matter from which the creative act draws its effects?"[38] But we have to insist that it is the existence of any substance prior to creation which the phrase *ex nihilo* rules out.[39] The Genesis account declares that the world and everything in it was brought into existence solely by the spoken commands of God. There is no suggestion that God took either a great big piece of "nothing," or little pieces of "nothing" and made them into somethings.

Does this mean that the idea of a creation "out of nothing" cannot be understood? Must we admit that the idea that only God existed at one time is really a leap of irrational faith? Must we assume with Professor Miles that the concept has no "cash-value," and that "we do not know what sort of occurrences would count as 'creation of God' "?[40]

Miles' conclusion is not inevitable. According to Professor Bertocci, an analogy of the idea of *creatio ex nihilo* can be drawn from an analysis of human free will. No matter how much conditioning and relatedness is involved in a choice, there is still the central reality of "creative change." This is best seen in character forming. At particular "choice-points" some new character traits, new directions or formulation, take place. These are really new departures; they are not mechanical changes from rearrangements of existing parts, nor are they evolved from present potential. They are creative choices of the human will which are not produced from anything which previously exists. In this context, Bertocci declares that the doctrine of *creatio ex nihilo* is, therefore, "not at odds with human experience, and especially that of forming character."[41] He allows that there are "differences of detail beyond human imagination and conception" in the case of creation, but Bertocci still insists that the creative act of God is not essentially different from the creative act of human choice. Free choices add new qualities and dimensions to personality. It is not a case of making something "out of" nothing. The old dictum remains true, *ex nihil nihil fit* (from nothing nothing is made). In both the case of God and man, the "agent" is present before the willed creative act. Bertocci says,

"Creation is a kind of change produced by a kind of being who pre-exists his creative act and is co-existent with his creative act, that is, maintaining his own identity as well as sustaining the creative process toward its goal, and to its goal when he is successful."[42]

Creation as an Act of God

To say that creation is an "act" of God implies that the language of the creation story is literal. The question is, "Can it be so used to convey any meaningful sense?" Many people today believe that a literal creative act of God is not simply false, but meaningless. But what is the structure of creation terminology? Paul Tillich says that it is to be regarded as *myth*. Braithwaite states that it is a *story*. But the idea that it is a *parable* seems to have the majority vote.[43] If we agree that it is simply parabolic, there is still the question of whether any actuality attaches to the concept. T. R. Miles is sure there is none: Donald Evans allows there is some sense of actuality indicated by the concept.

Miles calls creation-language a "theistic-parable," having no objective validity in any literal sense. He sets down three criteria which he believes reveal the parabolic nature of the creation story. First, he contends that whether it is literally true or false is not important. Second, he says that there are always actual things associated with the story, which clearly indicate whether it is a parable or not. Third, Miles holds that the most important consideration is that "as a parable" the concept of creation conveys an important message.[44] Giving "parable" an abnormal meaning, he thinks that the three criteria make void any notion of a literal creation.[45]

But if Miles' idea were accepted, the significance of theological discussion would be reduced to the mere projection of one individual's sense of value; it would make God-talk no more than a psychological process, an expression of the believer's own faith-attitude. That is not what the Christian theist intends when he declares that God created the world.

Donald Evans refuses to be pushed to Miles' conclusion, but he does agree that the language of creation is "parabolic." He makes the point that religious language has the character of self-involvement. Thus, the biblical story of creation is colored by Israel's experience of redemption.[46] At the same time he declares, "All biblical language concerning God as Creator is parabolic."[47] Causal language is applied to creation, which he maintains is "obviously parabolic."[48] For examples he refers to the figures of the potter[49] and the victor.[50] Is there no "core" of the divine action which can be properly called a creation in any literal sense? Evans does not think so. He argues rather that the facts must not be minimized, that there is a "reality" of God's creative action.[51] "The *reality* of God, or of God's action," he writes, "is not being denied; but what is *meant* by 'God the Creator' cannot be abstracted from human attitudes. Instead, if 'reality' is not merely a question of sheer existence but of *importance* to men, then surely the 'reality' of God is being strenuously affirmed by anyone who expresses the various parabolic outlooks concerning God the Creator."[52]

Any biblical concept of creation must acknowledge that God actually created. No matter how the language of the creation story is understood in terms of self-involvement, it is more than a statement about human attitudes. D. M. MacKinnon properly says that "to believe in Creation is to see the world in a certain way."[53] But that statement is only part of the truth about the statement "God created the world." In his dialogue with MacKinnon, Antony Flew correctly argues that any doctrine of creation worthy of the name regards God as "acting" to bring about the world. It is not enough to declare that by believing in creation the believer is merely giving a picture or a parable of his religious perspective on life. The question is: Is the statement that God created the world a factual statement of the world's beginning?

That is what we seek to establish; we want to say that the world has its beginning and its being, actually and literally, as a result of God's creative action. Even if we admit with MacKinnon that in stating that God "created" or "made" the world, we are using a familiar term to refer to what lies outside our experience, we do not consider them as empty terms when we talk about God's relation to the world. It may be just as G. S. Hendry contends, that our understanding of God must be distinguished from the ordinary processes of acquiring knowledge; for the Christian thinker does not so much know as acknowledge truth.[54] But at the same time we must maintain that creation can only be acknowledged if it is a fact. Let its language be described as mythical, parabolic, or perhaps more realistically, as poetic, it is nonetheless a mythical, parabolic, or poetic account of something which *actually* took place. Speaking of the world's existence as an act of God is not just adopting a theistic parable which forces us to take up a religious attitude toward the Ultimate Reality. By it we express the conviction that the whole universe was created by the willed act of God.

Christ the Center of Creation

The issue is then the basis upon which belief in creation as a divine act can be justified. Is it within a cosmological or a Christological context? Some believe God created the universe as a result of contemplating nature. Ancient and modern Thomists, who rely on the principle of analogy, base their faith in God as Creator on what they see in the natural order. Writers of this school begin with the cosmos and build up arguments for a Divine Cause and Origin of the universe by means of the theistic proofs.[55]

On the other side are those whose approach is Christological. Brunner, by linking the two views, has a foot in both camps. Brunner rejects Barth's complete repudiation of natural theology. He affirms a limited knowledge of God to be gained from His creation. "In the material world," he declares, "there is a mathematical order which bears witness to the thought of the Creator."[56] However, Christian faith arises mainly in the revelation of God in Jesus Christ."[57] It seems then that Brunner blends the cosmological and Christological approaches; or perhaps he sees cosmological through the eyes of the Christological.

But some take their stand exclusively on Christological grounds. Gästa Lindeskog declares, "If Christ is the center of the New Testament, the theology of Creation which was of such importance to the Old, must be interpreted Christologically."[58] Many who argue from this perspective contend that even Israel based her conception of the world-Creator on her deliverance at the Exodus. Barth inevitably takes a full Christological stance. "The fact that God has regard to His Son—the Son of Man, the Word made flesh—is the true and genuine basis of creation," he asserts.[59] The only reason for the world's creation was God's free love. This was "a genuine necessity . . . constituted by the fact from all eternity . . . [that He] willed to love the world, and did love it, that He gave His only begotten Son (John 3:16)."[60] The aim of creation is history, argues Barth. History is the arena in which the Triune God reveals Himself. Thus, "God wills and God creates the creature for the sake of His Son or Word and therefore in harmony with Himself, and for His own supreme glory and therefore in the Holy Spirit."[61] As Barth conceives it, "It is the awareness of *God* in Christ which finally sets men free to say that in Jesus Christ they have encountered the Creator of the world."[62]

W. A. Whitehorne suggests there may be obstacles for the modern mind which hamper full and free acceptance of the cosmic role of Christ. But the positive question is: "What is it that moves the believer to worship Christ as agent of the creation?"[63] Worship of Christ is ultimately prompted by the recognition that the sufferings of Christ show that the creative processes everywhere move by divine love. "It is unlikely that we shall enjoy a renewed faith in the Christo-centric doctrine of creation until the Holy Spirit moves men to a more distinguished practical response and gratitude and obedience in the ordinary business of living."[64]

This Christo-centered perspective of God's creation gives the Christian believer an elevated view of God's relationship toward the world. By centering creation in Christ we know that no matter how much evil influences it, it has not been wrenched out of God's control and care. The anchorage which faith finds in the reality of a Christ-centered universe is this: since He is the prototype of all creation, we do not live in a God-abandoned world. God is neither dead, done, nor gone. This reality gives meaning to all creation. It is in and through Him that all the potential of existence was made real.

Karl Rahner, using Aristotelian categories of thought affirms, "Christ has always been involved in the whole of history as its prospective entelechy."[65] In other words, Christ is prefigured in all history and in all creation. Christ the Word is the inner reason and purpose of all things, the reality of all that is. Thus, the universe is generally "good" because it is the product of God's commands in and through the Word. Mankind in particular is "very good" because it is made in the image of Jesus' own sonship. The whole system participating in God is still God's, because He has given it the gift of existence and bestowed something of His own goodness upon it. Thus, whenever a creature is concerned with the mere satisfaction of itself, conceiving of itself as existing by and for itself, it is falling away from God and is bent on its own destruction. But when the creature is unconcerned about its own existence, seeking to find itself in love through the creative love of God, then it is fulfilling the purpose of its creation and the high potential which God has bestowed upon it in Christ.

Augustine recalls being "kindled" with a "great ardour" in his early passion for wisdom by reading Cicero's *Hortensius*. He was to learn later that its only drawback was that "the Name of Christ was not there."[66] The Christian asserts that this Name is the key to the question of the existence of man and the world. The ultimate reason for everything is here. It is the only theological view which gives the existence of the world importance, and only the Christological view gives life its significance. In a very real and intimate sense this is God's world. It is other than God; yet it is of God and for God. Apart from God the world is nothing. God acts in and for His Son. Thus, the Incarnation as the "Word made flesh" stands as reminder that the world is not independent of God, not something alien in which He has no interest. "All things came to be (*egeneto*) through (*dia*) Him and apart from Him not even one thing (*oude en*) was made that has been made (*gegonen*)."[67] Christ, the everlasting Son of the Father, is the reason for and the goal of all that is. "For it was by Him that all things were created both in heaven and on earth . . . and He is prior to all, and all cohere in Him."[68]

The idea of God as the Creator in and through Christ is, therefore, the first and the last word for Christian faith. If its reality were left out, we would have an incoherent view of the universe. The fact that this is a God-created universe gives us hope for its renewal in righteousness as a new heaven and earth; while, at the same time, as P. T. Forsyth remarks, "The final key to the first creation is the second."[69] In the final analysis, a true view of the world comes from seeing it as God's world, while to have a right understanding of God is to know Him as world-Creator through Christ. Therefore, Aquinas is right when he says, "they plainly hold a false opinion who say that in regard to the truth of religion it does not matter what a man thinks about Creation so long as he has a correct opinion concerning God."[70] It follows that *error circa creaturas redundat in falsam de Deo sententiam* (an error concerning the Creation is false thinking about God).

Chapter 4

Providence

The doctrine of providence has fallen on hard times. Contemporary ideas oppose the confession that human destiny is divinely ordered. Modern life seems to render the notion of a God who controls and cares incomprehensible. The meaninglessness of life, the purposelessness of history, and the recklessness of nature, it is felt, speak against the affirmation that a Divine Being sovereignly rules the cosmos. Modern life and literature have united to make inhospitable the concept of providence for those without belief in a God-governed universe; while the thought and theme of God's rule over all has been blurred in the faith and message of the Church.

Contemporary Neglect of the Doctrine of Providence

G. C. Berkouwer speaks of the crisis of the providence doctrine in our century, and asserts that "the confession of God's Providence has become, now more than ever, a stone of stumbling."[1] Langdon B. Gilkey, reviewing the place given the doctrine in contemporary theology, asks, "Why has Providence in our generation been left a rootless, disembodied ghost, flitting from footnote to footnote, but rarely finding secure lodgement in sustained theological discourse?"[2]

Theology has too often allowed itself to be conditioned and colored by the contemporary outlook and has taken its cue from what prevailing opinion allows it to say. Thus the doctrine of providence has become evacuated of real significance in order to make it palatable to the modern mind. Nature and man are given credit for what the Christian confessions and theologies of an earlier day brought under the immediate action of God. The concept of secondary causes and the autonomy of man are invoked so as to remove the active God from the scene. Thus, men give God little to do, and they make the idea of providence merely a vague and general concern of God for His world. But a God who does nothing or only a very little is certainly not the God of the Christian faith; indeed, He is not even a pale facsimile of the Christian God. Modern man has lost the sense of God; with this loss, the awareness of His ordering of life's ways has disappeared.

Earlier Christian Faith in Providence

Without exception, the great teachers of the early Church firmly believed that God is active in His world; and this conviction was given the strongest statement by Augustine.[3] Throughout the Middle Ages, faith in God's providential ordering was undimmed, although more scope was given to man's freedom. Aquinas had certainty in God's overruling of all life's events.[4]

Reformation theology, too, held a robust doctrine of providence. Luther personally experienced the upholding and governing of God. He knew himself to be "spared, sustained and led" in a special and spectacular way. True, Luther made no claim to be able to explain to all what belonged to the *Deus absconditus* (concealed God): he had not eavesdropped on the Council Chamber of God. Calvin speaks of God's overruling as a "most useful doctrine."[5] He is emphatic that God controls all events, not only in the world, but also in the lives of every individual, and in the perverse no less than in the elect. With Augustine, Calvin was sure that "for the things which God rightly wills, he accomplishes by the evil wills of bad men," as well as by the good. Calvin declares that "providence extends no less to the hand than to the eye!" A footnote states that the French edition added the clarifying remark: "*C'est a dire, que non seulement il voit, mais aussi ordonne ce qu'il veut être fait.*" (He not only sees, but ordains what he wills to be be done.) Calvin, as Luther, does not claim to be able to simplify the doctrine of providence. Such a truth belongs to, what he calls, "the secret counsel of God." But the conclusion, he boldly affirms, cannot be avoided that "God wills the sin he also punishes, the suffering he also deplores, and even the damnation from which he seeks to save us."[6]

The Puritan writer, John Flavel, writing in 1678 speaks of "the duty of the people of God to meditate upon the performances of

Providence for them, at all times, but especially in times of difficulty and trouble."[7] Due observation to providence, he assures his readers, will overpower and suppress the "natural atheism" of the human heart.[8]

Modern man, however, does not approach reality with the same conviction that a divinely ordained purpose can be read from life's experiences. And with a "God" barely conceived as personal, the idea of a Divine overruling means little for much contemporary theology. The current agnosticism of society has afflicted Christian thinking; and Christian thinking seems to give a religious flavor to the "natural atheism" of the natural man. Without a living God to observe in providential activity, the Church has no answer of faith for contemporary man, who believes that this is a God-empty universe.

Weakening of Faith in Providence

Early faith in providence rested squarely upon the acceptance of God's special revelation; it was, that is to say, essentially biblical. But the rise of Darwinism in the mid-nineteenth century promoted radical reinterpretation of the doctrine; and more disconcertingly, faith in particular providential acts of God was lost. Darwin had assured his generation that there was no need to appeal to a God outside the natural order to explain the origin and presence of existing organisms. A large spectrum of contemporary theology was ready to adapt to this view. The question was posed: If the universe was not constructed according to a divine purpose, might it be moving toward ultimate perfection? Some theologians accepted this idea. By regarding purpose as the goal, rather than a plan that was followed, theologians presented the idea of providence as the ongoing movement of history, and they explained the Kingdom of God in terms of social progress, which they optimistically forecasted would be fulfilled in the near future. Confidence in the certainty of unhindered progress consequently became unrestrained, and the notion of a "genial providence" found widespread acceptance.

Inevitably in such a treatment, the problem of evil earned scant attention. In fact, evil virtually did not exist for those who lived cozy lives in country mansions attended by poorly paid servants, who followed them every Sunday morning to church to sing lustily, and sometimes lustfully:

The rich man in his castle,
The poor man at his gate.
God made them high and lowly,
And ordered their estate.

The thought may have comforted them, but it made nonsense of biblical faith. For contentment with what we have is not the same as contentment with what things are.

The attitude toward encountered evil was gay and buoyant. Evil was present like rugger and cricket, to train a gentleman. In the spirit of a true sportsman, even in this conflict he was expected to play the game. Above all, he must not be called "out." Gilkey has drawn attention to F. R. Tennant's confident assurance about the presence of evil. He regarded it, as was typical of his time, as necessary to moral health as a cold bath or vigorous exercise was to the bodily health of an Edwardian gentleman.[9]

All this buoyancy was soon to be sunk, however. It floated while the optimists of the time still daydreamed of social progress leading to utopia. For in the end, as Berkouwer observes, the concept "of a genial Providence is only a transfigured remnant of the doctrine of universal Providence."[10]

But as the moral dykes of history burst from the tragedy of two world wars, the dream became a nightmare; both God and man appeared to be swept away in the full flood. The notion of unhindered progress and the hoped-for ultimate realization of the brotherhood of man under the universal Fatherhood of God collapsed. The "intemperate optimism," as John Baillie designates it, of the earlier period, with its "Utopian illusions about the promise of the future" is "now taking its revenge upon us."[11] The upsurge of incredible and incalculable evils have made a mockery of that earlier gentlemanly optimism. In its place have come despair, chaos and nihilism. Certain modern poets have vied with certain modern philosophers in proclaiming the "tragedy," the "nothingness," the "meaninglessness," and the "absurdity" of life. Among the latter are the non-theistic existentialists who have been foremost in emphasizing the "emptiness" of existence. Sartre, for example, assures his audience, "There's no argument; I tell you, God is dead." And one after another, his character heroes, Mathieu and Orests, for example, move within a philosophic framework of unrelieved chaos.[12] Gabriel Jaspers, likewise, expresses the same tragic grimness and blames the poets of Christianity for failing to make acceptable the devastating finality of the absurd. They have included it "within the plan of Providence and the operations of Grace," and in this way have immunized men from "the vast nothingness of self-destruction in the world."[13]

We are called upon from many quarters to accept as the ultimate truth that life has no significance and history, no purpose. In such a situation the idea of providence has become quite meaningless. Man, as Christopher Fry contends, provides his own providence. He must adjust himself to his fate as best he can, and with grim heroics accept the absurdity of death. For is not "Human existence" after all, "being-for-the-purpose of dying."[14] Above all, man must rid himself of the "beautiful illusion" that there is a Creator of the world, a kind providence, and a life hereafter.[15]

A Criticism of Faith in Providence

H. J. Paton specifically criticizes what he considers the blandly cheerful tone of devotional writing on the subject of providence. He rebukes not only one of Cowper's hymns, in which he expresses faith in the sustaining providing care of God, but also the Psalms. Paton regards the Psalmist as either very lucky or very blind when he asserted that, although he was young and is now old, he has never seen the righteous forsaken or his seed begging bread. Paton pronounces such facile optimism a survival of primitive savage notions. It used to be the fashion, he allows, to speak of a special providence, and such a belief has been a comfort to "simple souls" who, Paton says, have never entered deeply into the religious life. The ideas of providence, Paton concludes, has no meaning, for the reason that there are no particular acts of God. The concept of a special care of God is merely another way of speaking of happenings, which we regard as advantageous to ourselves; to think otherwise, it is added, is not religion but superstition.[16] Paton's repudiation of the meaning and relevance of the doctrine of providence is, however, unjust to the deeply religious insight of these "simple souls." For it is precisely they who often have the acutest awareness of the real issues for faith. They move in the arena of life's actualities, and are keenly alive to its lures and lashes. There may be some theological problems which the "layman" may leave trustingly in the hands of the theological expert, but providence is not, as Brunner says, one of them.[17] The questions raised by faith in God's governing, guarding and guiding power and grace arise out of life as it is lived. And the "simple soul" who has been spared, sustained and led, cannot as Hazelton notes, doubt God's control and care.[18] Such a faith does not consider what is merely advantageous. Faith in God's providence, as Aulén stresses, has little in common with a eudaemonistic attitude which seeks to make God man's servant. It is the very theocentric character of faith which calls for the radical removal of all such eudaemonisms in the relation between God and man.[19]

The down-to-earth believer in divine providence is not insensitive to the turns and twists which come with soft feet, or to the sharp and stunning happenings which appear with threatening and frightening face. But he takes "the chances and accidents of history," writes Pollard, to be "the very warp and woof of the fabric of providence which God is ever weaving."[20] When the "simple soul" prays, "Give us this day our daily bread, and forgive us our trespasses," he unites the natural world with the moral and spiritual. He knows God is actively in charge of both. The prayer would be meaningless unless faith has the assurance that God wills and works in His total universe. For, "Prayer honours Providence," says Flavel, "and Providence honours prayer."[21]

Faith in God's Providence not Easy

Neither Flavel, in the seventeenth century, nor Hazelton, in the twentieth, allows his readers to conclude that belief in providence is easy to grasp or to maintain. The providences of God, says Flavel, "often puzzle and entangle our thoughts."[22] And Hazelton, while affirming, "The only cure for both moral ambiguity and emotional anxiety is faith in God as the Christian doctrine of Providence expresses it,"[23] is still compelled to acknowlege, "Belief in Providence may actually be harder for Christians than for non-Christians."[24] The latter may expect little from God; but to hold on to God when He is apparently absent or totally silent demands more from the understanding of faith.

Such an assured faith in God's continued rule and right stands far above the shallow optimism so often mistaken for providence by superior souls. These tough-minded persons of today prefer to detail their estrangement or debate about their despair. On the other side, the believer, the tender-hearted, is sure that life is not a haphazard affair. God is there—and here; for "in all providences, especially in some, He comes near to us."[25] Thus, the idea of Divine Providence is "also the absolute denial of the idea that the universe has no meaning," says Brunner, "that things only happen 'by accident.' "[26] Even if the conception of providence expressed in the "jazzed-up lyrics" of the modern chorus book seems crude and curious, the lyrics nevertheless declare that God has not abandoned His world. To sing, "He's got the whole world in His hand," is to voice a profound truth; for providence is, after all, "more a theme of faith than a doctrine," according to Clarke, "and faith may be much clearer than the doctrine."[27]

Fate and Providence

If we discount belief in God's special sovereign acts as so much wishful thinking, we misunderstand the drift of biblical theism, and we misread the requirements of a full-blooded faith. The only possible alternative to the Christian doctrine of providence is the naturalistic conception of life. The Stoic, like the Platonist, in earlier days, had no idea of a special interest of God in His world. He was aware of only a general providence, an impersonal world-reason lying unmoved and immoveable behind the causally determined, all-inclusive totality. For many moderns "fate is a powerful contemporary substitute for the providence of God."[28] Many read human destiny in terms of the finality and finitude and ultimacy of the tragic. The pagan of a bygone era saw Fate as, in some sense, the handmaid, if not the servant, of the highest of the gods. But now, with God dead, or at any rate, absent, Fate has taken the throne of the universe.

"Fate is offered to us as the only possible substitute for God—possible, that is, to anyone who knows what the world is about—and is recommended to fill the vacuum which God has left behind him."[29] The new paganism has deified Fate.

But the question is: Does the substitute satisfy the longings of an awakened spirit and hold up before the probings of an understanding mind? The fact is that Fate cannot permit any questioning of its working. It meets every attempt with a blank negative: there is no reason at all because all is without reason. Hazelton points out that fatalism cannot entertain the possibility of any "why?" One is spared in the midst of some calamity—but why? One is sustained in the midst of tragedy—but why? One is led safely through dangerous paths—but why? Fate has no answer, because life has no meaning. Thus is "fate a sort of providence-in-reverse, which is to say a malevolent, teasing parody of God's guiding, guarding, governing power."[30] But the man of faith views life in other ways. He does not, if he is an understanding believer, talk glibly of the "will of God," as if it were but a more religious way of speaking about fate. He knows himself, not as a cog in the chariot wheel of Zeus and a prisoner in an impersonal system. We do not say "Providence" by saying "Fate" in falsely spiritual tones.

For the Christian, Brunner writes, Providence "is only another name for the fact that God looks at me, and never ceases to look at me, at the same time with His glance embraces the whole, and unites His will for me with His will for the world."[31] Even a vague belief in a general purpose will give little comfort to the single individual. "Religion," says C.C.J. Webb, "cannot remain content with a mere *general* Providence which *cannot* be verified in the individual. The saying that "the hairs of your head are all numbered" expresses an essential characteristic of religious faith."[32] Fate rebuffs every attempt to get behind the experiences of life to seek some ultimate reason with a "Road Closed" notice. But the believer in God as Ultimate Relief and Final Demand knows it is not so; for him "What began as a negation therefore issues in a powerful affirmation," according to Hazelton. "Even though God's way were not known, his path was in the great waters. For it is Providence that says 'yes' to us through the implacable 'no' of would-be Fate; and this is not our 'yes' but God's, who guides and guards and governs everything—yes everything—for good."[33]

A Theme with Variations

Providence is, then, "a theme with variations": and anyone who would deal adequately with, as a justification of his faith in a God-ordained and God-ordered universe, faces big questions. He must, for example, reconcile, if he can, his belief in God's all-inclusive providence with his feeling of autonomy. Such a discussion, however, can become a theological parlor-game. This pitfall can be avoided if the discussion is limited to living experience. It is tempting, to be sure, to accept the easy solution of a divine determinism. But in this way one merely substitutes "God" for "Fate" in the interests of religion, in opposition to the popular paganism which substitutes "Fate" for "God".

Yet no view of providence can be admitted which denies the absolute sovereignty of God or the relative freedom of man. No understanding of providence is true which conceives of it in a mechanical sort of way. God's providential control of the world does not cancel man's freedom. It is, in fact, this very autonomy which is necessary for man's moral responsibility. Here compulsion is out of the question. Sovereignty and predestination do not annul the freedom of man which makes him a responsible being before God.

On the other hand, God does not surrender the destiny of the universe to His creatures. Actually, He controls through means which permit man's freedom. And our moral nature affirms our freedom. At the same time, a God who is not fully in control of His world does not meet the demands of faith. Consequently, while our nature assures our freedom, our faith requires a sovereign God. Both must remain. The final question, then, for any adequate doctrine of divine providence resolves itself into this: How can God's providence be regarded as the fulfillment of a divine plan?

This is a subject which, according to John Wright, fewer theologians than formerly discuss.[34] Yet it is an unavoidable question. The ready answer of both the Bannezian or classical Thomist school on the one side, or the Molinist, on the other side, does not convince. The former, regarding God's plan as eternally preestablished, conceive of man's freedom as "directed" infallibly to its fulfillment. The Molinists, grounding God's actions on His unerring foreknowledge, seek to allow for the free determination of His creatures in the extablishing of His eternal purpose. Neither solution, however, finally satisfies; for both make God's relation to the world static, clearly at variance with what divine revelation and experience reveal as His unfettered dealings with men. Both seek to answer the question: is knowlege by God of the free future acts of His creatures prior to His divine decree? The Bannezians answer, "No"; the Molinists answer, "Yes." But in both cases it is supposed that a necessary condition for the direction of Divine Providence is that God should know the "free futurities" of His creatures. But this may not be at all an essential prerequisite.

Divine Providence and Human Freedom

Both Scripture and experience teach us many paradoxes about God's ways with His people. It is basic truth that this is God's world in which He can freely act. God is not bound by some form of necessity. He is, as Moltmann describes, a God "whose freedom is the source of new things to come."[35] And human history is the theater of His activity. Those who experience being spared, sustained, and led by God have the assurance, too, that they have been spared for a good purpose, been sustained by a sure hand, and been led in the right way. A score of biblical passages attest that God is sovereign, and that His Word will accomplish His purpose and prosper in the thing for which He sends it.[36] At the same time, both Scripture and experience show abundant evidence that in some measure His plan is contingent upon man's response. Clear proofs exist for what Wright calls, "the *frustration* of God in the face of the 'free resistance' of man."[37]

Some things God desired of His people never came; hopes entertained were not fulfilled. Yet, throughout, God's sovereignty is not lessened or weakened. For one is aware of God's providential readjustments, of what Wright speaks of as the "divine adaptability" which characterizes His dealings with men. God clearly shows Himself ready to do some new thing, to make again another appropriate vessel to replace the marred one. God is, therefore, in His providential activity "an Almighty improviser." We must not, then, conceive of God's providence in any static sense. "The divine plan," says Maritain, "is not a scenario prepared in advance, in which free subjects would play parts and act as performers. We must purge out thoughts of any idea of a play written in advance, at a time prior to time—a play in which time unfolds, and the characters of time read the parts. On the contrary, everything is improvised, under the eternal and immutable direction of the Almighty Stage Manager."[38]

This does not mean God has placed himself at the mercy of man's caprice. For God has an overall plan for the good of His world, a plan to end all evil and establish an eternal order of righteousness. And that plan He will effect by the present overruling of all that every man decides to do. In this context, "His knowledge of events is," as Pontifex says, "always simultaneous with the events themselves."[39] Here we have the adaptability of God, "Hence, no matter what the free determination of the creatures may be," explains Wright, "God has antecedently determined what will be its result, how it will fit into the building up of the heavenly Jerusalem."[40] But this does not allow the conclusion that He has predetermined the free responses of man. For a "divine knowledge of individual conditioned free futures is not required in order to establish an acceptable doctrine of providence."[41] What is required, and what we know to be true, is that God can and does meet every contingency, even those brought about by man's free determination, so that they all promote His ultimate purpose; His ultimate purpose includes what is best for His people in their present as well as in their final destiny.

Along this line we can read one of the most significant demonstrations of God's providential overrulings in the Old Testament. The brethren of Joseph sold him into Egypt: they meant it for evil, but God meant it for his good. Their act was overruled by God to bless Joseph and to benefit many.[42] God has, therefore, the seemingly mysterious power of guiding free beings without negating their freedom. The freedom of man is accompanied by a higher sovereignty of God over men's spirits. God is greater than we think, and the mystery of providence is found in that greatness. We may be rightly suspicious, as George Santayana was, of those who proclaim that they have the key of all reality in their pockets. Those little gnostics, those circumnavigators of being, need to be told that we do not believe them.[43] "The *gloria* of God consists," says Barth, "in the fact that He is so powerful in relations to the creature; that He asserts Himself so thoroughly."[44]

Divine Providence and Human Suffering and Sin

Any doctrine of providence must face the problem of a theodicy; the problem, that is, of reconciling the thought of the love and righteousness of God with the apparent contradictory mass of evidence of human suffering and sin. We will discuss these issues later. Meanwhile, we must assume that this "shadow side" of creation, as Barth calls it, cannot be rationalized away, as does Leibniz by his statement that "this is the best of all possible worlds"; or rhymed away, as does Browning by saying, "God's in His heaven, All's right with the world."

The question must be asked: how can we justify God's providential rule in view of the evil, both natural and moral, in the world? There are, broadly, two historic answers to this question. The first, which we may designate the Deistic-Arminian view, is that God has left nature and men free of His continuous interference to fulfill or to falsify their destiny. The second, which we may call the Fideistic-Revelatory view, is that God's providential activity is guaranteed to His elect only; the sinful world being abandoned to a just condemnation.

The Deistic-Arminian View of Providence

Advocates of this idea contend for a certain loose-play within world events and in human life so as to exempt God from responsibility for evil. With this position they believe they are loyal to predominant scientific thought, on the one hand, and to the fundamental requirements of morality on the other.

The scientific climate today has focused for every man the concept of natural events. Contemporary thought characteristically gives these natural events credit for catastrophies in the natural order. The success of the empirical sciences has given the general impression that the universe is to be conceived as a great interlocking system of cause-effect relationships. Thus, any natural event can be linked to its preceding cause; no outside force needs to be considered. Thus, what was once referred to God is, for modern man, referred to "Nature." And within nature the complete explanation must be sought. Material upheavals in the natural order, which were formerly believingly attributed to the "will of God," are now traced to a convergence of causes within the system of things.

Many contemporary theologians have adopted this scientific view. They are satisfied to leave particular events to the action of natural causes, while still contending that God must be allowed responsibility for the general ordering of affairs. In this exposition of providence, God is certainly relieved of direct responsibility for evil, but at the cost of separating Him from the world and human life. Such a deistic view, while suiting the scientific mind, hardly meets the deeper needs of the religious spirit. For God is considered too remote to be real. And no view of providence can be finally satisfying which puts "nature" beyond God's constant care and control. For, as Brunner remarks, "Nature does not stand between us and God like a 'foreign body.' "[45]

Some philosophers of religion have sought to remedy this defect. They have made God near and active, but only by reducing the area of His operation and thus regarding Him as mighty, but not almighty. So E. S. Brightman, for example, impressed by the purposelessness of the cosmic process, reverts to the Platonic notion of a Divine Being not to be held responsible for such "waste and futility."[46] Like Plato, Brightman conceives of God as the author only of the good,[47] and declares that the hypothesis which forces itself on us is that of a finite God.[48]

It is, of course, futile to minimize the tragic realities of the natural order, to which Brightman is so sensitive. "These grim affairs cannot," as Camfield argues, "be eliminated by closing one's eyes to them."[49] Nevertheless, the hypothesis of a finite God deprives the believer of the certainty that God is great enough to control world events. "The Biblical writers," writes Carnell, "were fully aware of the presence of evil in the world, yet they confidently affirmed that the heart will know full satisfaction only when it trusts in a God who has a sovereign right to do things which appear to be contrary to human well being."[50]

"No age," says Martin Heidegger in his book, *Kant and the Problem of Metaphysics,* "has known so much and so many things about man . . . And yet no age has known less than ours what man is." Certainly the anthropological issue has become prominent in recent discussion. Freudianism, Existentialism, and Humanism, among other causes, have served to bring man into the center of the picture. Philosophy, sociology, and psychology, each in its own way, has become preoccupied with the problem of human nature and existence. Yet, while man remains as much as ever *homo absconditus* (man the mystery), the common understanding seems to emphasize that he is essentially a free being. The "freedom of man" has, in fact, become a sort of catch-phrase. Unique stress has been placed upon the notion of man as an "autonomous" and "creative" being. He is consequently a creature that can "make himself," "discover himself," gain "authentic existence," and the like. He is his own cause, reason, and source of action.

This idea of the ultimate autonomy of man has been particularly acknowledged in some contemporary writings. The purpose is to underscore man's freedom as the cause of his own failings and to accentuate his continuing responsibility for his acts. Since man is essentially free, God is in no way responsible for the evil man wills to commit or for the future which he can create. The idea of man's freedom over against God becomes for many the key to the riddle of man's nature.[51]

Brunner regards the scholastic distinction between God as *causa prima* (primary cause) and natural causes as *causae secundae* (secondary causes) as valueless and doubtful. He goes on to deny the propriety of applying the causal idea to God at all. There is, he argues, no such relation between the Creator and the creation, and more especially between God and human freedom.[52] Brunner evidently desires to free God from responsibility for, or implication in, the sin of man. He thinks that the notion of a pan-causalism distorts reality, and consequently he denies what he calls a "determinism from above," a causal action of God, which he regards as making human freedom an illusion. Yet, he can still say, "All that is, and all that happens, takes place within the knowledge and will of God. . . . Everything that happens has its final ground in God."[53] He does not, however, tell us how man's freedom to sin is harmonized with this declaration.

Brunner, in the same way as Berdyaev, sees God's active will as somehow standing apart from the human freedom to sin.[54] He leaves the impression that God is somehow enfeebled. He restricts divine overruling to the area outside natural causes and human autonomy. It is consequently hard to define the idea of the Divine Providence. Such an interpretation of God's interaction with His world certainly fails to meet faith's demand and need. In this exposition, Brunner has sapped the doctrine of providence of its strength and solace. But God's rule over all must be taken in its full seriousness and extent *over* all nature and *in* it; and *over* man's sin and *in* it.

The Fideistic-Revelatory View of Providence

Much recent theological thinking has distrusted reason in the matters of faith. This distrust of reason has arisen partly as a reaction to man's failure, during the era of optimism, to lay the foundations for an earthly paradise. Man's inherent goodness has been proven false. As a result, the subsequent period of pessimism has pronounced man as hopeless and helpless in the realm of the moral and spiritual. Thus, history itself has come to be regarded as the tragic catalog of man's failures, a telling commentary on man's inhumanity. The consequent tendency has been to abandon history to the devil.[55] No longer is it in any believable sense God's world with, "All things bright and beautiful." It is really sin's unrestricted domain. "God is not in the world" says Berdyaev. "There is nothing of God in the dull prosaic normality of the objective universe." It is thus no surprise to find him arguing that the traditional doctrines of providence are "dreadfully strained and artificial," and to charge that they are among the chief hindrances to a belief in God.

But the view that God has relinquished the world to the devil has two results. On the one hand, it sets forth "salvation history," the special sphere of God's activity, over against human history, the realm of the demonic. On the other hand, it restricts the knowledge of God to the knowing of God. Barth puts this second point sharply: "The knowability of God can be known only in the real knowledge of God." God is known in the revelation of faith, in a faith which is itself "created out of nothing," and a revelation coming "perpendicularly from above." With this goes an outright repudiation, especially in Barth's case, of a natural theology, which allows "the doctrine of a union of a man with God existing outside salvation."[56] Barth regards natural theology as "a game played with the natural man with a view of leading him beyond this preliminary step and placing before him the actual itself."[57] But Barth refuses to play the game. It is, he asserts, simply the naturalness of natural theology which commends itself to the natural man.

In the light of this understanding of human history as demonic, and of natural theology as repugnant, how is the doctrine of providence to be understood? Broadly, it yields the conception of providence as eschatological-soteriological, that is, concerning future salvation. By rejecting propositional knowledge of God, much has been made of the concept of God as *Deus actus* (God revealed in action). These acts of God, as acts of salvation, are referred to as *Heilsgeschichte*—"salvation history." The consequence is that God's relation to the actual world has been eschatologically conceived. The Christian view of providence, Brunner roundly asserts, is wholly teleological, related to the End, and determined by the End.[58]

By stressing the fideistic-revelatory formula, some have identified providence with salvation. Only as providence is "faith-centered" is it held to be Christian. Thus Brunner says that "it is only from the standpoint of Election that we can think of Providence at all."[59] Barth, too, having repudiated what he calls an "earthly forecourt theology or a Christian world-and-life view," declares, "Providence is nothing other than God's free grace, and God's free grace in Christ is Providence."[60] Barth even blames Calvin for compromising with natural theology.[61] But the fideistic-soteriological account prohibits all such objective speculations. "It is to be noted further," says Barth, "that in the knowledge of God's providence by faith there can never be any question of speculation or theory."[62] Much in this statement instantly appeals to the Christian spirit. But there are difficulties nevertheless. We need not pursue here the question which immediately arises concerning the place of reason in a religious theory of the nature of knowledge. Barth would have us exclude reason *in toto*, to leave us with the impression that the genuineness of our faith is the measure of its absurdity. Nor do we need to discuss in detail the natural theology issue. The modern reaction to the elevated place given to it in an earlier period is understandable. Barth has hailed Anselm as the high priest of the *theologia revelata* (revealed theology), with its principle of *analogia fidei* (analogy of faith), in contrast with Aquinas the patron saint of the *theologia naturalis* (natural theology) and its key category of *analogia entis* (analogy of being). Barth sees in the *fides quaerens intellectum* (faith seeking knowledge) of the Doctor Magnificus an outlook akin to his own.[63] Whether Barth is right in setting Anselm, the Doctor Magnificus, as the champion of faith over against Aquinas, the Doctor Angelicus, as the protagonist of reason is another matter which does not concern us here.[64]

It is, however, relevant to our subject to observe that if the method of knowing God's providence is restricted, then the area of His sovereign control will be reduced. Barth does admit that God's overruling extends to "those outside the covenant," but they cannot know it; for such a knowledge of God's providence belongs to faith. Gustaf Wingren pronounces Barth's doctrine to be "unbiblical," and contends that although Barth uses biblical language, his system is totally foreign to the Bible. His main error, according to Wingren, is that "he has removed the law as a power that rules over man before the preaching of the gospel appears."[65] John Baillie confesses that on reading Barth's works, "what struck me at once as unfamiliar was his insistence that mankind had no *knowledge* of God save in Jesus Christ."[66]

The main difficulty, however, in the fideistic-revelatory formula is that it seems to limit God's relation to man to the inward response of faith. But God's overruling is actual outside His particular acts of revelation. His saving activity takes place in the real spatio-temporal world; and the spiritual and physical are not separate and unconnected realms. God is both Creator as well as Redeemer; because He is Creator He is responsible for His world; since He is Redeemer He is able to act redemptively in His own universe.

If the world were, in the last analysis, hostile to God's action, all certainty for faith would be gone. Only a God who is sovereign in the universal whole can institute a salvation having mundane repercussions for world history. God is not sovereign within the terms of the grace-faith relation only. "If we are to avoid this fatal spiritualizing or interiorizing of Christianity, which relinquishes not only the whole external world of nature and history but also, in effect, the first two persons of the Trinity in favor of the third alone we must, it seems to me, be able to make theological statements about God as the providential Lord of objective natural and historical events, even if this means the overhauling of our existentialist epistemology."[67]

Knowledge of Divine Providence

The problem of how one gains the knowledge of divine providence remains, therefore, a matter of vital importance. Is it based on the nature of the creation or on the nature of salvation? Is it discoverable from the contemplation of nature or from the analysis of experience? Put historically, the issue is whether providence is to be regarded as a "mixed article" or a "pure article" of faith. According to Thomism, ancient and modern, providence is one of the mixed articles because it is a truth discoverable within general revelation. Knowledge of providence is a conclusion open to men in general as they behold "the glorious harmony of the cosmic totality." The purposeful character of the universal order reveals an over-arching design. This understanding of providence, characteristic of historic Roman Catholic theology, is regarded as abstract and theoretical by many Protestant writers.[68] In the opinion of the latter, such a conception of providence is virtually identical with the stoic doctrine of Fate and has no place in the authentic Christian message.

In repudiating the view that an idea of providence can be gathered from a contemplation of cosmic order, these teachers contend that a belief in providence derives from the Christian experience of forgiveness. "In the cross," says Bavink, the Christian believer "has seen the Special Providence of God. He has, in forgiving and regenerating grace, experienced Providence in his heart."[69] In this sense it is a "pure article" of Christian doctrine.

The emphasis on experience as the ground of faith in providence has been sharply stated by H. H. Farmer. The believing man has his own unquenchable assurance of the divine purpose shaping his destiny and bringing him to respond in awareness of the love of God.[70] Wendland, to whom Farmer is heavily indebted, maintains emphatically that faith in providence starts within the experience of personal guilt and divine grace within the individual's life. "Christian faith in providence" he writes, "becomes a reality only for one who has experienced the redemptive love of God directed to him personally. It becomes clear to him, as he looks back over the past, that the seeking love of God is traceable in all the complex circumstances of his life. Faith is certain that as in the past, so too in the future this holy Divine love will surround us."[71] Without this experience of grace, without fellowship with God by prayer and thanksgiving, belief in providence is simply unattainable. Wendland speaks of belief in providence as "a believing certainty which must be always gained anew by means of ceaseless inward labor and active obedience to Divine tasks, and in full view of all our bright and dark experiences."[72]

There is, however, an obvious corollary to this way of understanding how a knowledge of providence arises, which has the logical effect of extending the area of God's activity. For the one who reads in his own experience the undoubted evidence of God's overruling will not regard himself as having a monopoly of the divine concern. He will not find it hard to believe that others, who as he, have been brought into the kingdom of God, are also the subjects of the same sovereign superintendency. Nor, indeed, will one whose experience has made vital for him the reality of providence stop there: he will not regard, as did Leibe, that only those who have been apprehended by the grace of God, the elect, are the objects of God's concern. God, after all, is not limited in His control of life's affairs. And from his own assurance of the divine arranging, the believing man conceives of God's providence including those who have never sought His grace, even those who resolutely refuse it. But to those who have come to faith in His government, God's ruling presence will be more intimately real. To all, even those still alienated, His power and purpose remain.

This means that in the last reckoning nature is not hostile to human endeavor; for God is the Lord of nature. Mark Rutherford's Mrs. Snale sees nature's ways cruel, not with the ferocity of the tiger, but with the dull insensitivity of a wagon wheel which runs over a man's neck as easily as over flint. But this interpretation fails to properly read the signs. For nature is not so much hostile as neutral. And its neutrality is but another name for justice at the heart of things. Christ used the very impartiality of nature as proof of the perfect heavenly Father, whose unsought blessings fall equally on the evil and on the good. Thus, God's providential government of the total order takes account of all men, and especially the race of man as a unity. While the idea of human solidarity has a dark and forbidding aspect, from another point of view, it has been the means of untold blessing. "Racial unity and solidarity are vitally connected with the spiritual leadership of Christ. The benefits of his mediatorial work flow out to men because he is one with mankind."[73] And these blessings flow out for the good of many who neither know nor care about Him.

The man with a living awareness of God's providence cannot help seeing that His overruling action takes place in the present world. He does not restrict it to an *eschaton* (last time). He is well assured that all creation is under the authority of God. "Unless we are to abandon the conception of providence altogether," says C. S. Lewis, "and with it the belief in efficacious prayer, it follows that all events are equally providential. If God directs the course of events at all then he directs the movements of every atom at every moment; 'not a sparrow falls to the ground' without that direction.

The 'naturalness' of natural events does not consist of somehow being outside God's providence."[74]

In this living faith in providence the religious man finds the deeper meaning in the moral argument for the existence of God. Here it acquires real content and significance. For evidently, to the man of faith, life has religious and ethical value. And the existence of such values are seen to relate to God on the one hand, and to the world on the other.

The evidence of value, that, for example, some things are worthwhile, that life has a purpose, and that there are good and evil, assure a living faith. The awakened consciousness knows that a Spiritual and Ethical Reality is necessary to fulfill man's spiritual and ethical nature. Nothing in the "here" and the "now" ultimately satisfies the need of the spiritually and ethically awakened soul. To discover what is adequate, man must press beyond the present world. He must find God in whom he finds rest and hope. And yet he needs God in the "here" and "now": but if God can meet his soul's demands, as his experience testifies that He can, then He must be in control of the world order wherein man's spiritual and ethical nature finds its fulfillment. If the world were ultimately hostile to man's religious and ethical life, then there would be no guarantee that these needs of man could be met. Because the religious and ethical life operate in the spacio-temporal world, then it is essential that faith be assured of a Spiritual and Ethical Being who causes the material realm to be suited to spiritual and ethical actions.

Man lives in a natural order, and upon its regularity his very life depends. Because of this, even the religious man is not exempt from those physical contingencies which are "natural" in that order. Providence, that is to say, does not work against that order for the protection of the good man and the destruction of the bad. But the natural arrangement provides the sphere for spiritual and moral development and training. From one point of view, the natural and the supernatural may be set against each other: but from another, these two different worlds may be seen to complement each other. The Christian, as any other, must live in the natural order and be subject to its regularities and requirements. But while he must read the behavior of the world in "naturalistic" terms, he can also see it from, so to speak, the other side—from the divine perspective.

Here we have what has come to be known as the Principle of Complementarity made popular by Niels Bohr. Thus, what form the human side finds its explanation according to the laws of physical causation, the man of faith can see from the divine side as the operation of God's providence. This does not entitle the believer to claim to be omniscient; for we walk by faith. While, therefore, "The Christian doctrine of providence teaches that the whole of history stands under an ultimate divine control," says John Baillie, this does not mean, he rightly goes on to assert, "that the Christian is able to trace the working of God's hand in it all, but he can trace in some events which have become what we have called paradigmatic for him, having what Whitehead called an 'elucidatory power' which casts light upon the rest. Nor does it mean that all that happens is the result of God's direct ruling, so that no room would be left for the free actions of his creatures, but rather that he can and does so 'overrule' these as to make them subservient to his ultimate purpose."[75] One needs, then, as Flavel contends, the "spiritual eyes" to discern the providences of God.[76]

When, however, the idea of providence has been raised into the cold atmosphere of reflective thought, difficulties and apparent contradictions begin to appear.[77] Yet the believer remains convinced all things do work together for his good. In the most tangled events of his life, he still stands in the faith that God will use seeming evil for his ultimate benefit. Even in those bewildering happenings he encounters, he knows the hand of God somehow remains. He is convinced that what he calls the chances and changes of everyday experiences have their place in God's providential scheme.[78] Physical things as well as spiritual; happenings which seem accidental, no less than events which seem diabolical, are not outside God's control but are altogether orchestrated by God for the fulfillment of His good purpose for us.[79]

Such a faith, we need to insist, based on man's experience "remains, and must remain, the affirmation of a mystery, so far as the manner of its working out in and through the infinite complexity of events in this universe is concerned. It is an affirmation of faith and not of sight; it arises primarily out of the deep insights and necessities of the soul of the man as God calls it into awareness of Himself and its own significance, and not from any observation of the general course of external events.[80]

Objective Basis for Belief in Providence

The fideistic-revelatory view of providence has, and must ever have, a strong appeal. It evokes a response from the awakened soul. With this, however, comes an obvious danger of placing the emphasis on the personal and the inward: it results in virtually equating theology, the study of God, with epistemology, the theory of how we know, by making doctrine identical with the reality of the encounter or the measure of the response. But it is inadequate to restrict man's knowledge of God to the limits of his awareness; nor, indeed, is it possible to locate man's experience of God in the bare structure of the "I-Thou" relationship; nor, yet, is there such a thing as a "naked" or "unmediated" experience. The faith-encounter or the faith-experience, whichever term is preferred, cannot be a mere inner feeling.[81] Encounter *with God* is essential, an experience *of God*: there must, that is to say, be some authentication of God. It is, therefore, within the context of a documented revelation that a full faith in providence can be reconciled and a full providence doctrine verified.

"Providences in themselves," says Flavel, "are not a perfect guide";[82] they must, he insists, be tested by the biblical word. The Bible has the final attestation that God *could* come redemptively into our human situation because He *has done* saving acts of judgment and mercy in history. It is in the context of the truths of God's revelation that, according to John Oman, the four "veils" which hide from our eyes the meaning of life's mysteries are lifted. They are the veils of ignorance, sin, weakness and evanescence (disappearing like a vapor). "By four great doctrines," says Oman, "they are taken away. The veil of ignorance is removed by the Incarnation, the veil of sin by the Atonement, the veil of our weakness by Grace, the veil of our evanescence by Immortality."[83]

It is clearly impossible, therefore, to restrict the Christian doctrine of providence to those characteristics which can be verified and vivified within individual experience. Many phases of the biblical account of God's overruling lie outside such a possibility. No Christian experience can, for example, attest either the *arche* (beginning) or the *telos* (end) of God's providence in history and nature, which lies outside the range of personal experience. Here the Christian believer can only accept the account of God's dealings with His world that has come down to us. Consequently, what the Christian knows of providence in the experience of faith is not the full measure of faith's knowledge.[84] Faith's subjectivity has its assurance and certainty in faith's objectivity.

Thus, while Christian faith in providence begins in experience, it is not thereby limited to an analysis of experience. "We do not stand on the fact of our experience, but on the fact *which* we experience."[85] And the fact we experience is the fact of God declared in Christ. It is on the Christ-Fact that faith finds sure ground; for here is pictured, in clearest focus and form, the divine overruling of history by God. Thus, the ultimate certainty of God's control of His world cannot be based on or limited to the testimony of experience. "Which is the way of the Spirit—subjective illumination with its shifting lights, or objective revelation in an ever-fresh and growing experience? Is today's vagrant insight or yesterday's apostolic inspiration good for today and forever?"[86]

If no organized church, as Forsyth maintains, can live without a normative Bible, a formative gospel and a positive Word, neither can the individual believer. He needs these, not only as the cause of his experience, but also as a check upon his experience; not only for his illumination, but also for his instruction. This means, with reference to the issue of providence that, as a final fact, a total Christian doctrine of God's overruling must be essentially biblical.

Certainly I must experience the reality of God's care and concern for me and over me if belief in God's providence is to ring true at all. But the context for the experience, the context of the nature of God of whom I have become gratefully aware, is assured only in God's self-revelation. The God whose providence we have experienced must be the God whose saving action we read in the history of our redemption. We cannot stop short at an account of providence that is a mere inference or deduction from experience. We must get behind experience to God, to God in His self-disclosure, and in the conviction that it is Himself He unveils. We must certainly meet God in relationship, but the knowledge of God who sustains and governs is not secured by a mere questioning of that relationship. God has spoken as well as acted; what He does for us must be strenghtened by what He has said to us.

Providence and Action

The danger in using the concept of "providence," even if used to represent God's overruling, is that it wears the aspect of the impersonal. Some who speak of "providence" have hardly any idea of God. For them, providence is almost an equivalent for "good luck," with a horseshoe rather than a cross as its symbol. Precisely at this point we see the essential difference between luck and providence. The impersonal character of fate stands as against the personal nature of the Christian doctrine of providence. Both beliefs may agree in the conviction that a power outside ourselves controls man's ways and destiny; but while fate is implacable and blind, divine providence fully recognizes the free actions of man. It is a significant characteristic of the great believers in God's overruling that they have not given way to inertia. It is, in fact, "a curious historical phenomenon, often noted, that Calvinism, in which the central tenet was an omnipotent and omnipresent Providence, produced—contrary to strict logic—a release of human energy. Providence proved a stimulus to action, rather than a paralysis of despair."[87]

In any right doctrine of providence the attributes of God must not be severed, as though God were somehow torn by conflicting desires. "Observe," says Flavel, "the sweet harmony and consent of the divine attributes in the issue of Providence! They may seem sometimes to jar and clash, to part with each other, and to go contrary ways; but they only seem to do so, for in the winding up, they always embrace each other."[88] In this regard, it is helpful to note the declaration of the Psalmist, "Mercy and truth are met together: righteousness and peace have kissed each other," finds its immediate context in reference to the providential arrangements of God for Israel's deliverance from Babylon.[89]

Providence and History

Historians have too often read history in terms of one aspect of God's nature, thus distorting the evidences for His interventions. We have observed how some theologians have virtually given the world to the devil.[90] In harmony with this conception, certain modern historians tend to view human history as a series of judgments. There is, of course, sufficient data for such an account. One after another, nations drunk with power have collapsed. In this sense, history itself is a judgment of God; it appears that God "has only to withhold his protection and let events take their course—'I will hide my face from them, I will see what their end will be'—and the penalty comes from his formidable non-intervention."[91] The truth here is that sin brings its own judgment and frustration.

But if some would interpret God's providence in history solely in terms of judgment, others would interpret it solely in terms of mercy. So Roger Shinn, for example, says, "Hence the Christian doctrine of providence in its deeper forms cannot be primarily a theory of historical causation. It is rather a confidence that God's grace is sufficient to any occasion, that he cares for his people in the midst of the contingencies which buffet their lives, that he is the Lord of History—not the main efficient cause. The final aspect of providence . . . will be known less in the rise and fall of nations than in a divine grace which may be found whatever the course of events."[92] But unless the dark and forbidding aspects of national and natural events are equally under God's overruling, then it is not easy to discern the reality of the providential operations of divine grace in the individual life.

We sometimes find it difficult to see the actions of God as gracious in all the operations of providence. Yet the eye of faith will discern, in all the ordering of events, something of His goodness, but not to the exclusion of His justice. For in the reckoning of faith there is the affirmation that with mercy and with judgment the web of life is woven. "It would be a quite inadequate Christian reading of providence," says Beach, "to affirm that the final form of God's munificence is the limit he sets to the power of evil, his making the devil to tremble, and his scattering the proud in the imagination of their hearts. For God is redeemer, and the intention of his chastisment is restoration. History under his rule is the story of continued judgment, but also of continued promise and hope."[93]

This truth in the context of God's providential overruling of events for the people of God means that, "However contrary the winds and tides of Providence at any time seem to us, yet nothing is more certain than that they all conspire to hasten sanctified souls to God and fit them for glory."[94] And in the last analysis is that not the right reading of providence according to the biblical witness of God's sovereignty over the natural order, the events of history, and in His acts of grace? It is our conviction that it most certainly is.

Chapter 5

Miracles

The question of miracles is again being debated. For a long time miracles have been rejected by skeptics and neglected by Christian apologists. Miracles were the *Streitfrage*, or the main point, of controversy in the nineteenth century. There were good reasons for the disagreement then. It was an era when the omnipotence of science was virtually undisputed, when Newtonian physics had made it seem that the world ran by itself and that it could function by its own inherent laws without any further aid from God. There was no room for miracles. How could God, who was generally recognized as the Creator, interfere with the inevitable course of nature. The impossibility of such intrusions, what we can call miracles, is expressed by Alexander Pope in his Essay on Man:

> Think we, like some weak prince, the Eternal Cause
> Prone for his favorites to reverse his laws.

God cannot change things. He cannot alter the movements of the universe. Darwinism imprisoned the world even more firmly in the straight-jacket of fate. Fredric Harrison and T. H. Huxley preached the gospel of unhindered progress with virtual religious fervor. Scientific understanding of the world made popular the view that a divine interference within the cosmic order was impossible.

Hume Called the Tune

Besides all this, Hume was quoted as having knock-down arguments against any who dared suggest that miracles happen.

Hume had made it appear that the worst theological fallacy was the claim that God, when He wished, could play fast and loose with the laws of nature.[1] In fact, it was Hume who chose the ground of debate in the earlier apologetic for miracles. Christian writers who accepted Hume's definition of a miracle as the violation of the laws of nature were embarrassed by their counter-arguments. By regarding miracles as intrusions of the Divine Being to change the laws of nature, they seemed to breach the causal order. They found it difficult to prove their case because of their inability to show how the universe could continue on its ordained course in spite of these divine interferences. The general tendency was to appeal to the operation of some unknown higher law or to speculate that miracles were the natural result of physical laws already at work.

This apologetic stressed that miracles take place in the natural and physical order but that they are unusual occurrences which stand out. Miracles were seen as a proof of God's power to convey truth to man. By them He revealed the divine source of the truths which He had given to man. But this idea of miracles as a violation of the natural chain reaction became nearly impossible to defend in the climate and opinion of the last half of the nineteenth century. Many felt that it was no longer reasonable to justify the "natural miracles." Therefore Christians began emphasizing the moral miracles which they regarded as a realm free from the reign of unbreakable laws. Thus, in the end, the reply to the skeptics' assertion "nothing miraculous" was that there are certainly "moral miracles." Therefore, they left the physical world—the world of natural science—outside the interference of God.

However, the odd thing was that both Hume and Darwin had actually undermined their own position by the way they had stated their case. Hume argued that a miracle is so contrary to all human experience that it is more reasonable to disbelieve all of the testimony for them rather than to hold that they actually took place. But Hume's argument involves a glaring *petitio principii*. A miracle, Hume maintained, is contrary to human experience; by human experience he means personal experience. It is a fact that we have not witnessed a miracle in the authentic sense of the term; but others claim that they have. To make one's own experience the measure of all human experience would mean to rule out the acceptance of any new fact. The general experience to which Hume appeals is, after all, merely negative. But the positive testimony of one man who witnessed the commission of a crime cannot be rebutted by the assertion of any number who were not there and declare that it could never have happened. Negative testimony can never neutralize the positive without rendering all human testimony void.

Hume falls into the self-contradiction of seeking to discredit faith in human testimony by using as his proof only the general experiences of men which we know through testimony. How can we be so sure that such testimony is true? We do not know that something is true merely because it has the majority vote. But we are not now concerned with a consideration of Hume's arguments. They have been reiterated and rebutted throughout history, only to deepen the skeptic in his skepticism and the believer in his conviction that if Hume did more than any other unbeliever to shake faith in the miraculous then there is no knock-down disproof of miracles.[2]

A self-contradiction also undermines the Darwinian thesis. In explaining the presence of new species, he stressed the concept "mutations." But these beneficial jumps from the original stock, he admitted, are without explanation. Contending that they occur by chance is only another way of saying that they are unpredictable; they do not act according to fixed laws. This does not mean that they are miraculous in any proper use of that term. But it does suggest that the assertion that all nature acts according to unbreakable laws is vacuous.

Miracles and the Scientific World View

The old definition of a miracle as the violation of the order of nature, which Hume used to deny their possibility, and which was accepted by Christian apologists to their later frustration, has had to undergo certain changes in the context of the modern understanding of the world. The idea of the laws of nature as fixed and unbreakable no longer holds. It seems to be an axiom of recent thinkers that natural laws are not to be regarded as statements about the ultimate structure of the universe. In fact, the relationship between scientific theories and the actual physical world appears far more distant than originally supposed. Stephen Toulmin has taught us to believe that scientific theories are "maps" of the real world.[3] R. B. Braithwaite sees them as "models."[4] In general, then, scientific theory and law can be likened to maps or models produced by the scientific observer, during his investigation of phenomena, that he might gain some understanding of the world in which he lives. Of course, this does not mean that the map or the model is a pure invention or mere subjectivity. It receives a sense of objectivity by what the investigation of the physical world conveys. Nonetheless, the map or model is not an absolute account of the nature of things. It has no ontological status. It is a map or model built from the scientist's empirical generalizations, and conditioned, in some measure, by the state of existing knowledge and observational techniques. This means that the map or model cannot be taken as the final word. Future discoveries may necessitate new theories. There is, therefore, no reason to be intimidated by the straight-jacket conception of the universe, since modern scientific understanding of the laws of nature has shown such a view to be unreasonable.

Yet even if the laws of nature are, as Swinburne says, "corrigible,"[5] this does not mean there are not well-established generalizations, "laws of nature," which account for much which goes on in the world. It is in relation to these established generalizations that the occurrence of a "counter-instance" can be pronounced impossible. But, on the other hand, if there are good reasons for affirming that such a "counter-instance" did occur, then can that "instance" be pronounced a miracle, taking place as it does in a map or model of the universe whose general features and outline remain unaltered?

Such well-established generalizations do not, therefore, make the world safe against miracles. It is, in fact, only because nature in general is regular that we can, so to speak, "identify" a miracle. The hints we get from our scientific maps and models suggest that the ultimate nature of reality is not that of an interlocking system of cause-effect relationships. For, as C. S. Lewis contends, man's rationality is the tell-tale rift in nature which shows that there is something beyond and behind her. Man's thinking, which seeks to construe a total system, cannot itself be brought into the system. It requires an explanation in terms which allow more than the natural. Human thought is evidence of the ultimacy of a Higher Thinking. It suggests that the final nature of reality is personal. If, therefore, above and beyond nature there is One who, as Final Thought and Final Personhood, controls the regular course of natural events, is it not surely open to Him to inaugurate irregular events of the type called miracles? Such irregular actions we may regard as God's short-cut methods, a quick way of fulfilling His purpose for the sake of man. They are not a series of arbitrary acts or disconnected raids on nature. Nor are they acts done, so to speak, behind nature's back. Certainly, a "miracle" is "caused" by God's direct action, yet when once introduced it comes immediately within the context of nature and obeys her "laws." As C. S. Lewis explains, "If God creates a miraculous spermatozoon in the body of a virgin, it does not proceed to break any laws. The laws at once took over. Nature is ready. Pregnancy follows, according to all the normal laws, and nine months later a child is born. If events ever come from beyond Nature altogether, she will be no more incommoded by them. Be sure she will rush to the point where she is invaded, as the defensive forces rush to a cut in our finger, and there hasten to accomodate the new-comer. The moment it enters her realm it obeys her laws. Miraculous wine will intoxicate, miraculous conception will lead to pregnancy, inspired books will suffer the ordinary processes of textual corruption, miraculous bread will be digested."[6]

Natural Explanation of the Miraculous

Nowell-Smith questions the contention that miracles are "above, contrary to, or exceeding nature," and as such are beyond natural explanation.[7] He agrees that scientific theories must change, but stresses that the scientific method remains constant. Thus, he argues, while it is true that miracles cannot be explained in present day scientific theory, it is not obvious that they cannot be investigated by the scientific method. And if they can, he concludes, then they belong to the order of the "natural" and may someday be explained in new, strictly scientific terms. Nowell-Smith cannot see how miracles demonstrate the existence of a divine order. If God's acts are detectable, then a generalization about them can be accurately predicted. But such an admission can only make the so-called supernatural a new department of the natural. "The supernatural," he writes, "is either so different from the natural that we are unable to investigate it at all, or it is not. If it is not, then it can hardly have the momentous significance Mr. Lunn (his opponent in the discussion) claims for it; and if it is it cannot be invoked as an explanation of the unusual."[8]

It is not our purpose here to examine this criticism of a miracle by Nowell-Smith, except to note that it is set in the form of a dilemma, and as such may be countered by the construction of another which will appear equally cogent. If the supernatural is different from the natural, then it can explain the momentous events of a special character called miracles; and if the supernatural is not actually different, but is simply another department of the natural, then it can only account for understandable naturalistic events. But the supernatural is either different, or it is not different: if different, then it can be appealed to as an explanation for such special events called miracles; if not different, then there are no inexplicable events. Nowell-Smith does indeed admit that there are what are termed miracles which cannot be explained by present-day scientific theory. He can only suggest that they can be explained in principle, and possibly will be understood in the future. But this escape affirmation hardly supports his basic contention that a miracle, so-called, can be subjected to a naturalistic explanation.

Miracles as Non-conforming Events

I. T. Ramsey defends the nature of God's actions in the natural world by analogy with the difference based on observation, which, he holds, is discernable in ourselves.[9] We are all aware of a "general" activity which characterizes ourselves and our world in all ordinary observable situations. This "first-order activity," as Ramsey calls it, is observable, and is, therefore, open to scientific investigation. Our "particularized," or, "second-order activity," on the other hand, arises through involvement in actual situations. This is, however, a private awareness, and as such, is not open to scientific generalizations. Awareness of this particularized, second-order activity, comes only through involvement; it cannot be inferred. Since this sense of personal quality is non-objective, it cannot be described in impersonal object language. Its "proof" lies in the actual experience when a situation "takes on depth." Examples are frequent of situations suddenly taking on a new dimension—when the crust of human experience is broken and previously unnoticed meaning and significance are revealed. It is then the "ice breaks," the "penny drops," the "light dawns."

Ramsey applies this distinction between impersonal first-order and personal second-order activity to God's twofold relation to the world. He sees a miracle as an event which witnesses to, and is the occasion for, a personal, second-order activity of God. "What is a miracle?", he asks. He answers that it is "a non-conforming event, a *miraculum* whose non-conformity, whose oddness, evokes, gives rise to, what we have called a characteristic theological situation. With a miracle, a situation, 'comes alive,' the light dawns, the penny drops."[10] It is, then, when the universe takes on the sense of the personal that we have what is called a miracle.

There are, of course, obvious weaknesses in this apologetic for miracles.[11] The distinction between impersonal and personal activity, which our own experience is said to verify, is taken as substantiating a similar distinction in the mode of the divine activity. But this surely begs the question. The whole subject of analogy from the human to the divine is here raised: and this is an issue so much debated that it is unsafe to use it as the foundation upon which to build such an edifice. If, however, we are only aware of our second-order activities by experience, then it is difficult to see how *we* can be so sure of God's second-order activities that we can transfer to Him distinctions claimed to be discoverable in our human activity.

Left as it is, Ramsey's account of the miraculous yields this conclusion: only as man discerns in a situation what he interprets as an activity of God is there a miracle. Such a conclusion would mean that a miracle may give us some information about the adequacy of our own spiritual insight; it does not give us justification for distinguishing between different modes of God's activity.

Ramsey does, of course, seek to avoid the difficulty by substituting the idea of "disclosure" for "discernment." But this alone does not provide adequate reason for singling out any special event as a miracle. Ramsey refers to the "oddness," and the "non-conformity" of the event; but here again he does not meet the requirements of the situation. For the "disclosure situation" turns out to be identical with the non-conforming event: that is mere tautology. The "oddness" lies precisely in the fact that a situation yields the awareness of God in a personal way: that is what is called a miracle. But there is no reason God's personal activity should be limited to special events; for the regular processes of nature can certainly produce the awareness of such activity. Despite the problems, there is undoubted value in Ramsey's approach. It reminds us that God's activity cannot be reduced to a neat, uncomplicated formula. But more particularly it underlines the limitations of objective scientific abstractions to give a total explanation of all events. Ramsey refuses to have God imprisoned in a network of causal relationships.

In similar fashion, Emil Brunner contends that we should eliminate the fiction of a pan-causalism, which would exclude God from His universe.[12] It is only, he argues, in the sphere of what is called "dead nature" that the strictly mechanical and causal idea can be carried through. The facts of our own human experiences mark the limitations of causality in our relation to the world. The reality of our own freedom points to that of the Divine, wherein human freedom has its ground and its goal. Divine freedom, says Brunner, "is only in the freedom of revelation, the miracle of the *supernatural* revelation in its perfection: the miracle of the Incarnation and Redemption. And this miracle of the divine revelation is the real *miracle* of which the Bible speaks. And the so-called *miracles*, those of the Old Testament and those of the New, are only the *accompaniments* of this one miracle of revelation, the miracle of the Coming of God to man."[13]

Both Ramsey and Brunner are anxious to find a place for God's activity in an ordered universe. And they do so by contending, as Barth says, that "we cannot hypostatize the concept of law."[14] They reject Hume's idea of miracles as an interference with the laws of nature, in the sense of their being a break in the series of causes. At the same time they see the theological significance of believing in God's miraculous action in the universe.

Miracles and Religious Faith

The religious purpose of what is termed a miracle is especially stressed by recent writers. They generally admit that miracles cannot be explained by natural law. Thus, for example, H. H. Farmer begins his treatment of the subject by seeking to remove the idea of the miraculous from the sphere of the mechanical. For Farmer, then, a miracle is essentially revelatory, an event in which and through which a man realizes God is active toward him personally. In a miracle God meets us both as absolute demand and final succor. Farmer sees a miracle as conveying an awareness of the supernatural, of God, as Active Will, operative within events. This means for Farmer that the wonder and awe evoked by the miraculous event is not due to its cataclysmic accompaniments, but to the sense of the "numinous," the awareness of the presence of God it inspires. God's approach to the soul explains the "arrestingness and inscrutability" of the revelatory event.

Farmer declares emphatically that this understanding of miracles prevents the necessity of seeking intellectual justification for them. They are revelatory events; therefore, the discovery therein of God speaking personally cannot be defined either in terms of, or be dependent on, our knowledge of natural processes and relationships. Thus, "each man's miracle and revelation must be his own."

Yet, not all revelation as divine disclosure can be interpreted as miracle. When God comes redemptively in revelation we have what can properly be called miracle: and more specifically, when God's relief is felt as something intensely personal and individual, the word *miracle* becomes inevitable and appropriate on the lips of the religious man. Farmer underscores his conviction that miraculous events take place through the initiative of God in an ordered universe. But this does not mean that they upset in any way the causal relationship. Because God is immanent in His world, He is able to coordinate every new event in His total workings.

The one serious difficulty in Farmer's view is the way he seems to have robbed miracles of any real objectivity, offering them to the subjective judgment of the person involved in the Divine-human encounter.[15] And this deficiency H. D. Lewis has sought to remedy. He claims that to define a miracle merely as a supernatural event is too wide.[16] He agrees that the normal use and association of *miracle* must involve reference to the religious factor in the determining of events. There must, however, be something more specific than this. This "something further," according to Lewis, which sets miracles apart from other events, is some characteristic measure of deviation from the normal course which events would have taken, due to some religious factor other than the process of revelation itself and the effect this naturally has on other events.[17]

Classifying a miracle as religious experience generally seems appropriate. But these questions remain: Is the criterion—deviation from the normal course of events—sufficient to identify an event as a miracle? And who is to be judge of this? How is the deviation to be understood in relation to the normal course of events? By what right do we refer to "deviation" as a direct act of God? For by a miracle we surely mean more than some abnormal event that inspires a religious response.

So far in our discussion we have determined that no treatment of miracles can be finally satisfactory which does not relate them to the scientific view of the world, on the one hand, or which does not give effective account of their religious purpose, on the other. In the light of these facts, we can proceed to consider the case for miracles. In doing so, we will say something first about the concept of miracle in general, and then about biblical miracles in particular.

A General Definition of a Miracle

In broad terms, a miracle is a specific act of God in His own world. Those who believe in a personal and moral Creator and

Sustainer of the universe expect miracles. If we fully acknowledge man's moral consciousness and the testimony it bears to the moral nature of God, it would seem most fitting that God should make special interventions into the natural order for the sake of those moral beings who stand in need of His grace and help. The very essence of the Christian world view says that God, as personal and free Spirit, has a moral end in view for man and the world. And we cannot imagine that He is helpless to fulfill His divine purpose.

Thus, the faith of the biblical theist includes the conviction that the unity of nature, far from being a system of physical causes and effects, is a free system of ends. The reality of miracles is certainly confirmed in the Christian's own experience of God. He has become aware that a supernatural power has taken hold of his life; he does not, therefore, find it difficult to accept those miracles to which the Bible gives witness, since they provide the context which secures and assures his own experience of divine grace. They have significance for him because they are woven into that revelation of God which is related to and relevant for his own life.

The one who has entered into a living awareness of God, as ethical personality, is confident that there is more than a closed system of nature. He recognizes a supernatural order, beyond and within the mundane order. The term *supernatural* certainly carries ambiguity, as, indeed, does the root word, *natural*. One may say in a genuine sense that all God does is "natural" to Him; for whatever He does is according to some method of His own, and in harmony with His own nature. Every such act of God belongs to the wider system of His rational activity. Yet, however right it is to insist that all God's activities are normal, rational, and intelligible, we cannot afford to discard the word *supernatural*. There are still those activities of God which are "outside" the "natural" course of things. It is these acts of God we refer to as "supernatural" and "miraculous."

We may define a miracle, then, as an event brought about by the immediate agency of God, in contrast with His ordinary method of working. Although such an act appeals to the senses, it is yet performed for a specific religious purpose: it is also of such a nature that it does not disrupt the causal order, while the total laws of nature, even if they were fully known, would be unable to account for it.

The Religious Purpose of Miracles

Wendland declares that "no miracles are ever experienced by unbelievers."[18] In the context of religious experience, he insists, one finds their independent, unique, and real significance. Only faith sees God working and hears God speaking in any event. The *mirabile* (marvel) of the *miraculum* (miracle) has significance for the religious life.

The New Testament certainly does give us the warrant for stressing the necessity of this subjective personal faith in order to see God active in an event. The miracles of the New Testament are no stunning and silencing wonders. They are signs of God's presence and evidences of His divine purpose, and can only be read as such from the perspective of faith. At the same time, we must insist that a miracle is not just a mere religious reading of any and every event. It is, of course true, as A. N. Whitehead says, that "every event on its finer side introduces God into the world."[19] From that point of view, R. G. Collingwood is right in maintaining that miracles "are a standing testimony to the deadness and falsity of our materialistic dogmas."[20] But he is wrong when he urges that the meaning and purpose of a miracle is lost "if we regard it as unique and exclusive."[21] Collingwood seems to regard a miracle as something which takes place in the eye of the religious beholder. "To the religious person," he writes, "it is surely true to say that nothing exists which is not miraculous. And if by miracle he means an act of God realized as such, he is surely justified in finding miracles everywhere."[22]

But this is not what the theistic believer means by a miracle in its precise and proper connotation. We have concluded that a miracle is performed for a religious purpose, and that only by faith can one see something of that purpose. Because, however, the religious man can see something of God in every event, this does not at all mean that everything is miraculous. For that would empty the term of its significance. A miracle is a special act of God, performed for a religious purpose certainly; but it is an act, nevertheless, which is "unique and exclusive" in itself. A miracle is not the religious reading of every event, but the religious appreciation of a special event—brought about by the immediate agency of God—by those whose eyes are open to His ways in His world.

A Miracle as an Immediate Act of God

Those who say a miracle belongs to a higher order of nature, and as such, is only an indirect work of God, object to the assertion that a miracle is an immediate act of God in His own world. This higher order, to which a miracle is referred, is declared by some to be completely unknown and by others as being partly understood. This appeal to the operation of higher law or laws leaves the so-called miraculous event still within the realm of nature. Though the appeal does seem to give some deference to the notion of natural laws, it is, in the end, only a guess designed to make the idea of miracles less offensive to the scientifically minded. By thus accommodating the concept of a miracle to natural law, one robs it of its essential meaning. Even an atheist may believe an extraordinary event which happens through the intermittent action of some unknown law, provided he is satisfied that the alleged law has a place in *rerum natura* (the nature of things). Belief in unknown laws does not call for any special act of God any more than a sudden appearance of a comet or meteor within the terrestrial orbit.

The case for miracles is no better if the miracle is conceived to be the result of obscure physical activity with which we are only partially acquainted. This idea merely pushes back the divine working further into the organization of the system. All miracles have a natural side; but with that granted, the case for miracles is not thereby weakened, for still a miracle would evidence the extraordinary work of God as immanent in His world. Granted this close action and reaction between the living and personal God and His world, miracles become credible. For God, as immanent in His world, can impart new impulses, which originating from His immediate activity, take their place in the cosmic organism. But although these impulses arise from within, they have their origin and operation not from the mechanism itself but from the immediate action of the immanent God.

And God can do new things. He does not run in a rut. Unlike Ixion at his wheel, God is not bound hopelessly to the cosmic process. He is certainly not incapable of making some unique and dramatic manifestations of His power. Such new demonstrations are possible because God did not exhaust Himself in creating the world. God is at hand to meet the needs of His moral creatures. Miracles are possible since they are objects for which the universe is built. In a dynamic universe, of which the living and personal God is the core of its energy, results brought about by the immediate action of God cannot be quickly ruled out. The simple fact is that since God is esteemed by religious faith to be living and personal, and not a mere force or the sum of cosmic processes, miracles *are* possible. They need not be regarded as spelling out "monster" as Emerson said, but rather as bearing witness to other aspects of the divine character otherwise unknown and unrecognized.

Miracles and the Laws of Nature

The evidence for the uniformity of nature must not be allowed to exclude God from His world. For without order there could be no miracle. Miracles presuppose law; and the importance of miracles is proof of the existence of nature's uniformity. But uniformity is not mechanism, for nature is a vast realm of life and meaning of which human existence is a part, and of which the final unity is God. Nature's ways may be thought of as "habits of will" and its regularities as the regularities of freedom. We must, therefore, as William James urges, rid ourselves of the mechanical and the impersonal view of the ultimate.

The realities of everyday life, the free activities of thought, choice and love show plainly that much cannot be brought under the dominion of inevitable law. These realities occur in a uniform world without violating the natural order. Man can act freely in an ordered world. He can produce results by exercising his volition, results which would otherwise not have been. Choice cannot, therefore, be thought impossible with God, the source and cause of that voluntary ability in man; God can act immediately in and work directly on that system of nature which He has Himself created and now sustains.

A disorderly universe would be repugnant. And the believer is convinced that God has not created a disorderly world. Important as it is for the scientist to approach the world as an ordered system, he must not overextend the idea. The idea of uniformity can so dominate the mind that one comes to accept this as the full and final truth, regarding all that exists as a great mindless machine of interlocking natural events. But if naturalism were, indeed, the final fact, then there would seem to be no reason to trust our convictions that nature is uniform. If nature is all, how did we come to believe there was anything else? The very unnaturalism of naturalism almost appears as evidence of its inadequacy.

While God's miracles are said to be extraordinary, they are not therefore arbitrary. His miracles do not appear to be occasional stabbings of nature by a God wholly outside its system. Miracles are not God paying visits in bewildering disguises, now and again, to an alien territory. Exclusive emphasis on the divine transcendence led the Deists to regard "miracles" as arbitrary interferences by God with the created order. Some modern writers, who unlike the Deists have no stake in denying miracles, are bothered by the concept of the Divine transcendence in relation to the miraculous.

Thus, Mary Hesse, for example, declares that more "difficult to understand from the scientific point of view is theological talk about the specific acts of a transcendent God," than talk of miracles defined as violations of the laws of nature. She reckons, in fact, "The fundamental problem is not about miracles, but about transcendence."[23] This is certainly true if God is conceived of in terms of bare transcendence. But the Christian theist does not admit that the world is, so to speak, unhinged from God or that God is altogether outside it. It is, of course, true that when reference is made to a miracle from the point of view of transcendence, such ideas as "interference" or "intervention" by God in the natural order arise. But even though the world as God's creation must have a certain independence and autonomy, it still depends upon God. As a created entity it is other than God, and yet as His creation it has its continuity in Him. And only in the context of these twin facts does the idea of miracles have justification.

Thus, in the theistic view, and in particular in the Christian view, the cosmos is independent of God; and the essential goodness of the cosmos is reflected in the fact of its freedom and autonomy and in the value that separates entities and individual beings hold in themselves. Yet, by reason of its independence, the world is distinct from God, and being such, He must reveal Himself to the world in an indirect manner. "But yet if God is to show Himself, He must somehow remove the veil that the cosmos constitutes, and break through the natural processes. But to break through all the time would be to destroy them and to mislead men, for the strangeness of the miraculous and its rarity reflect the otherness and transcendence of God. To be always breaking through would constitute a cheapening of the vision of God that the miracle provides."[24]

This does not mean that God only acts occasionally in His world. For the truth is that He is ever active in the universe He has made. The God of Christian faith is not the "Unmoved Mover" of Aristotle. He is a God truly capable of dealing in a personal way with His human creatures, since He controls the whole world. He is indeed Lord of the ways of nature and the winds of history. He is not remote from His world, "on the limits far withdrawn." He is immanent in the universe and incessant in His love for His creation. And because He is, it does not seem improbable that He should act for good cause, as occasion demands, for the blessing of man whom He has made for sonship with Himself. Allowing, then, "the close and intimate fellowship of God with man," "it becomes less strange that God's activity in the world could vary in particular ways according to the requirements of His personal dealings with us. The Fatherhood of God has for the Christian much to do with belief in miracles."[25] A world created by God, when combined with the right understanding of creation, has room for miracles.[26]

And miraculous acts of God require no greater exercise of God's power than does His providential upholding of the ordinary processes of nature. For a God who is omnipotent, *more* or *less* have no meaning. The fundamental question is not whether He has power, but whether His purpose requires a miracle. The fact is that miracles give us as much evidence of God's gracious restraint as they do of His sovereign power. They may often be seen as a check upon His judgments, as acts of grace in His plan of redemption for mankind.

The modern scientific view of the world presents a startling paradox. On the one hand, it makes it more difficult to believe in miracles and on the other much easier.

Some imagine that the extension of knowledge must finally eliminate the element of mystery from the world. All will eventually be explained, and no room will be left for God. But the Christian believer need not be perturbed by the growth of knowledge, for he does not believe that God is to be confined to the dim mists of mystery. He need not, therefore, retreat to the God-of-the-gaps hypothesis in order to find space for God in the universe. For God is as necessary for, and as present in, the "explained" as He is for and in the inexplicable. God cannot be reduced to areas of the unknown, which may diminish year by year with the advance of science. God is certainly above and beyond all; but He is no less in and through all.

Yet, we realize that the more we learn about the universe, the more we discover how much there is unknown. The farther men penetrate the immeasurabilities of space, the more they learn of vaster realms still unreached and unexplored. We are unveiling the greatness of the universe, its profundities and immensities. With this enlarged view, the idea that it all came about by chance, by a stroke of luck, appears all the more impossible and incredible.

Thus, all naturalistic theories are revealed to be pathetic gropings of unbelief. Far more fitting to the requirements of the situation is the Christian doctrine of the cosmic Christ through whom God has created all things and in whom they hold together. For all nature is needed to reveal Christ; and Christ is needed to make all nature holy. He is the canvas on which the world is painted, as He is the frame in which it is set. Here we have what Augustine called the "secret metaphysic" through which the man of faith can keep his perspective right in a scientific age. In Christ the significance of miracles must be sought. To say that a miracle is an event without scientific explanation is not to say that it is without any explanation. It has its final reason in the purpose of God and is an instance of His direct and special act in the world He has created.

The Identification of a Miracle

What criteria can be used to identify the alleged miracle? No simple answer exists. It used to be popular to declare that a miracle is an act beyond the power of man to bring about. In an earlier age this seemed an adequate mark for recognizing a miracle, and was considered in itself as conclusive proof of their actuality. But the advance of science has rendered this criterion inapplicable. For what once was supposed to be beyond the power of man is now commonplace. It is not possible to state categorically what is beyond the power of man: and even if it could be shown that some event were not within man's ability to perform, the judgment that it must be a miracle does not necessarily follow. For it might be an event of the natural order, the cause of which is not yet known. The transition, therefore, from the proposition that an act appears beyond the power of man to the conclusion that it must be a direct act of God is precarious.

But if it is insufficient to identify a miracle as an act beyond the powers natural to man, perhaps a moral criterion may be more suitable. Can we then identify a miracle as an act of God performed for the specific good of His creatures? This would seem a sound principle by which to mark out a specific act of God in His world. For, as G. F. Woods observes, "Though the miraculous acts may be infrequent, they may be in line with some unchanging purpose which is good."[27] We, too, would want to give some weight to this factor while recognizing the difficulties it holds. There are questions here left begging. Why, for example, should there be ills in the world which need remedying by occasional acts of God? It almost appears that the moral criterion merely focuses attention upon the enormous sum of moral disorders in the world. And if a few are indeed helped by a miraculous act of God, does not this accentuate the huge number remaining whose needs are not met? And why are so few healed? The apparent shortage of the miraculous acts of healing calls for an explanation. If the one case draws forth the special interposition of God, then why not others? And why not all? Evidently, therefore, "We cannot be quite sure that an unusual event is a divine miracle because it is congruous with the purpose which is morally worthy of approval."[28]

We are consequently driven back to declaring that a miracle must be judged within a religious context, and there identified. This is not as feeble a conclusion as may at first appear: it is, rather, what we should expect from the nature of the case. Faith must be exercised to designate a specific act for which the scientist as a scientist can offer no explanation, a miracle. It is faith that discerns God immediately acting in the situation. What from the scientific point of view cannot be accounted for, from the religious perspective is directly "caused" by God.

It is, therefore, evidently impossible for anyone to identify an act as immediately brought about by God unless one has some prior idea of the God who acts. If a man "has no idea of God prior to observing the act, it is not intelligible how he can attribute the act to God. It seems more probable that, in observing what he takes to be a miracle, his belief in God is confirmed, and his idea of God is modified."[29]

A Word about Biblical Miracles

The Bible uses three main words to describe God's extraordinary acts, which we call miracles. One class of terms emphasizes their striking, or unusual, character.[30] The New Testament uses the word *teras*, literally "a portent," in this context.[31] Another class of terms stresses the power displayed in the works: the New Testament word here is *dunamis* (power).[32] In John's Gospel, especially, the miracle is referred to as a "sign" (*semeion*), which clarifies the theological significance of the event. But whatever word is used, the main fact about the biblical miracles is that they belong to the context of God's saving purpose for the world. They are part and parcel of His revelation, and as such proclaim to faith the reality of the living and personal God. Thus, the miracles of the Bible events dramatically unveil God's essential nature as the One who redeems and guides His people. They are not, therefore, mere freakish displays of supernatural powers, nor yet mere evidential additions to His revelation.

In the Old Testament, miracles show God's character as "a just God and a Savior" (Is. 45:21). Without miracles the God of the Jews would be an abstraction: in and through His miraculous acts He is revealed for the great and gracious One He is. Significant, then, is the fact that these extraordinary works of God are coincident with some new movement in His progressive unfolding of Himself. They cluster, so to speak, around special occasions such as the deliverance of Israel from Egypt.

It is, therefore, inevitable that at the time of God's fullest and final revelation in Christ, the Word becomes flesh, there should be associated wonders, mighty acts, and signs. So the miracles of the Gospel are integral to the record. They are not there to entertain the reader or even to magnify the main Figure of the story. Remove them and they leave inexplicable gaps: delete them from the account, and we are left wondering why such a Person did not, on occasions befitting His intervention, act in some such way.

Although the miracles of the Gospels are related to faith, they were not performed to evoke faith. Jesus consistently refused to give signs and wonders to compel belief. At the same time, the miracles of Jesus directly and eloquently testify to the fundamental truth of the Christian faith, that Christ exhibited powers which are characteristically Godlike and Divine. For unlike the men of God of the Old Testament, He performed His mighty works in His own right and name. They stand, therefore, as evidences of the special office He claimed toward the human race, namely, that of Savior. He proved He was such by the acts of a Savior.

The miracles of Jesus display the fullness of His Lordship over God's world. There is no evidence of a limitation. He stilled the tempest, healed the sick, raised the dead, and cast out devils. Every sort of need and occasion came under His control. In no place and at no time did Jesus show Himself unequal to the demand: there was never a situation beyond His power. Thus, the miracles of Jesus reveal His kingdom, and demonstrate His dominion. They show the superiority of the spiritual over the material, even though some of His miracles were themselves of a physical nature. In this way they declare the oneness of God's world; they assure us that His redemption affects man's total life. The miracles have a specific eschatological character as Messianic deeds of salvation. Even the so-called nature-miracles, while they reveal the present sovereignty of Christ over the world, point also to the end when all nature shall be renewed at the coming of the Son of Man.

This means that it is the Person of Christ who makes the Gospel miracles credible. The character of Christ compels us to believe that He performed the deeds through God. Thus the miracles have their significance in the context of God's acts of self-disclosure, and so nourish faith in God by demonstrating that He acts, not by remote control, but in an immediate and direct way for the saving of mankind.

But no one can read the Bible without realizing that extraordinary acts of a miraculous character can be performed by evil men and false prophets. Such wonder-workers are described in both the Old and New Testaments.[33] Therefore, one must ask if there are any criteria to distinguish the true miracle from the false? Some ideas such as these may be appropriate.

A true miracle is done for some definite purpose. There is always some religious and revelatory end in view. The general run of *Wundergeschichten* (miracle stories) is that of a mere display of the dazzling and spectacular for its own sake. Thus the false miracle has the nature of a "portent." This may be why in the New Testament the term *teras* (wonder) is always associated with *semeion* (divine sign), to stress that only significant portents are properly direct acts of God and consequently true miracles. Further, a true miracle harmonizes with the whole panorama of God's unfolding self-disclosure. It does not stand out as inappropriate and unfitting. The miracles of Jesus are particularly characterized by spontaneity and restraint. They arose "naturally" out of the occasion and never appear to be engineered. Yet, while they were performed in response to human need, and as a manifestation of Christ's compassion, they are not scattered about indiscriminately. A true miracle has a relationship to faith and gets its perspective from that standpoint. The stunning wonders performed by evil men and false prophets point away from God, focusing attention upon the human actor.

The question, then, about biblical miracles becomes a question about the acceptability of the biblical *Weltanschauung* (world view). In the context of biblical theism, the demand for other evidences for their actuality will be less stringent. If another and opposite world view is one's presupposition, then, of course, much more logical and historical evidences will be required to verify their actuality. Swinburne explains, "With one *Weltanschauung* (world view) one rightly does not ask much in the way of detailed historical evidence for a miracle since miracles are the kind of events which one expects to occur in many or certain specific circumstances. The testimony of one witness to an occurrence of the kind of miracle which in its circumstance one would expect to happen should be sufficient to carry conviction, just as we accept the testimony of one witness to a claim that when he let go of a book which he was holding it fell to the ground. With another *Weltan-*

schauung one rightly asks for a large amount of historical evidence, because of one's general conviction that the world is a certain sort of world, a world without a god and so a world in which miracles do not happen."[34]

The question of particular miracles is asked with the assurance we have in the Christian gospel of a supernatural activity of God for the sake of man and his salvation. In the New Testament the miracles are mainly subservient to the saving work of Christ. They are to be understood in the light of His redeeming action. They are not isolated events, and their "unnaturalness" is not generally adduced as proof of their divine origin. The miracles of the Gospels are revelations of Christ's own person.

All the miraculous acts of God find their significance and their sanction in the "Grand Miracle" of the Word made flesh. "Every other miracle," writes C. S. Lewis, "prepares for this, exhibits this, or results from this. Just as every natural event is the manifestation in a particular place and moment of Nature's total character, so every Christian miracle manifests at a particular place and moment the character and significance of the Incarnation. There is no question of arbitrary interferences just scattered about. It relates not to a series of disconnected raids on Nature but the various steps of a strategically coherent invasion—an invasion which intends complete conquest and "occupation." The fitness, and therefore credibility of the particular miracles depends on their relation to the Grand Miracle; all discussion of them in isolation from it is futile."[35]

But as the Incarnation shows us God's movement into the human situation, so the Cross and Resurrection of Christ reveal God's plan within history for man's salvation. The man who has a personal consciousness of sin and a living experience of forgiveness through Christ, his living and present Redeemer, is in the best position to enter upon a study of miracles. Such a person already has personal assurance of an "intervention" of God into human history, which does not in any way abrogate the causal system. Christianity, it has been claimed, cannot be proved except by a bad conscience. This fact every Christian believer could confirm. He has entered the living experience of divine grace through the reality of a disturbed conscience. He would agree that God's greatest act is His breaking in to restore grace into human lives, an invasion which does not disturb the connections of nature. And since the natural and the moral cannot be "sundered as with an axe," God's miraculous activities in nature, for which He has a moral purpose, likewise do not interfere with the cosmic arrangements.

In the end, it is by a miracle we are redeemed into an understanding of the miraculous. Only the one who has experienced a miracle can believe a miracle.

Chapter 6

The Problems of Prayer

Prayer has meaning and significance only in the context of the theistic view, that this world is the creation of the living and personal God, over which He rules and in which He acts. Since God is Personal Being, He can hear man's prayer; since He is the Living God, He can respond to man's asking. The idea of God as One who answers prayer rests, then, on the one hand, on the theistic view of God in His relation to the world; and, on the other hand, on the biblical view of man as made in the image of God. Man is a personal being, made for fellowship with God. He is, as Brunner says, a "theological being"; as such the attitude of prayer is proper for him. Prayer is not extraneous, foreign or incredible to him. It springs from man's awareness of himself as a dependent being. Thus, man is by nature a requesting creature, and God is by nature a responding Being. Out of the coincidence of these twin facts, the reality of prayer springs. The asking man and the answering God meet in the act of prayer.

It comes, therefore, as no surprise to learn that the practice of prayer is not only a feature of most religions but also an attitude which is in some measure natural to man. It is a fact that most children pray. It seems to be an instinctive activity with them. The young child resorts to prayer for its cash-value or its therapeutic usefulness. But whatever the drive which stirs this natural reaction, its creative center is the conviction, feeling, or hope that something will be gained by it, either for oneself or for another.

Questioning the Instinctive

Apparently, children naturally pray. However, the developing youngster soon questions the pragmatic value or the therapeutic usefulness of his infantile reactions.[1] He learns that random and instinctive activity must be challenged and sometimes curbed. He remembers when he was afraid in the dark; now he knows that there is nothing in the dark to frighten him. He has learned that reactions admittedly proper to the early period of infant development are no longer admissible. He has left the primary school behind and is now in the sixth grade. He is no longer an infant, subject to primitive reactions, but a growing lad capable of finding reasons.

This conflict arouses questions about the worthwhileness and worthiness of prayer. He recalls how he used to beg under covers for some Great One to make the darkness depart. Time and again he had asked for this and that; but they had not come. So the question arises, What's the use? Is it really any good praying for someone to be made well? Does he not know now that all one can do is leave the matter in the hands of the doctor, and with a bit of luck the patient will recover? But if the sickness is beyond the doctor's help, then all the praying in the world will make no difference. It is a case of cause and effect: and that is all there is to it. As far as the result is concerned, to pray or not to pray is *nihil ad rem*, nothing to the point.

Even if prayer is considered a mere primitive reaction, it cannot on that account be summarily ruled out as unheeded by God. Some prayers, from the point of view of the spiritually aware and alert, appear naive and crude. But this does not mean they are necessarily unheard and unanswered by God. For is not the incarnation of the Son of God a standing reminder that God the Almighty stoops to our human ways. God does not assure an answer for the prayer offered in high sounds and sonorous tones, with the conception of God all square. The New Testament presents enough evidence that the halting and lisping request of battered and broken humanity is heeded by the living God. The bruised reed He shall not break and the smoking flax He shall not quench. The sobs and sighs of a needy soul beckon God's grace, which, in the last analysis, is His debt to Himself.

To say this, however, we do not wish to encourage the notion that prayer is a sort of Alladin's lamp, which anyone can operate at will once he has learned the secret. Certainly the Bible assures us that if we ask anything in faith we shall have it. This promise offers limitless possibilities. And we need not dismiss the promise as embarrassing, as Alec Vidler would, calling it a venerable anachronism. Yet such an encouragement is not to be bandied about as a sort of "open sesame" to anyone and everyone to try their luck at getting every whim satisfied and every wish fulfilled. Huck Finn had problems on this point. He was told he could get whatever he wanted just for the asking. But it did not work. So he not unnaturally gave up the whole business of praying.

But prayer is not just the easiest way to get every natural want supplied. As long as a person's prayer is purely instinctive, he merely puts faith in the act of prayer as such. The reality of God is not vitally present. If prayer continues as a primitive reaction, one will resort to prayer only by way of an occasional ejaculation or hardened form of continuous incantation. But this kind of prayer is barely distinguishable from superstition or magic. Prayer, we must remember, depends largely on its role in the life of the person who offers it. If prayer is an isolated occurrence or an extended performance, having little or no relation to the character and conduct of the individual before or after praying, it can hardly be called prayer.

Bonhoeffer tells of his experience during a heavy bombing raid on the concentration camp where he was held prisoner during World War II. One of his fellow-prisoners, "normally a frivolous sort of chap," according to Bonhoeffer, panicked at the possibility of immediate death. "O God, O God!" was all he could mutter. Bonhoeffer confesses that he could not bring himself to offer any Christian encouragement or comfort to Him. His prayer, in Bonhoeffer's judgment, was merely an instinctive reaction born out of sheer fright. Bonhoeffer only felt obliged to assure the pathetic man that the bombing ordeal would not last long.[2] Bonhoeffer did not suppose that such exclamations, wrenched from someone in a tight corner, truly constitutes prayer. That is not truly prayer, he contends, which has no significant relation to the person's life after the danger has passed.

Although we can understand Bonhoeffer's hesitation, it still remains true that the instinctive reaction of appeal to God for help is a basic factor in prayer. For the Christian gospel does not destroy man's native traits; it takes hold of them and channels them into higher and holier ends. It is the fact that man is a social being, built for "togetherness," which is the fundamental reason for the existence of the Church. The grace of God takes hold of man's gregarious instinct and directs it into new and richer experiences of *koinonia*, or fellowship in Christ. The Church is not a random alignment of isolated individuals: it is a living unity of redeemed people in one Body. In turning to the One, a man does not turn away from the many, but quite the reverse.

The same factor is true in the case of prayer. The awareness of the Father-child relationship with God through grace gives the instinctive reaction to pray new meaning and deeper significance. True prayer, then, while possessing all the characteristics of a natural response of a dependent being to a prayer-situation, is enriched, in the experience of faith, by an elevated sense of worthwhileness. Prayer no longer vaguely refers to a someone in whom one half-believes, and of whom one has no assurance that He hears and can answer prayer. Only within the experienced reality of God in Christ can one be certain that prayer is not a useless and fruitless activity.

Yet, even here faith sometimes reflects and questions. At such times, tensions arise between the warm assurance that the God known personally and redeemingly in Christ must and does answer prayer, and the reflections and questionings of reason as to whether indeed He should and can.

Jesus and Prayer

Jesus, the Christian believer's supreme authority in the affairs of the soul, found no difficulties believing God does hear and answer prayer. He could address God as His Father, the Lord of heaven and earth. For Him, Father, not fate, was the final fact about the universe; and to the Father nothing was impossible. However, Jesus did specify obstacles to prayer; but they were all on man's side and of man's own creating, such as lack of faith or perseverance. In contrast with Him, we who are so earth-bound find difficulties of another kind, difficulties as either the spectator or the participant in prayer. Certainly "the problems about prayer," writes C. S. Lewis, "which really press upon a man when he is praying for dear life are not the general and philosophical ones; they are those that arise within Christianity itself."[0]

The Meaning of Prayer

But what precisely is prayer? Some use the term so widely that it seems to be synonymous with religion in general. The essential feature and nature of religion is an awareness of a relationship between a man and a Being he believes to be God. Although prayer may indeed kindle an intense and vivid sense of the divine presence—also the central note of religion—it goes beyond these moments of conscious communion. Prayer is an element in religion, it is not all that is meant by religion. For the believing man prayer is, as it was for Jesus, to love, to labor and to live for others; prayer, however, cannot be identified absolutely with any one of these activities or with all of them together. The idea of prayer is robbed of its essential distinctiveness if it is defined merely in terms of moral activity.

Even to equate prayer with religious experience fails to pinpoint the meaning of prayer. For in our most intense moments of religious experience, the human initiative is virtually absent; or at least the clear consciousness of it is. It seems, for example, in the experiences of Paul, Augustine, and a host of others, that they were somehow apprehended by God. The initiative was altogether from God's side. And however speedily they responded in prayer, it was not in prayer, or, as a result of it, that they experienced divine grace. In prayer, by contrast, the initiative is more obviously with the worshipper; for, as H. D. Lewis observes, "Prayer is not what happens to us, but what we do, notwithstanding that it is in a context in which much is done to us."[4]

On the other hand, to identify prayer with certain outward physical postures overly restricts the definition. To kneel, to close the eyes, and to bow the head are not necessities of the prayer act. True prayer can be offered without these articular features: and, equally, prayers can be sung as well as said.

What, then, do we mean by prayer? The term is often used to cover a wide variety of activities and attitudes characteristic of the prayer act. In its most general meaning it refers to the idea of the soul's communion with God. This communion takes three forms: there is meditation, in which the soul ponders the goodness and glory of God; there is adoration, in which the soul, as it were, becomes lost in rapture in the thought of God Himself; and there is contemplation, in which the "eyes of the soul" open, so to speak, toward the supermundane and the eternal.

But these three aspects are in a sense characterized by a less personal awareness. They operate in a third-person context, God being the object of the prayer. Intercession operates in a second-person relationship, in which man becomes the object and its central and distinctive note. Here we have what Brightman calls, "the loftiest type of prayer";[5] or, "the very heart of prayer," as H. H. Farmer puts it.[6]

Prayer as Conversation

Psychologically, prayer is in the form of conversation. But does the conversation accomplish anything? Emerson pronounces prayer to be the soliliquy of a beholding and jubilant soul: it is the spirit of God declaring His own works good. But this makes the effect of prayer merely subjective. One who believes in the efficacy of prayer certainly intends more than this. He is convinced that prayer is useful, not simply because it arouses religious feelings, but because it assures actual results.

The believer contends that prayer is an asking of God for blessings on oneself or for others, to which God, as He thinks fit, can and does respond. The believer knows needs have been met through prayer that would not have been met without it. J. H. Paton, however, does not favor this claim. He agrees that it would be inhuman to forbid a mother to pray for her sick child or even to forbid men to pray for themselves or others in time of danger, but he stresses that nothing can be accomplished, either for the sick child or for those in danger, because of the prayer. Although the prayer of the mother can have no effect on the child's health, he does console her with the assurance that it may "do her good."[7]

But this is not at all what the believer holds to be the facts. He does not regard prayer as the releasing of a subjective safety-valve. He considers himself to be talking to God who has an interest in his affairs and who can do something for him. Prayer, he knows, is active, objective and social: the very conviction of its worth whileness requires a particular view of God, man and the world.

Paton's summary dismissal of the effectiveness of prayer does, however, force the Christian believer to consider the skeptic's denial that prayer has any effect upon conditions in the objective world. It also compells him to reflect upon the questions which the reasoning of faith poses.

Difficulties in Prayer

Problems regarding prayer press from two sides. Unbelief proposes problems, and faith itself asks questions. For while blind unbelief is sure to err, it is also true that blind faith is soon to erode. Faith may laugh at impossibilities, but it cannot ignore difficulties. In some respects, the problems arising from the denials of faith's reality are akin to those which arise from faith's conviction. The skeptic's criticisms, however, are often directed against the instinct to appeal to God for help in a dangerous situation, rather than against prayer as the spontaneous act of one who knows God in the fellowship of faith. For this reason, the skeptic and the believer are sometimes at cross-purposes: they both talk about prayer, but they are not talking about the same thing.

With these observations in mind, we will seek to do two things: first, we will deal with some of the difficulties connected with the claim that prayer is effective, and then, in the next chapter, we will make some statements on the language of prayer and end that chapter with remarks on the issue of unanswered prayer.

Early in the history of the Church, theological objections originated against the idea of intercessory prayer. Origen, for example, in a treatise on the subject, had to contend with the dilemma reiterated through the centuries: if it is right that we should have the blessings for which we pray, then God will grant them without prayer, and if it is wrong, then He will not, and cannot, grant them at all. Augustine and Chrysostom, each emphasizing in his own way the doctrine of God's predetermination of all events, had to face the problems which the idea of intercessory prayer causes in this context.

In one of his Donellan Lectures, *On Prayer*, of 1877, J. H. Jellet declared, "Inconsistency with the character of God, inconsistency with the laws of nature, inconsistency with experience—these were the objections alleged, early in the eighteenth century, against the supposition of the Divine interferences, and these are the objections urged still."[8]

In the statements of Origen and Jellet, two broad types of complaint surface against the meaningfulness of prayer. These may be designated as the ethical-theological and the philosophical-scientific. And we will now condiser the main thrusts of the arguments involved in these dualistic terms.

Ethical-Theological Objections to Prayer

When the first term of this dualistic designation is emphasized, it focuses our attention on problems that arise from a supposed regard for the ethical nature of man; when the second term is emphasized, it points to the difficulties concerning the relationship of prayer to the believer's own understanding of God.

1. *Prayer destroys self-reliance.* Emerson made it fashionable to repudiate prayer as an attitude inappropriate to man's dignity. He argued that man should not ask God for things; that would betray discontent, distrust and show a lack of self-reliance. The objection has continued: prayer nullifies man's self-dependence; begging weakens character; God helps those who help themselves.

Of course, these declarations hold elements of truth the believer should consider. For some quietists seem content to sit down with arms folded and feet up, and to reiterate the slogan, "Prayer changes things." Prayer does indeed change things, but not with this attitude. The greatest folly and gullibility is to neglect immediate duty in the pretense that prayer will work magically to bring good results. To pray for safety in a gas-filled room when it is possible to burst open the door or window would be sheer stupidity. We all know men who have made necessary practical readjustments and have, without prayer, prospered as a result; while others, in spite of their prayers have failed and have landed in misfortune.

Yet, when it is understood that it is not a case of *either* definite action *or* definite prayer, but a case of *both/and*, the critic's objection is crippled. Prayer is not a way of getting things done easily and cheaply. To think of prayer as an escape from necessary duty is to view it as magic. Prayer is, rather, the means and the method of securing the Divine cooperation so that our best endeavors may be more efficiently executed. By prayer, a power not our own is assured in cases where we would be otherwise helpless. However, there are times and places where prayer is the only effective action. The documents of faith show innumerable times when the resources of human labor have been exhausted, and only the prayer of faith has produced the required result. In such extremities prayer has had its opportunity. Thus, while there are occasions and situations where *Ora and laboura* (you must pray and work), there are others in which the only and adequate action is to pray.

2. *Prayer is essentially immoral.* The same argument further claims that petitionary prayer, if it did in fact work, would create unjust and improper results. The notion that blessing can be had in a seemingly cheap and easy way offends our moral good taste. It sounds like something for nothing; they have not labored, and yet they benefit.

Everyday experience, however, testifies that social life is so structured that each of us continuously receives countless benefits for which we have not expended one atom of energy. And intercessory prayer is totally in harmony with this arrangement of social order. If, by its means, blessings are bestowed on those who have not labored for them, this harmonizes with the principle which runs through the total cosmic arrangement. We must not suppose that when petition is made on behalf of others that the requested benefit will be mechanically imposed. The special favors of God come only to those who willingly appropriate them and meet the conditions out of which they arise.

The issue has, however, been pressed that the idea of one's welfare depending on another's inclination to pray is rather precarious. In some moods, says H. D. Lewis, it seems a formidable objection to suppose that a person should be allowed to suffer or lack because of my neglecting to pray. For "my prayer for myself or others, or my neglecting to do so, seems so far removed from the normal conditions of well-being and mutual help as to seem a rather pointless or irrelevant condition. To leave scope for me to help people is one thing, to allow their fortunes to turn on whether I pray for them is another."[9] In spite of this, however, Lewis asserts that prayer is the life-center of our relationship with God, which spreads out into the experiences of others and gathers them into its influence. "It is," he says, "when we know or meet one another in our prayers and prayerful living that we have the finest relationship with one another, bound together in the union of our bond with God."[10] Lewis believes that prayer has most prominence where the personal relation between God and man is strong. He therefore sees no impropriety in contending that, especially when God is known to be particularly present in Christ, "it is not very strange that the extension and sanctification of this in the whole life leads to the granting of certain things simply because they are brought before God in humility and resignation and faith, in our most sacred communion with God."[11]

3. *Prayer is childish.* If it were true that asking God for things is only a form of childish begging, then intercessory prayer would be lifeless. Making request of God, it is said, is an attitude more suited to the stage of the spiritual nursery; it is quite unbecoming in the religiously mature, who should be characterized by the calm spirit of contentment with life as it is.

But such an idea of prayer is altogether out of harmony with a biblical faith. It is at odds with the character of God, which reason and revelation demand as the ultimate source of all that is. This idea of prayer disregards the character of man, created in the image of God, whose highest good is found in glorifying God and enjoying Him forever. It seems certain that the measure of faith's conviction in the reality of the living God is the measure of faith's assurance concerning the usefulness of intercessory prayer. It is, indeed, in the act of petition that the essential identity of human personality is secured and preserved. Prayer is dialogue. "Real prayers," says Ferré, "are person-to-person calls,"[12] so that the more spiritually mature a man is the more he will seek the face of God in petition for himself and others. In petitionary prayer the full grown man reveals his spiritual maturity. Petitionary prayer is not in the least at variance with that serenity of soul which should characterize those who have confidence in God. Petitionary prayer and trustful poise are not contradictory. Rather, prayer is "the nearest approach to God and the highest enjoyment of Him, that we are capable of in this life. When our hearts are full of God, sending up holy desires to the throne of grace, we are upon the utmost heights of human greatness."[13] This declaration does not deny that there is a sort of frantic utterance from even religious people when facing difficulties. Their cry seems to betray a lack of trust and smacks of the jittery. But this could well be, as we have argued, the immediate and indistinctive reaction to a prayer-situation. But the truly believing man will not stop there. The fact is that quite often the same sort of reaction escapes some professed atheists who have encountered an unexpected jam; but in their case it goes no further. "The criterion of true prayer is that it should be the expression of nobleness in the man who prays. It is the spiritually mature reaching upwards."[14]

It is the spiritually mature, then, who pray. Was it not for this very reason that Jesus, as the greatest and the mightiest, prayed as no others have done? And never did He "stoop to encourage apron-string prayers."[15] Rather, He taught that the "surest way to mature is to pray; the truest way to gain objectivity is to pray; the fullest way to relate our lives to the world is to pray."[16] Petitionary prayer, therefore, is far from being the evidence of distrust; it is really inspired by confident faith in God, as it is increased by it. The offerer of such prayer sees a purpose higher than his own. He is ready to defer and to refer all that he asks to the divine will. His petitions are permeated with a devoted trustfulness; he conditions all his requests on the three-fold proviso, "Hallowed be thy name; Thy kingdom come; Thy will be done." Here are, what C. S. Lewis calls, the "festoons" upon which every petition is hinged. Such provisos, such festoons, do not empty prayer of all reality. Nor are they kept in reserve as a sort of apologetic escape route from the demand of unbelievers, who require evidence that the prayers have been answered. When petitionary prayer is offered in the context of these provisos, it gains depth and measure, for the "festoons" do not "obliterate the plain public sense of the petition, but are merely hung on it."[17] The fact, explains Farmer, is that "the man who is in the habit of bringing petitions to God because he believes that his heart's desires are of interest to God and can, through prayer, be linked to a larger wisdom and more effective power than his own, is in a better mood for accepting whatever happens than a man who has schooled himself never to ask for what he desires at all."[18] The man who has made a practice of seeking God's face will gratefully accept what God gives in answer to prayer. In and through the activity of prayer, faith is enlarged and enriched.

4. *Prayer is self-interested.* Critics have repeatedly argued that prayer is fundamentally selfish, because the individual's own desires and needs are in the center of the picture. We have already agreed that some believers do sometimes give the impression that they conceive of God as a sort of magician, who can produce, as out of a hat, what their whim or fancy craves. But this is unlike what the informed believer would regard as a true view of prayer. Also, the charge that because the "self" is focused, therefore praying is a selfish act, is psychologically and spiritually false.

Prayer is indeed an act of asking; but like any act of asking, it is the essential "self" that asks. But this does not mean that the asking itself is selfish. In man's relation to God, the self is not obliterated but redeemed and released. There is, therefore, no just reason why the desire for well-being should not be present in true prayer. The man of faith is not necessarily selfish to ask God for something relating to his own well-being, although his prayer is specifically concerned with himself. If such a prayer is offered with the spiritual provisos that relate to the divine will and glory, then it has been purged of the crudely selfish and the falsely egoistical. "So that far from making an attempt to drag down the Divine will to the level of his own, the man who prays is lifting up the human will to the Divine."[19]

When, therefore, petitionary prayer is thus lifted into the realm of the Divine will and purpose, it has become rightly directed toward personal well-being, because it is essentially theocentric. For its plea is not one's own standard of moral excellence, and its spirit is not the stoic attitude of self-adulation, and its purpose is not some desired form of self-advancement. It is concerned with God and His stake in us; His purpose with us; and our services for His kingdom and His honor. "Of all considerations the most important is that we pray bowing ourselves to God's perspective rather than insisting on our own."[20] If, then, "petition be, on its subjective side, the expression of the soul's profound interest in its own highest self-fulfillment—an interest which we have insisted is not in isolation from but is rather the underlying unity of the most specialized activities of life—and, on its objective side, is the expression of the awareness of God as final succor, then the eudaemonistic element (desire for personal well-being) is not only unavoidable, but also eminently proper."[21]

Furthermore, intercessory prayer is more often "other-regarding" than "self-regarding." "This kind of prayer has less of the ego involvement and produces a wholesome psychological effect upon the petitioner. No higher function of man can be imagined than unselfish concern for others; its therapeutic effect is tremendous. Many instances are found in the Bible and also in the testimonies of Christians of how God works on the mind and heart of the person for whom intercession is made."[22]

After dealing with ethical objections, we come now to consider the other side of the two-pronged criticism of intercessory prayer. We face questions posed in the context of conceptions of God with which the Christian believer has the profoundest sympathy.

5. *Prayer is unnecessary*. Reasoning from the biblical premise that God's loving wisdom is over all His works, some have concluded that intercessory prayer is superfluous. For since God knows what is best for His creatures, He will do the best possible for every one of them. Since He is no reluctant or restricted Deity, He will fully give all things needful. To ask God, therefore, for added blessings, either for ourselves or others is to show dissatisfaction with His way and to express disbelief in His loving concern.

But we can surely reply that, while we most certainly believe that God is wise and loving, it does not follow that He will dole out His gifts in fullest measure to all men alike and apart from conditions. The best that God can do for a man is not some fixed, self-evident quantity He arbitrarily dispenses. The best possible parent does not press upon his child all he would bestow if he knows it is not desired or appreciated. And it is in prayer, in genuine petition in the spirit and mind of Christ, that an individual reveals that state of heart in which God may entrust benefits specifically requested. It may indeed be that God does give His best possible to every man without prayer, for He makes His sun to rise on the evil and on the good. But the best possible that God, as faithful Creator, assures without prayer to every man may not be the best possible which could come to any man if He really prayed.

Christ Himself declared that your Father knows what you need before you ask Him. Yet none emphasized more than He, both by practice and precept, the value of intercessory prayer. For Him there was no incongruity in the fact that God knows all, and yet we may ask for anything. Petitionary prayer is not the denial of God's loving purpose and wisdom. For the idea of prayer is neither to inform God of our needs of which He is ignorant, nor to ask Him to change His mind or methods to suit our liking.

God's best gifts are not given apart from our asking. Man is, after all, a being of moral freedom; he is not a machine requiring repairs, parts and lubrication at the owner's discretion. He is a creature who can appropriate God's gifts. Man has the capacity for asking, just as we believe God has for bestowing. True petitionary prayer springs from the meeting of the Divine and the human; the will of God to give and the will of man to ask. The heavenly Father does give good gifts to those who ask Him.

It is, in fact, through prayer itself that man is drawn into that attitude in which his fundamental need may be met. In the end, man's greatest need is not for things but for God Himself. Some specific need may begin the operation; but real prayer issues in a deeper communion with God, in whom the soul finds an abiding satisfaction. The prodigal of Luke's Gospel was driven back to the father's home by hunger. An empty stomach opened his lips in petition. But he needed the shelter, stability and relief of his father more than the fatted calf. Yet it was the physical need which sent him back. But in the end, the restored fellowship was more important to him than the prepared feast. So it is with God and us. He leaves us with needs—needs which can only be met when we come to Him and ask; but in the very asking we begin that communion with God which is the soul's greatest need. "Thus is it with our petitions addressed to God for the supply of our needs, whether spiritual or temporal, there is a very real and definite purpose. If, without the intervention of prayer, every need were supplied, we would place ourselves in a false position. A life of imaginary independence, with all its disorganizing influences on a nature formed to find the true center of its being in God, would supplant the true sense of dependence on Him, of fellowship with Him, and of gratitude toward Him. And, with the loss of that sense, the real powers by which the noblest forms of action, endurance, and progress are sustained, would be undermined."[23]

To suggest, therefore, that petitionary prayer is unnecessary in the economy of God's gracious dealing with man is to miss the point. Prayer is essential to the fulfillment of the divine purpose and program. It is "part of the soul's response to the challenge and invitation to become *through* cooperation with Him a personality more and more fitted *for* cooperation with Him: it is one of the things by which, under earthly conditions, the soul grows in stature as a son of God and in readiness for that which in its consummation transcends earthly conditions altogether."[24]

6. *Prayer is meaningless*. Early in Christian history debate arose concerning the alleged conflict between petitionary prayer and God's overruling. Antagonists asked if God can really do anything new for us if all is predetermined.

This argument, when fully elaborated, rests upon the presupposition that the sovereignty of God and the freedom of man cannot be reconciled. But, maybe, as we have indicated elsewhere, this is not so.[25] At any rate, we do not believe that God has set rations for His creatures, or that His purposes are fulfilled in total disregard to man's freedom. God's sovereignty is a sovereignty of love; His love offers itself to man's free response, a free response itself awakened by the operations of grace. In God's over-arching plan and all-embracing love, man's free actions have their place. On man's side, prayer is the cause of definite and specific blessings. On God's side, prayer and blessings are linked in the wisdom and grace of His divine purpose. Thus, prayer, far from being an attempt to coax God to revise His ideas and to alter His intention, is a factor which He has always taken into account for the good of man and the accomplishment of His will.

A genuine Christian philosophy does not view God as a remote and transcendent Being unconcerned with anything but His own eternal Selfhood. Just as a valid Christian epistemology does not conceive of Him beyond all knowledge and only dimly apprehended by analogies and negations. But God is, as Pestalozzi says, our nearest neighbor. And since knowledge of Him is personal, prayer to Him is conversational. A true Christian theism sees God immanent in His world. He is "above all," yet He is not out of the reach of any.

Fundamental for the practice of petitionary prayer is the assurance of the providence of God, the conviction that the world is not out of bounds to Him. Through the movements of human history runs a divine purpose. All the unforseen changes and chances of life are under the control of His all-embracing love. Nature and history are both operations of His manifold works. God is interested and active in the sphere of the mundane; for the believer that is most fully and clearly demonstrated in the incarnation of the Son of God. In this fact and act the believer sees the union of God with His creation, which silences all doubts about His care and concern. All things, including the affairs of our lives, are working toward the fulfillment of His grand design.

Prayer has effect when based on this conviction of God's providential ordering. God is at hand. Prayer begins with firm confidence in the goodness of God. Out of this grows the assurance that blessings, spiritual and temporal, may be sought and received, not just for their own sake, or, yet for ours; they are sought for the sake of the outworking of that ultimate purpose of God to which the believing man has given his cooperation and his consecration. Petitionary prayer is a means to this higher end.

Prayer, then, finds its perspective and validity in the context of faith's awareness of God as livingly present. The essential reality of the Christian gospel is that God has lost nothing of His glory by taking a full interest and involvement in our poor state. To listen and to respond is the very essence of love: and God is love. God's perfection and transcendence are not compromised by His concern for man's affairs—a concern so full and generous that He took upon Himself the burden of our sin and shame. "If," therefore, "we find ourselves able to accept this, we ought not to find insuperable difficulties in the notion of petitionary prayer at the level, which I have called for the sake of convenience, the theological one."[26]

Philosophical-Scientific Objections

We do not need to be disturbed if petitionary prayer is dismissed from the standpoint of Hegelian or Spinozan philosophies of impersonal monism. Hegel's absolute idealism leaves no room for the reality and continuity of human personality, thus allowing prayer only subjective value. But the Christian experience of God sharpens the sense of personal worth; this belief lifts prayer into the realm of a face-to-face conversation. The integrity of human personality receives its highest confirmation in the act of petitionary prayer.

Spinoza's cosmic necessitarianism would render the idea of petitionary prayer null and void. All that *is*, exists by an eternal necessity. No new thing can be immediately produced by God for the attainment of a divine end, for that would be to destroy the perfection of God. No fresh element can be introduced by the prayer of faith. What is *is*, and must be accepted *as it is*.

But there is an inherent contradiction in Spinoza's system. He has sought to prove that freedom is an illusion, and yet he wanted his thesis accepted. But what if man has no power of choice? Spinoza asked people to agree with his view. If, however, such assent is possible, then freedom is certainly real: and if freedom is real, then, can it be denied to God, of whom man, as a free agent, is made in His image?

God is the Ultimate Unconditioned, bound by nothing but consistency with His own nature. And because He is so, the way is open for petition to be made to Him; for He is free both to inspire confidence in Himself and to answer the requests made to Him.

7. *Prayer is not scientific*. The more specifically scientific area today presents objections which are thought to be crippling to the idea of petitionary prayer. For the modern mind, taught that the world is a closed-system, the affirmation that prayer brings about new results seems impossible. In a context in which such concepts as, "the reign of the law" and "the conversation of matter" are dominant notions, the thought of prayers being answered from "beyond" the natural world-order appears arbitrary and capricious. To suppose that God could answer every human petition, varied as they are, and often contradictory, would be to upset the rhythm of the cosmic processes.

Such thoughts have weighed so heavily upon many thinking persons that they have abandoned whatever belief they may have had in the validity of petitionary prayer. Or, if they continue to repeat requests, they pray with the vague belief that it may at least do themselves good by keeping alive the spirit of thankfulness, and by reminding them that there are values in the world other than brute material ones. But the uncertainty that God can act in the world has bred in many serious minds a degeneration of faith in a prayer-answering heavenly Father.

If a person continues to pray without the conviction that answers can come from on High, he will inevitably end up in philosophic hypocrisy: or, if that drift is avoided, it can only be by the departmentalizing of the mind. Such an attitude can only create an unbearable tension and introduce a dichotomy between a basic skepticism, which has no certainty that God can do anything, and the continuing performance of a mere religious habit. In the end this is bound to initiate a conflict which dulls the spiritual awareness and destroys the wholesome balance of personality, which vital religion claims to sustain. It would be far better to end such a practice, since it demands some measure of spiritual perception, than to continue it for the sake of custom or appearance. If doubt has squeezed the very life out of the habit of petitionary payer, the only right course seems to be to cease vain repetitions and to take stock of the situation; if one looks coldly and calmly at his position, he may be able to renew his faith in prayer's usefulness and in the God who can act within His own universe.

We have argued throughout the earlier chapters that the spiritual realm is not finally separate from, and independent of, the natural; both somehow unite and coalesce in and under the one ultimate Divine Personality. This view provides a context for a system of principles in which the actuality of petitionary prayer and the validity of the scientific view of the world can be held together. Admittedly, we cannot offer a final solution, nor, perhaps, an acceptable explanation of the interconnection of the physical and the spiritual spheres.

Many apologists have sought to allow for the possibility of answers to prayer by introducing a dichotomy between the world of the scientist and the realm of faith. The scientist is confined to the natural order, fettered by the law of cause and effect. Faith, however, knows a higher sphere, the free and spontaneous world of the spirit, in which inviolable necessity has no place. Although H. H. Farmer does not, as did Schleiermacher, put the two realms in this absolute juxtaposition, he still contends that "God's initiation of events relevantly to individual situations, if it is a fact at all, falls within the area of reality which transcends the scientific interest and method."[27] But if such severance of the physical from the spiritual were allowed, it would restrict true prayer to requests for "spiritual blessings," since only these lie outside the realm of natural causality. In this sort of apologetic God is permitted to act in the sphere of the moral and the spiritual: but He cannot interfere with the physical and external.

This fundamental antithesis between the natural and the spiritual cannot, however, be accepted. For God is God of both realms, and they are both one under Him. If, therefore, He can answer any prayer He can answer all, for what are termed "spiritual" responses from God are no less acts of His volition which have physical consequences. And these physical consequences occur in the sphere of nature, which God rules according to His own laws.

And the theistic believer is sure that this is an orderly universe. For a lawless universe, as Farmer observes, would be a godless one.

It is with the knowledge that he lives in a causally related world-system that the believer proclaims his faith that God does answer prayer. By so doing, he is denying that answers to prayer introduce disorder into the cosmic arrangement. He does not believe God breaks the causal principle. God acts purposefully within His ordered events to answer the requests of His children in a manner consistent with His own wisdom.

The knowledge that nature works in a regular fashion does not void the possibility of God responding to the pleas of His people. In fact, it is because of the constancy of nature's behavior that we are able to "identify" God's special responses to the prayer of faith. Faith knows that the living God works, and that He works in response to the intercession of His children. He does that which is new; yet He acts in and by His own laws, which are, in the last reckoning, the expression of His will. "Prayers . . . are not magical causes: they don't like spells act directly on nature. They act on nature through God."[28]

In the activity of prayer, in the conviction that God hears and answers, faith enters its clearest protest against those learned systems of philosophy which deny purpose and the ability to respond to the Ultimate. For if God is considered helpless in His world, if He cannot answer man's requests because He has imprisoned Himself in His own laws, then what meaning can be given to man's spiritual quest at all? If indeed God is hindered from responding to human appeals because causal relationships are so fixed that He cannot act, how can anyone receive a benefit from parent or friend? In this case, all ideas of generosity and kindness would be a pathetic mockery; and to exhort people to be kind and generous or to blame them for not being so would be hideous nonsense.

But prayer has its own "laws"; in a "prayer-situation" God can act for the fulfillment of His own end in the giving or withholding of requested blessings. It would be an extraordinary thing if God were denied that freedom of action which our own experience shows belongs to human beings. Man can certainly express purpose in a universe of law without any violation of the causal system. In the realm of human relationships people receive benefits every day simply because they asked for them, and yet none is aware of a denial of our psychological and moral freedom. We "interfere," we might say, with the order of nature and cause results which would not have otherwise taken place. Each is conscious of some measure of autonomy. The whole story of deterministic philosophy has not yet advanced an adequate reason to explain away this sense of freedom. It would seem, therefore, incredible to deny to God, in a measure infinitely beyond ours, this power, of which we as His creation are so surely aware.

Chapter 7

The Language of Prayer

In this chapter we will consider the concept of prayer as a talking to God and how this concept influences the language of prayer. When the believer prays he certainly does consider himself to be in conversation with a Someone who is "other than," and "outside," his own consciousness. He does not think he is just talking to himself, that he is asking and answering his own questions, as he might, for example, say to himself, "Now where did I put that pen? I know I had it a moment ago." The one who mutters thus to himself knows very well what he is doing. He does not really believe he is addressing an actual existing other, and he does not expect to be answered by someone else.

Prayer as a Talking to God

But the one who prays does believe he is talking to God. For such a one prayer is not like an internal dialogue; it is in the form of a conversation with Another. Yet the man of faith will acknowledge that sometimes his praying was in fact no more than a talking to himself. He was at such times merely uttering words and repeating statements; but God was far distant. There have been occasions, he will admit, when he did not "get through" to God. But he will lay the blame for such failures at his own door. There were priorities he had not got right or sins he had not confessed. The Bible itself, indeed, has many illustrations of prayers which missed the mark for reasons such as these. It refers to those who uttered words which were little more than a form of self-approving soliloquy. In our Lord's story of the Pharisee and the publican, the former is depicted as standing and praying with himself. His praying was a talking to himself; it was not truly a talking to God, although the term "God" was used almost apologetically in the preface. The proud and pathetic Pharisee composed an ode of self-congratulation in his own honor: and his praying rang the changes on the personal pronoun.

These experiences of the man of faith and this illustration of the Pharisee show by contrast that true prayer is focused on God and is addressed to God, with all the characteristics of asking and requesting. It is, of course, a fact that "one cannot infer from the form of language the existence of the being to whom it is said to be addressed," yet it is certain that believing people do consider themselves to be talking to God when they pray.[1] To understand what prayer is, one must therefore take his stand within that wider context of religious beliefs, in which prayer arises. The one who is unsure regarding God and His ways in the world is hardly likely to reach a true verdict respecting the validity and worthwhileness of prayer. For the question of whether one is really talking to God or not is really and finally a religious question. It is not one which the philosopher as such can properly decide. In fact, the philosopher misconceives his task if he assumes it as his province to determine whether contact is made with God in prayer.

To ask whether a man is or is not talking to God is to ask whether he is or is not praying; for prayer is by definition a talking to God and can only be meaningfully discussed as such.

But how is such a concept to be understood? We all know what it means to talk to another person, to a neighbor, to a friend, to a stranger. Is prayer just another instance of talking to someone else? The answer is *yes* and *no*. It is certainly a form of talking; but it is a talking *to God*. "Hear my prayer, O my God"; herein lies the difference that makes all the difference. The nature of our talk is conditioned by the character of the one addressed. Now prayer is another instance of talking, but not of talking to just anyone. It is a talking to God, "and the divinity of the object addressed determines the nature of the talk."[2]

Does, then, the difference lie in the fact that the Other is not present in the same manner that humans are? To this we must first answer *no*, although it will be immediately qualified by a *yes*. Certainly God is not present as humans are; for God is God and not man. He is not One among the many; not even *primus inter pares* (first among equals). No man has seen God at any time, and even the heaven of heavens cannot contain Him. God is "other than" we are. As God He is sovereignly real in every place; omniscient, omnipresent, omnipotent. He is fully present everywhere. So then, does prayer as a talking to God mean that He must be thought of as present in the same way that humans are? The answer is emphatically *no*.

But if one asks if He can be understood to be present in some way humans *know*, the answer is *yes*. This point has been well made by C. S. Lewis. "To put ourselves thus on a personal footing with God," he writes, "could, in itself and without warrant, be nothing but presumption and illusion. But we are taught that it is not; that it is God who gives us that footing. For it is by the Holy Spirit that we cry, 'Father.' By unveiling, by confessing our sins and 'making known' our requests, we assume the high rank of persons before Him. And He, descending, becomes Person to us.

"But I should not have said *becomes*. In Him there is no becoming. He reveals Himself as Person. For—dare one say it? in a book it would need pages of qualifications and insurances—God is in some measure to man as man is to God. The door in God that opens is the door he knocks at. (At least I think so, usually.) The Person in Him—He is more than a person—meets those who can welcome or at least face it. He speaks as 'I' when we truly call him 'Thou' (How good Buber is!).

"This talk of *meeting* is, no doubt, anthropomorphic; as if God and I could be face to face, like two fellow-creatures, when in reality He is above me and within me and all about me. That is why it must be balanced by all manner of metaphysical and theological abstractions. But never, here or anywhere else, let us think that while anthropomorphic images are a concession to our weakness, the abstractions are the literal truth. Both are equally concessions; each singly misleading, and the two together mutually corrective. Unless you sit to it lightly, continually muttering, 'Not thus, no thus, neither is this Thou,' the abstraction is fatal. It will make the life of lives inanimate and the love of loves impersonal. The naive image is mischievous because in so far as it holds unbelievers back from conversion. It does believers, even at its crudest, no harm. What soul ever perished for believing that God the Father really has a beard?!"[3]

It is our contention, then, that while we cannot say that God is present to us precisely in the way that other humans are, He is yet present in ways that humans know. In the very concept of prayer as a talking to God, the believer expresses his conviction that the Ultimate Factor in the universe is in some authentic sense personal and as such is able to hear and respond to His requests. It is in this context of trustful regard for God that prayer has its meaning. But we can only trust in one who occupies a position of "overagainstness" in relation to us. The other must, so to speak, be "out there," and have independent reality as a free moral agent. He must, that is to say, not be compelled to act under the sway of some impersonal force.

The belief that the other possesses freedom to act on our behalf is an essential element of trust. Thus, the "overagainstness" of the other accompanies the recognition of His ability and readiness to help. There can therefore only be trust in a God who is believed to be "there" as an actual Existent, yet One who, in spite of His otherness, is not indifferent to us. Because He is God, He can make absolute demands upon us; since He is God, He assures us maximum power to meet His demands. He is therefore a God worthy of our trust, as One to whom we can talk. Consequently, "to understand the language of prayer," writes Phillips, "which in this case means understanding what it means to *ask* God for something, one must take account of the relationship within which prayer is made. The point is not that God cannot answer the request *unless* there is a spiritual relation between the believer and Himself, but rather, that in order to understand what we mean by asking, receiving, and thanking in this context, one must understand the spiritual relationship."[4]

Does God Answer Prayer?

This question can only be finally answered in the context of faith. It is not one upon which unbelief can seriously judge. And yet there are confessing agnostics, who have dogmatically denied that God answers prayer. As a typical example in this regard, one may refer to the discussion of the subject by T. R. Miles. Setting his critique in the context of linguistic philosophy, Miles proceeds to examine the proposition: "God answers prayer." It yields, he suggests, two constituent declarations: a) prayer sometimes produces results, and b) these results are caused by God.[5]

Miles readily admits, as far as the first case is concerned, that it is not possible to assert categorically that there are no instances of a connection between prayer and certain results. He nevertheless contends that only by a thoroughgoing use of the empirical method can the validity of the statement be established. He thereupon calls for a controlled experiment to statistically prove or disprove the claim. His idea is to set apart two wings of a hospital. In the one, ordinary methods of treatment are used; in the other, these methods are supplemented by prayer. In this way, Miles contends it will be possible to find out for certain whether prayer does in fact produce results. Admitting the practical difficulties of his suggested experiment, Miles is emphatic that the question of whether prayer does work can only be decided in some experimental manner.

But there are snags in Miles' contention, apart from the practical one he allows. To call for a controlled experiment is an old rue; and because it has the ring of sincerity it is point-making. Yet it is obviously absurd. Miles seeks to forestall further criticism by repudiating C. S. Lewis's assertion that such a method of assessing a connection between prayer and actual results is irreverent and a blasphemous tempting of God. But is not Lewis surely right in his position? For was not some such suggestion made to Christ Himself to prove His relationship with God by demonstrative results? But He rejected the demand outright. In so doing He made clear that statements of faith can only be verified within their own context and according to their own standards. For unless religious experience is granted independent validity in its own field, and the theoretic reflections about it are considered in the context of this basic acceptance, then all discussion about religious issues will be irrelevant to those to whom religion is a living affair.[6] To talk, therefore, of a controlled experiment as a method to judge the validity of prayer-claims is a failure to take account of this elementary fact; for to "understand religious judgments we need to understand religious interests."[7]

Miles will not allow any validity to the second element in the proposition: God answers prayer.—He discredits the claim that any results are caused by God. He discounts the idea of God being dragged in as an "Extra Entity"; and to credit "activity" to God is, he thinks, to make God a sort of "para-psychical" person. Indeed, all talk of God is inappropriate, for no statement regarding God can be of what God is. God is beyond all our classifications; all we can do in the presence of the ultimate and mysterious is to adopt the "way of silence." This means that prayer-language, the language of commitment and dedication, may be retained as subjectively useful; but "pseudo-causal" prayer, as he calls it, is not possible.

It is hard to be sure whether Miles regards himself as engaging a real enemy or not. If he is, as H. D. Lewis explains, "merely tilting against those who have a crudely anthropomorphic view of God—as a Being up in the skies for example—then the most we would complain about would be that he is wasting his time, most of all in talking to Christians today. . . . But if Professor Miles merely wishes to enjoy himself attacking preposterous theological windmills we might leave him to it. The trouble is that when he, and many like him today, have disposed of crude misconceptions which they take to be common, they conclude that there is nothing left but "parables" and ways of viewing secular facts. We may have to use the language of parable and metaphor in religion, but the reference all the same is to something we take to be real. God is not a fact in the sense of being part of the world He sustains, but does it make sense to say that we believe in Him unless we take Him to be some kind of reality?"[8] We would answer Professor Lewis's question and say: it makes no sense whatever. God is some kind of reality: the kind that can and does answer prayer. According to Pascal, "God instituted prayer in order to allow His creatures the dignity of causality." There are two methods whereby results may be brought about by God—namely, work and prayer. Both are alike in this respect—that in both we try to produce a state of affairs which God has not (or at any rate not yet) seen fit to provide "on His own."[9]

The Problem of Unanswered Prayer

For the remainder of this chapter we will make some comments on the vexing question of unanswered prayer. For many this is the most urgent issue of all on the subject. Some have been so plagued with doubts about God's seeming unconcern and lack of responsiveness that they have virtually abandoned the practice of petitionary prayer. They may still seek to keep up a nodding acquaintance with God; to bid Him "Good morning" and "Good night" at least. But those who still affirm that God does answer prayer face the criticism that their claim is only a case of wishful thinking. Critics say it is but another instance of the "pathetic fallacy"; of the natural tendency to attribute motives and causes where they do not apply; to mistake coincident events for purposes; to dogmatize that there is only one explanation for a result when there may be a thousand. All these objections finally focus on two main questions directed to the believer: how do you know that God has answered your prayers, and why are some left unanswered?

Some meet these objections by contending that God says, "Yes," to all our prayers; others suppose that He says, "No," to some of them.

The former maintain that God has not refused to answer any of the believer's prayers; they say everything is answered according to the way things turn out. The prayer, for example, was for health, but it was not given; yet strength was found to bear the ordeal with fortitude. For the critic, this sort of answer is of course troublesome, in that it can never be falsified. There is always a let-out: what was asked for was not forthcoming, but something was received. We, however, are not able to adopt a solution so neat, which must appear to the objector to be merely evasive. It is not, it seems to us, in the interest of religion to defend the thesis that no prayer is left unanswered and no request unheeded. In fact, this "all-answer hypothesis," as we may call it, if accepted, would lead to some odd conclusions.

What are we to say, for example, if a believer who prayed for safety on an airplane trip was injured in a crash? Or another who asked for life was overcome by death? This latter instance would certainly be an extraordinary alternative.

This does not mean, however, that sometimes prayer cannot be seen in this light. Jesus prayed on the Mount of Olives that the cup might pass from Him, but it did not; instead He found courage to endure love's utmost limits for humanity's good. The apostle Paul prayed that the "thorn in the flesh" might be taken away, but it was not. Still his prayer was heard, and he was given grace sufficient to bear whatever it was.

It is important to recognize that in some cases God does not, for His own purposes and our good, answer our every specific request, but instead assures us of His grace to deal with the situation. However, we must openly admit that this is not always so. Some prayers appear to remain unanswered. Yet this does not justify that God does not have the divine right to meet our requests with a blank negative. He has that right; and He could use it. But in the context of rational debate, the problem is to identify both the negative and the positive instances. With regard to the negative cases we are asked how we know that God has said, "No." God, it seems, has said, "No," because we have not been able to identify a "Yes." But is not this, it is replied, mere evasion and escapism? And the question is further pressed; for how long must prayer be offered before one finally concludes that God has decided on a refusal? Here the ancient sigh acquires a new meaningfulness and relevance: "O Lord how long shall I cry for help and thou will not hear?"[10]

Can we ever really be sure that God has answered, "Yes"? May it not be a coincidence? H. D. Lewis refers to an oft told tale: a small boy, taught that God answers prayer, kneels behind a hedge and asks for a toy. A passing farmer overhears the petition, contacts the lad, and out of kindness or perversity supplies the money to meet the boyish wish. Lewis does not think that the logic of faith is much strengthened by stories of this kind. And he refers to certain other counter-suggestions which could be made by unbelievers to such an instance. For example, the meeting at the time might have been a coincidence—experiences of this sort are not rare; and the farmer could have given the money in response to some irrational whim—for people do act this way. Considering the case of someone "given up" by the medical expert and who prayed for himself, or was prayed for by others, and was restored to full health, Lewis underscores the difficulty which such instances present. What, for example, is to be said about the many "negative instances?" For there "seem to be enough negative examples to leave the explanation open, to attribute the recovery of the patient, if not to some subtle psychological influence, at least to some unknown factor which may, or *may not*, be religious."[11]

With regard to the negative instances, Lewis seeks to reduce the area of the problem by pointing out that some prayers are falsely so-called. They may spring from selfish and unworthy motives. Prayer is not, he insists, without its moral and spiritual conditions. Nor indeed does the efficacy of petitionary prayer "involve the expectation that such prayer will invariably receive an explicit answer." Looking at actual historical instances in which answers to prayer have been claimed by recognized men of God, Lewis sees an impressive correlation of such occurrences and the awareness of a peculiar enlivening presence of God. This consistent correlation carries, he believes, its own apologetic; at the same time it brings to faith a strong encouragement that prayer is not vain. Professor Lewis has certainly dealt honestly and suggestively with the problem of unanswered prayer; and we fully agree with much of what he has said. But maybe it will help if in our final paragraphs we approach the problem from a slightly different angle.

Factors Involved in Intercessory Prayer

In the act of intercessory prayer—as in any act of asking—three factors are involved. There is (A) the person who does the asking; (B) the one asked; (C) the act of asking itself. The right combination of these factors makes prayer effective. Reasons, therefore, for unanswered prayer can be found in any one.

We begin with (A)—the first party in the relationship—the petitioner himself. We must consider the desires which prompt his prayer; the attitude with which he prays; and the purpose for which his prayer is offered. All these, or any one, will affect the acceptance or rejection of a man's petitioning. Where self-interest dominates, that man has no right to expect anything from the Lord. Jesus refused to answer a gruesome request of His disciples that fire should come from heaven to destroy those who rejected His appeal. Many prayers simply cannot be answered, because they are offered out of twisted desires, selfish motives or for some unworthy end. "The major premise of effective prayer is a sense of worth," says Professor Vergilius Ferm.[12] This, however, is not a sense of our self-attained worth, as if God must meet our demands since we have some right to command Him. We have no such rights at all, except that God has invited us to ask of Him. God is not at our beck and call. The magician may adopt the attitude of coercion; but the attitude of prayer is that of a requesting.

Yet a "sense of worth" is essential in the man himself. For it is written that if we regard iniquity in our heart the Lord will not hear us.[13] Maybe we should distinguish between a "sense of worth" and a "sense of worthiness." The latter is something which no man apart from the grace of God can ever have. The Pharisee of our Lord's parable thought himself *worthy*, while the publican confessed himself of enough *worth* to God to ask for forgiveness. The man who considers that in himself, and of himself, he is worthy of God's attention has shortened the range of his prayer to the area of his own self. And to such a man God has nothing to say. But the man assured of his worth to God, who knows that God cares for him, can ask in faith and hope. Yet even he will not on that account assume there is anything automatic in the relationship between his praying and the blessings he requests. For he will admit that he is sometimes unclear as to what he should ask and confused as to what is best. The man of prayer will then be the first to acknowledge, in the light of faith's hindsight, that some prayers could not have been answered; he will even thank God that they were not. The fault is not in God but in himself.

Still there is the Other Party (B) involved in the prayer-situation. There is God: and God has His rights. His desires, attitudes, and purposes must be taken into consideration. To offer prayer for the fulfillment of our own ambitions and aspirations, without reference to God's glory and will, rightly earns the divine rebuff. And even a prayer which is free from the crudely selfish, or a prayer which is most devout and spiritual, is not on that account necessarily the sort of prayer God could always answer. God's will is best; only in this context can that which is best for us be understood and sought. Yet even to the most holy of men the awareness of God's will is not consistent. And what seems to be within His will is not always so; still, if God is good enough and loving enough and great enough to be addressed in petition, He is also to be entrusted with the answers. Prayer is offered on the strength of God's character: He loves enough not to grant those requests which His wisdom sees would either not be for our good or within His purpose.

There is also the other factor in the prayer relationship, the asking itself (C), or perhaps more properly, that which is asked. Some petitions made by indeed devout, pious persons are so trivial, so thoughtless, so general, that hardly any answer could be expected or seen. Common sense and experience tell us that the nature of a request significantly affects the response. A prayer that would give us a privileged position, where we would be assured preferential treatment at the expense of others, is not likely to be answered. God does not relieve us of duty and service in any such magical way. Certainly we can and should bring all things before God in prayer, for no detail of our lives escapes His concern. But we do not need to pray for something to be done for us which we can do ourselves—for something to be provided which we can secure ourselves. What an odd world it would be if God did in fact answer every prayer, even those offered sincerely enough; how chaotic it would all become. But God would not be God, and the believing man would not have a rounded personal relationship with Him, if He did.

There may, then, be some things we can never have without prayer: but it is not possible for any to get everything; for that would be to make such a one better than he is and to empty faith of an essential ingredient. Faith is not believing in prayer as a means of having every need met: it is believing in God who can answer prayer; it is believing in God sometimes when there is nothing else to believe in. Yet there are some things God will only give with prayer; and it may even be that for some individuals He has added certain results with their praying. This answer is for them alone—for their good, the good of others, and for God's glory. But there are other blessings general to man for which He has not made prayer a condition; for does He not make the sun rise upon the evil and the good alike? Some requests He could not grant because of their nature—not because they are intrinsically impossible, but just because they are absurd or improper. To pray, however fervently, let us say, for the sudden exodus of a particular ethnic group from our country so as to avoid disruption and inconvenience would be a prayer God could not answer. Some prayers come to nought clearly because of something amiss in the party who makes the petition; and some because God being God knows what is right and best; and some, doubtlessly, because their very nature rules them out of consideration.

Yet the believing man is still convicted that God can and does answer prayer; his conviction is assured by his awareness of the living God and authenticated in the experience of personal relationship with Him in faith.

Chapter 8

Natural Evil

The problem of evil is inevitable. For if the world is indeed God's world, and if God is what Christian theism proclaims Him to be, then, how can we account for the presence of evil in it? A world created by an omnipotent and good God would surely show exclusive evidence of the four values: happiness, truth, beauty, and goodness. Instead, the presence of the counter disvalues of pain, error, ugliness, and sin are overwhelming. How can such a state of affairs be explained? This is the issue with which we are to be concerned in this and the two following chapters.

The problem of evil can be approached from two points of view. On the one hand, when man is in the center of the discussion, the question concerns what philosophers refer to as moral evil and theologians refer to as sin. On the other hand, when the world as such is being considered, the question is that of natural evil. Moral evil, then, is that which makes man uneasy in his relationship with God; natural evil is that which makes him unsure in his relationship with the world. The most serious issue is to reconcile the theistic view of God in His relation to the world with the fact of natural evil. It appears on the surface that God can be held more directly responsible for natural evil than moral evil. The world, after all, is not of man's origination; it is something "given." And however much man has been able to master nature's forces he seems unable to eliminate the possibility of disaster, suffering and pain. Thus, while the presence of moral evil may be charged to man's account; that of natural evil cannot.

The problem of natural evil is generally occupied with the issue of suffering and pain. The terrible reality of human suffering is too poignant to need any powerful demonstration or pictorial description. In a world made small by speedy and easy communiction, we are aware as never before of what C.E.M. Joad refers to as "the obtrusiveness of evil."[1] It is hard to evade reflection upon the problem. Some have sought to minimize its reality with the easy optimism which is content to point out that the world has more happiness than misery. But even if such mathematical calculation were admitted as accurate, this would neither make the problem any less real, nor easier to understand by those who suffer. Victims of suffering would be bound to ask, "Why should I be the one who suffers? Why, indeed, should there be any suffering at all in God's world?"

Contrary Reactions to the Experience and Fact of Suffering

The presence of natural evil in the world has, from the religious point of view, induced almost opposite attitudes in many. On the one side, some find the experience of suffering an obstacle to faith, while others use the fact of suffering as an argument against faith. On the other side, some are inspired to faith through the experience of suffering, while others view suffering as an argument for faith.

Those whose suffering has led them to protest against the natural order may ask, "Why should such things be?" And they cannot be convinced that a good God with power to prevent pain can be in control. There are well-known biographies of men and women for whom the experience of suffering has hindered faith's awakening. And there are, besides, numbers of ordinary folks in whom suffering has smothered all possible belief in a God of goodness responsible for life's affairs.

Others, from a reflective rather than from an experimental standpoint, have used the fact of suffering as a refutation of belief in God. Hume's underscoring of the apparent nonpurposeful elements in the universe is well known. For him, the presence of so much undeserved pain counts decisively against belief in a God all-powerful and all-good. Antony Flew similarly argues that such an abundance of suffering and purposelessness in the world makes it impossible to believe in an almighty moral Being responsible for its existence.[2]

In opposition, however, have been those in all ages who have found in their suffering an inspiration to faith. Quite often the greatest sufferers have been the greatest believers. Many would confirm the sentiments voiced by VonHügel in the letter, "To a Friend in his Last Illness." He wrote: "Looking back now I am grateful for nothing so much as for this—that, given the suffering and trials which God then sent or permitted, He also soon gave her (our dearest Gertrud) a light, far more vivid and continuous than it used to be, and an evergrowing acceptance and active utilization of it, as to the place, meaning and unique fruitfulness of such suffering, thus met (as it were) halfway, in the mysterious, but most certain, most real scheme of the deepest life and of God."[3] VonHügel does not write in sonorous generalizations about the "nobleness of pain," or of its "uplifting effects." He was aware of what he calls the "apparent sterility of suffering which adds the final touch of trial to our pains." But he can still affirm that "God is more living and real than all suffering and all sin."

The anti-theistic assertion so often made, that no one deeply aware of the devastating effects of natural evil can still believe in God who is finally good and omnipotent, does not square with the empirical facts. More often it has been true that sensitiveness to evil has developed *pari passu* (simultaneously) with faith in such a Being. Men of deeply religious commitment have always been foremost in realizing the presence of natural evil and the seriousness of the problem it presents. In fact, as has been said, "The more wholehearted our belief in God, the deeper our revulsion from evil, the greater our compassion for suffering."[4]

The very presence of evil, instead of being an argument against belief in God, is rather an apologetic for theism. Good and evil are not, as C. S. Lewis says, on all fours. Badness is not even bad in the same way that goodness is good. Evil is not the final fact, since it is essentially parasitic in character. "Evil preys upon the good, but the good preys upon nothing. Now there is much good in the universe as well as much evil; and, in the long run good shows itself to be the stronger, as the slow but indisputable progress of the human race bears witness. It is this consideration which rules out the hypothesis that the ground of the universe is morally evil, and which, as far as it goes, favors the position of the theist."[5] In an irrational and nonmoral universe there would be no problem of evil; it is precisely because the world is essentially rational and moral that evil becomes a question. Because truth and justice are more fundamental, more in harmony with what we conceive the nature of the ultimate to be, we can pronounce any deviations therefrom to be unhealthy in a social context and unholy in a religious one.

Theism and Natural Evil

Since the believer does acknowledge the existence of an all-powerful and loving God he finds the problem of evil on his hands. The atheist certainly cannot avoid reflection upon the presence of a "something" which causes distress and unhappiness, but he can find some satisfaction in the notion that nature is just like that, or that "surd evil" is a necessary element in the developing process and will be shed in time. But all "theistic schemes of thought are confronted with one great and apparently insoluble difficulty—the fact of evil. The difficulty presented by this fact is felt with acuteness varying directly with the completeness of the conviction that God is good. If reality consists only in happenings, void of all purpose and tending to no goal, it may then be impossible to understand it at all, but at least there is no special difficulty about the occurrences described as evil. Whatever causal processes are recognized to exist are sufficient for these events, as for others. The very fact that evil is felt to be a problem even by many of those who avow no theistic faith, is evidence of the natural tendency of the mind to seek some explanation of the world in other terms than those of purely mechanical causation. But as soon as that principle is pronounced insufficient, there is no alternative recourse save to the principle of purpose; and if that be adopted the difficulty represented by evil at once appears."[6]

J. S. Mill, in his famous *Essay on Nature*, sought to throw doubt upon the existence of an omnipotent Being by arguing from the apparent imbalance in the apportionment of good and evil. Suffering and happiness, he supposed, should be exactly proportioned to a person's good and evil acts, so that no human being would have a worse lot than another who deserved worse. The idea is not of course new: the people of the days of the Old Testament prophet Ezekiel thought that God was mismanaging things. A perfect justice, they imagined, would weigh men's acts as in a balance. They assumed the Lord's ways were unfair; God reminded them that it was their own thinking that was at fault. The evil consequences they were observing were not the consequences of injustice at the heart of things but consequences of their own evil deeds.[7]

This must not be taken to mean that there is a direct relation between a specific case of natural evil and a willful wrongdoing. Few people would consider it improper for the deliberate transgressor to suffer for his crimes. The trouble is, however, that the wicked seem to get off scot-free. The instances where evil acts appear to bring no penalty often appear to threaten the moral government of the world. One may also be disturbed by instances where the innocent suffer without apparent reason.

In the light of such damaging evidences, can a man persist in the belief that a world in which such things can happen was created and is controlled by a God of love and power? If there is a God at all, it is argued, then, either His love must be defective or His power inadequate, or both, to allow all this tragedy.

The problem of suffering has ever been, and still remains, a tormenting reality. It has presented men throughout the ages with a challenge to seek some answer to why it should be so. The various answers which have been given can be classified under general headings; and by doing so we will be able to see how each fares when critically examined. We will begin with what believers consider is the least acceptable and ascend to what appears to us to be the most probable and reasonable.

The Unrealness of Natural Evil

Some have maintained that suffering and pain are illusory. This thesis has broadly taken two forms—a religious and a philosophical. The religiously oriented view has vogue among the Christian Scientists, who are apparently supported by some rather vague psychologists. For such suffering and pain have no objective reality and validity; they are mere states of mind.

It must, of course, be granted that there is such a thing as purely mental suffering, suffering for which no physical cause can be found. But it is another matter to assert that every instance of suffering is such a case. The heart-rending cry of the tortured or the agonizing moan of a child crushed by a car, for example, cannot be explained away like this. To seek to do so is to affront our intelligence and to make a mockery of the sobs and sighs of those who suffer. To suggest that human suffering is unreal is to suppose that the God of all truth has let man, created in His image, go on from generation to generation being mocked and deceived by a tragic illusion. That would virtually make God a party to a most ungodlike joke.

Besides, such a notion leaves too many questions begging. If evil is unreal why should good be supposed to be real? And why, too, should that which is mere illusion bring such heartbreak? And how can one understand the origin of an illusion so tragic which has universal impact?

From a philosophical standpoint, a number of teachers, mainly non-theistic pragmatists like John Dewey and R. W. Sellers, and logical empiricists like A. J. Ayer, refuse to regard good and evil as objectively real. They are rather, it is maintained, values and disvalues of conscious experience. The sources of good and evil are considered neutral and have no value as such. As these neutralities work out in experience they are designated either good or bad. Heat, for example, may be regarded as a neutral entity, becoming "good" when it warms us and "bad" when it burns us. But this rather trite observation does not answer the question: *why* suffering? It merely makes it unreal by reading it in terms of the artificial valuations of experience. Few, as F. R. Tennant observes, will find "comfort in the supposition that evil is an illusion of finite and temporal experience, an inadequate idea, or an appearance which would dissolve away if only we see *sub species temporis* (from the perspective of temporality). The problem of evil is raised by the world as we find it and is not solved by diverting attention to otherworldly cognition of a world-order other than the phenomenal and temporal."[8]

The Minimizing of Natural Evil

If the problem of evil cannot be explained (away) as illusion, maybe its force will be lessened by fixing the boundaries of its presence.

There are two prongs to the argument which seeks to reduce the effect of natural evil. On the one hand, it is contended that since animals do not really feel pain as do humans, there is consequently far less suffering in the world than at first appears. On the other hand, it is suggested, with the same conclusion, that physical pain cannot be stigmatized as evil because it has no moral overtones.

It may indeed be true that animals do not feel pain as does the higher species of man. However, they certainly behave as if they do. Animals show clear evidences of pain reactions. Maybe the difference between their experience and ours is that they do not reflect upon the fact. As McPherson says, "They have the pain but not the problem."[9] But just because animals do not apparently discuss the morality of their suffering, we have no right to say that there is nothing evil in their experience of pain. The very fact of the frustrations they exhibit at such times provides data for the problem. Man is prone to interpret animal reactions to unnecessary pain stimuli as evil. And if it is still insisted that the animals are really immune from suffering, the question remains: why should God allow His intelligent beings to be the victims of the delusion that animals do not suffer? Since we regard animals as sentient creatures, we are obliged to regard them as subject to suffering; and it is the apparent unnecessary horror, which so often attends pain reactions in the world of nature, that constitutes the problem of evil.

But what about the idea that physical pain cannot be called evil because it has no moral overtones? There is a sense in which it is true. If, for example, I cut my finger by accident, the action itself may be neither moral or immoral. It may well be that much pain is amoral. But even so, the experience of pain may have moral consequences; and the fact of the pain may raise questions of moral judgment.

Yet, if we suppose that three-quarters of the pain is merely physical, the question could still be asked: why should the other quarter cause such torture of mind and anguish of spirit in God's world? To suggest that mere physical suffering is no great cause for concern is to be left with the odd conclusion that an infant bruised or burned presents no real problem, while the parents' grief does. The fact of the matter is, however, that it is sometimes harder to be sure which is the worse evil, the mental or the physical. Professor Joad argues that most of us, if forced to choose, would opt for pain of mind or humiliation of spirit rather than physical torture. In most cases, however, there is no such alternative, since the two are so bound up with each other that it is not possible to experience one singly. It would seem, then, that the attempt to minimize evil, by belittling physical pain does not hold up.

The Usefulness of Natural Evil

If, then, neither the view that natural evil is unreal nor the view that it is less extensive than supposed can be taken as solutions to the problem of evil, perhaps, something may be said for what we may designate as the usefulness of natural evil. One of George Macdonald's stories pictures the bitter exclamation of a woman flung into an unexpected horror. "I wish I'd never been made." Her irritation was received with the quiet retort of her friend, "My dear, you're not made yet. You're only being made—and this is the Master's process." This dialogue depicts the thesis that seeming evil works for our final good, and that good somehow depends upon the existence of evil. Augustine classically expresses the idea by declaring that God would never have permitted evil if He were not strong enough to draw good from it. Also, Keats's well-known remark explains that pain and trouble are necessary to school an intelligence and to make a soul.

These two ways of stating the case have received modern restatement; the Augustinian by Jacques Maritain and the Keatsean by John Hick.

Maritain, closely following the bishop of Hippo, declares that it is in the "order of the goods of grace" that there should be read "the greater good par excellence" for which "are ordained absolutely speaking, simpliciter, all the evils that God permits, evil of fault and evil of suffering." Maritain argues that "this greater good, simpliciter" deals not primarily with the good of the universe or of nature. It does not serve the perfection of the machine of the world but supremely the goods of grace and glory and in the person-to-person love which unites created agents to God and to one another. In bringing about this result, evils are compensated by a "good incomparably greater." Yet there is also a second benefit, for, "the permission of evil for a greater good applies also in the domain of temporal history." Both good and evil progress simultaneously—wheat and weeds grow together. But the progress of the good is greater, "for everything considered, the good is certainly stronger than evil."

We live, then, in "hope"; yet, surely, since evil is ultimately for the sake of good, a hope which believes "that from social evils which revolt us, from slavery, from misery, from the power of great monsters which devour the individual person, from the barbarous conditions in which so many of God's creatures live, human history will emerge not only with the cessation of these evils, but with the increase of the goods of humanity—so that the spirit may gain ascendancy, that the unification of the human race may come about under the sign of liberty, not of a herd confrontation, and that all men may have access *free of charge* to the elementary goods of human life."[10]

Our concern here is not with Maritain's eschatological hope and vision, and whether it fits in with the biblical faith. But it is surely right to ask, if such a view of evil can really satisfy the reflective mind. Was all this evil needed to bring out the good? And there is a residue of evil which does not seem to be for anyone's good at all; some experiences of suffering and pain do not strengthen faith and make a life. Certainly, not every instance brings happy results out of all our afflictions. In the end, this does not seem to matter in Maritain's message, for the blessings and benefits that man cannot distill from evil, God will dissolve into non-being. As Maritain puts it, "He whose Name is above every name, the eternally Victorious is certain to win the game finally; He wins it at each instance, even when He seems to be loosing it."

Hick seeks to reconstruct an explanation in which natural evil has usefulness in nature. But first, he rejects "the cosmic picture sketched by St. Paul and completed by Augustine" as being nothing more than a "product of the religious imagination."[11] Granting that this "basically authentic history" approach was the only way open to them, and may still be "mythologically satisfying," it can, he argues, no longer be maintained in the light of scientific, moral, and logical objections. It comes unglued on the scientific level by reason of the demonstrated fact that natural "evils"—earthquakes and the like—were there prior to man's emergence. And the policy of punishing others for the sin of one man he considers immoral: while the notion that sin resulted from the free act of a perfect being is, he believes, incoherent.

Consequently, Hick contends that there is a better way for a theodicy, a defense of God's goodness in view of the existence of evil. He starts with the idea that man did not appear on the earth as a finished product, a perfect article, who somehow, but not unwillingly, got tripped up. He thereupon elaborates, "a two-stage conception of the creation of man." On the one hand, he is the product of a long evolutionary process, by which he has become capable of the infinite. This stage was easy enough for the divine omnipotence, for in the process, the "man-to-be" was largely the subject of divinely organized processes. But the second stage, in which the "man-that-had-come-to-be" attains perfection as a child of God, is a long, laborious process. This cannot be done by divine fiat, "but only through the uncompelled responses and willing co-operation of human individuals in their actions and reactions in the world in which God has placed them."[12]

God's supreme purpose is to fashion many, indeed all, sons for glory. He has made the world as a place best fitted for this end. The world is, therefore, to be seen, not as a once-for-all perfect and now sin-disrupted world, and not even as the best possible world in and of itself, but as the one most suited to God's plan for man. The theodicy, therefore, that will satisfy is, according to Hick, that which sees the world as a vale of soul-making. God's plan for mankind determined the sort of world He has made. He did not create a "hedonistic paradise"; for the chief end of man is not his own pleasure but that he should glorify God. Thus, the world is not for man's enjoyment so much as for his discipline and perfecting unto the fullness of the stature of Christ.

To think, therefore, of God's relation to the world on the model of a human housing pet animals in a cage is to miss the point of the divine intention. It would be humane to make the pets' quarters as pleasant and healthful as possible. But man is not an animal pet; he is a responsible being. The thesis is, then, that the world as we know it, with its quota of purposeless events, is best fitted as "a vale of soul-making." Man came into the world "at an epistemic distance from God," [without divine knowledge] as a product of natural evolution. And this is his "fallenness." Hick specifies his view as Irenaean, in contrast with the Augustinian in which evil is regarded as lack of the good stemming from man's misuse of his freedom. The Irenaean type of response to evil, fully blossomed in Schleiermacher, is "eschatologically oriented, finding its clue to the meaning of evil in the hoped-for fulfillment of God's purpose for his creation in an infinite, because eternal, good which is such as to satisfy all that has occurred on the way to it."[13]

This chapter will not discuss Hick's criticism of Augustine's account of the origin of sin due to man's misuse of his freedom, which he pronounces "self-contradictory and unintelligible."[14] Our concern is with his solution of the problem of natural evil. His fundamental thesis, that the evil in the world is all for man's good, somehow does not ring true. It is hardly comforting to tell a man who has just broken his neck that it is good for his soul. Of course, it may be; but that would be because of the man's attitude in his misfortune. But it would be difficult to convince him that that was the reason for it. Dr. Hick envisions a world which has been magically freed from all the harsh realities, and yet he tells us that only in a world where natural evil has a place can virtues like love and courage have any meaning. A heaven in which virtue did not reign supreme would be no heaven at all. He finds it difficult, however, to show how virtues can exist without the opposites—which he considers necessary in this vale of soul-making. And he cannot show why such excess of natural evil was required to help man on his upward way. It almost seems, as Donald Mackinnon remarks, that "if the 'world is a vale of soul-making' it shows many signs of being a badly botched job."[15] Hick is certainly not unaware of the seeming excess of suffering in nature, but when he has said all he can by way of mitigation and justification, he acknowledges defeat. He thus takes refuge in "the positive value of mystery."[16] Whether, however, this is a fitting conclusion for a theodicy which promised so much is another matter.

Yet, others regard this positive value of mystery the final solution to the problem of natural evil.

The Mysteriousness of Natural Evil

Julian Huxley asserts "that the life of the less-civilized half of mankind is largely based on trying to find an answer to a wrong question." And he expresses the opinion that "there are a number of questions that it is no use asking because they can never be answered."[17] This position has, it seems, been assumed by several recent writers on the subject of natural evil: the question itself is really absurd and, as such, permits no answer. We can only fall back on "the positive value of mystery."

C. A. Campbell does not regard moral evil as a problem, since he sees no difficulties in crediting sin to man's misuse of his free will. The problem of evil, however, is not, he contends, the problem of sin, but that of suffering.[18] Traditional solutions assume that God's nature can be grasped by the finite mind of man. It is supposed that we speak factually about God when we talk of Him as all-powerful and all-good. But this is not so, for all statements about God are symbolic, according to Campbell. If God is not, then, literally omnipotent and moral, does not the question, how can a powerful and good God create and allow natural evil, become meaningless? Campbell is convinced that it does. Consequently, "the whole project of seeking to 'explain' or 'justify' the world which God creates is in principle absurd; indeed irreligious, since it implies that mere finite minds can plumb the depths of the creative Mind, and thereby denies in effect the immensity of the gulf which the truly religious man must always acknowledge as separating the creature from the Creator."[19]

Evidently, then, it is folly and faithlessness to seek to frame the question as to why there should be natural evils. Rational theism allows such an issue to be raised just because it conceives of God in literalistic terms; but for Campbell, God is quite beyond all such. Thus, the "real solution to the problem of suffering, it is suggested, lies in seeing that it is not a problem that can have intelligible meaning for finite minds at all."[20] The endeavor to justify the ways of God to man is not, he asserts, "for supra-rational

Theism a question that it is difficult to answer. It is a question that it is ridiculous to ask."[21] Evidently, then, according to Campbell, it is the height of folly to talk about the problem of natural evil. To the sufferer who begins to frame the inevitable question, the finger indicating silence must be raised: "Mum's the word! for we are supra-rational theists and do not listen to silly questions!"

In line with Campbell is Berdyaev, who states that "traditional," or "positive," theology cannot deal with the problem of evil. For God is really beyond all rational statements and must be thought about "symbolically and mythologically."[22] "It is obvious," says Berdyaev, "that God is 'beyond good and evil' for on 'this side' of it is our fallen world and certainly not God. God is above the good. And there cannot be in Him any evil that is not this side of the distinction."[23] Man has, therefore, according to Berdyaev, his ultimate origin in the abyss of mystery—in "primeval uncreated meonic freedom." His essence is freedom, and this freedom is not God's gift but exists as itself eternal. The world and man are the offspring of "fathomless non-being." "Fathomless freedom springing from non-being entered the created world, consenting to the act of creation. God the Creator has done everything to bring light into that freedom, in harmony with His great conception of creation. But without destroying freedom He could not conquer the potency to evil contained therein. This is why there is tragedy and evil in the world; all tradegy is connected with freedom."[24] The ultimate basis of all, says Berdyaev, is a mystery which merges into the last Mystery of the Divine Nothing. This meonic, uncreated freedom which gives man his essential nature, is itself a mystery.

"Mystery, docta ignorantia, have a profound significance. The whole meaning, importance and value of life are determined by the mystery behind it, by an infinity which cannot be rationalized but can only be expressed in myths and symbols. God is the infinite mystery that underlies existence—and this alone makes the pain and evil endurable. They would be unendurable if the world and men were self-sufficient, if there were nothing beyond, higher, and deeper and more mysterious. We come to God not because rational thought demands His existence but because the world is bounded by a mystery in which rational thought ends. Consequently, all systems of positive theology are esoteric and do not touch upon the last things. Mystical negative theology brings us closer to the final depths. The limits to rational thought is set by a mystery and not by a taboo."[25]

Mystery, then, is the ultimate of all; as such it lies beyond the realm of logistics. The discrimination between good and evil belongs to the sphere of morality. But God is beyond such distinctions: therefore, questions about His relation to good and evil cannot be answered and should not be asked. Good and evil have an origin in time and have been preceeded by a state of being, "beyond," or "prior" to their coming to be. Good and evil are correlatives; good came about at the same time as evil and disappears together with it.[26] This means, Berdyaev declares, that "the tormenting problem of evil is not to be finally solved within the confines of the phenomenal world."[27]

To seek an answer to the question of evil is, therefore, futile, since no answer can be given; all is ultimate mystery. No wonder Berdyaev could not tolerate the person who thought he had all the answers.[28]

We accept the fact, as H. D. Lewis explains, that mystery surrounds all ultimate questions.[29] However, a religion of all mystery is impossible. We cannot appeal to mystery to make sense of a contradiction. When challenged to explain the presence of those natural evils which seem at odds with the belief that "God is almighty and wills the good of a creature," it really will not do to reiterate, "it is a mystery."[30] The fact is, however, that Berdyaev is not finally consistent with his own thesis. He seeks to bring relief to the sufferer by assuring him that God is a partner in his ordeal; tragic conflict, he insists, belongs to the very nature of the inner divine life.[31] All love brings suffering with it, and yet only love conquers suffering.[32] God is, then, the One most involved in our human sufferings. He shares the ills and pains which afflict us because of the natural evils which belong to the world. In saying this, Berdyaev does, of course, declare a profound truth. God is not remote from our agonies and heartaches. Yet, it is not very obvious how he himself can, having censured positive theology for intruding into the mystery of the Divine Being, so confidently pronounce God to be Tragic Deity. Nor are we able to understand why evil, conceived of as relative to good, should be so utterly incomprehensible.

The Naturalness of Natural Evil

Numerous writers seek a solution to the problem by advocating what we may refer to paradoxically as the naturalness of natural evil. The common denominator here is the idea of "evil" as somehow built into the constitution and structure of the physical world. There are, however, considerable differences in the way the details of the thesis are worked out. But they would seem to fall broadly under two main headings. On the one hand are those who regard natural evil as a direct consequence of the world's existence as a created actuality; on the other hand are those who see natural evil resulting from the influence of man's self-chosen moral failure upon an "imperfect" natural order.

Dom Pontifex illustrates for us the first of these ideas. "The possibility of evil is," he suggests, "inherent in creation."[33] Evil is lack of perfection. A perfect creation would have been impossible, for the concept is really a contradiction in terms. God is the one and only perfect; there cannot be another beside Him. There is, of logical necessity, a limitation attached to what is created. "A creature's power is limited, because it does not possess powers that other creatures have; God's power is unlimited because, being the Creator, he possesses not only all the powers that any creature possesses, or that any conceivable creature would possess, but even more than this."[34] This limitation of the creature over against God provides the possibility of evil; for the knowledge that we are limited implies the potential for frustration.

It is here, according to Pontifex, that a possible explanation for the existence of evil may be found. God is certainly omnipotent, but to suppose that even He could create another perfect being is to fail to grasp the precise meaning of His all-powerfulness. The presence of another perfect being would destroy the idea of God as uniquely perfect. In the structure of a created entity "the possibility of evil is unavoidable, an unfortunate necessity."[35] "Creation is a becoming, a gradual process in which there is a stage of imperfection before perfection is reached. But where there is imperfection, frustration is possible, and under certain circumstances it may be unavoidable."[36]

Pontifex does not claim that his explanation is the last word; not necessarily the "true" one; but it is at least a "possible" one. But his claim that creaturely limitation is the cause of natural evil can hardly be said to cover every case of its manifestation. It is not obvious, for example, why earthquakes should be attributed to such a cause.

D. H. Doig agrees that a certain quota of evils may stem from such a source but insists that it does not account for their sum total.[37] He suggests that there is something paradoxical about creation. It is the result, on the one hand, of the free and positive act of God, and yet, on the other hand, it exhibits the fact of His "negative withdrawal." Consequently, ambiguity exists in the world. Pain, for example, is not all evil; sometimes it is due to man's own fault and folly, but sometimes it warns of a more deep-seated danger. Yet the innocent still suffer; natural evils like earthquakes can only be attributed to "the ineluctable asperity of nature." Doig points out three causes for the existence of evil. The first is man's sin; the second, his ignorance and immaturity; and the third, "the hardness of nature," which causes "the frustration and unpleasantness of pain to have its emotional effects on the sufferer and others here as elsewhere."[38] Doig seeks to do justice to the first of these causes by suggesting that while disease and disability may not be the consequence of immediate and individual error, they may well be the result of collective error of mankind. He prefers, however, to see pain as a natural consequence of human limitation.

Doig does not, then, seek to explain the presence of evil by a single principle. He may be attacked on this score by those handy with the Occam razor. But his conviction that pain in general is inherent in the world as it is links up with that of C. S. Lewis. Lewis maintains that "the possibility of pain is inherent in the very existence of a world where souls can meet."[39] He calculates that man generates four-fifths of his suffering; after all, man, not God, makes bayonets and bombs. Such suffering is due to man's misuse of what may be called neutral entities—entities, that is, which could be used alternatively for his benefit. "The permanent nature of wood, which enables us to use it for a beam, also enables us to use it for hitting our neighbor on the head."[40] It is hardly fitting to blame God for the evil results of such a misuse. To suggest that He should not have made wood hard, because it produces, when deliberately used, a stunning effect on a man's head, is sheer folly. Nor can it be seriously maintained that God should step in every time and change the hard nature of wood to something soft like wool before actual contact with the head!

Lewis demonstrates that a world in which suffering is inherent is not out of harmony with the concept of a morally omnipotent God. He distinguishes between, what he designates as, absolute or intrinsic impossibilities and the relatively impossible. Intrinsic impossibilities can never be done even by an omnipotent God. God, for example, "cannot give a creature free-will and at the same time withhold free-will from it."[41] All things are certainly possible to God; but intrinsic impossibilities are not things but non-entities. The situation is otherwise in the case of the relatively impossible:

here some things are made impossible only because certain conditions have not been fulfilled. No fulfillment of conditions, however, can bring about the absolutely impossible. Thus, God's omnipotence means that He has power to do all that is intrinsically possible, not to do the intrinsically impossible. Lewis accordingly concludes that suffering must be possible in a world in which the highest possible moral values may be realized. For such a world must be an orderly world, and order depends upon things as they are and not otherwise. Even though God may occasionally "interfere," by what are called miracles, to modify the behavior of phenomena, it is still intrinsically impossible for Him to change the permanent nature of things as He has made them and yet leave them the same.

This is an undeniably ingenious attempt to justify the presence of suffering in God's world. Nonetheless, the application of the principle is limited. It certainly cannot be extended to cover cases of evil within the order of nature. It will not help much for a brokenhearted mother, in anguish over her suffering child, to be told that this is because of the way things are. It is all very well "to accept the universe"; but the question persists: why should it be a universe that permits such things?

The other way of stating the idea of the naturalness of natural evil is to argue that happenings in the natural order *become* evil in consequence of man's moral failure. This thesis gained classical exposition through Schleiermacher; although, according to John Hick, the idea runs back as far as Irenaeus. For Schleiermacher, what is now designated natural *evil* acquired evilness in relation to man's "fall."[42] The order of nature was not altered by the incoming of man's sin: earthquakes, pain, and the like, existed before man's arrival. But it is in the light of man's transgression that such happenings are defined as evil. When man had attained the status of a moral personality he was able to judge certain natural events as having ethical bearing on his life. When sin entered, that which was always there became, under God, the occasion of man's punishment. Viewed objectively and scientifically, then, natural evil is not due to man's sin; but viewed subjectively and religiously, it is to be regarded as both the effect and the penalty of man's sin.

George Galloway likewise maintains that "sin supervenes on an order in which natural evil already exists."[43] He is sure that moral evil is due to man's free agency, but he believes the prior presence of natural evil made possible man's wrong use of his freedom. Natural evil is then "the soil from which moral evil springs."[44]

Galloway is emphatic that "neither the view that sin is implicated in the nature of the finite being man, nor the view that it proceeds solely from the will and its power of free choice is by itself sufficient. . . . The natural evils which flow from man's finite nature, if they do not directly create sin, at least furnish the conditions which make it possible: while the specific character of sin itself is due to the agency of man's will."[45]

Neither Galloway nor Schleiermacher make clear why, prior to the incoming of sin, what is termed natural evil should have already existed. Apparently it would have existed because of the finite nature of created existences and the inherent deficiencies of an order which is in a state of becoming. Galloway admits that "when we ask at what point in the evolution of the human species natural was transformed into moral evil we are putting a question to which no definite answer can be given."[46]

The theologians, Dorner, Delitzsch and A. B. Bruce, argue that such a view by no means eliminates God from the scene. This view must rather be taken as evidence of the far-reaching wisdom of the Creator, who framed the world with a plan for the eventual incoming of moral evil. The constitution of the created universe has, therefore, always been designed in relation to sin. It did not, so to speak, enter as an unforeseen accident. In making the world, God was not blind to what was to be or unaware of the sort of choices man might make. He thus constructed His world as the most suitable abode for a race of morally infallible creatures, supplying everything necessary for their moral decision and discipline. On the one hand, there were happenings in the natural order which man would come to regard as evil in the event of his wrongdoing. On the other hand were manifold forms of good, which could reveal the faithfulness of the Creator and be the means of calling men back to repentance and of assuring pardon, restoration, and hope.

This account of natural evil is formulated in the context of a rigid doctrine of evolution and depends on the validity of its basic principle. More recent writers, following the lead given by Whitehead, Lloyd-Morgan, and Hartshorne, conceive of evolution dynamically rather than statically, and propose an explanation of natural evil in terms of incidents in the evolutionary process. This view acquires compelling statement from de Chardin and Pittenger, among others. The world, as such, is conceived to be in a state of process; it is itself a process. These process theologians virtually regard God as the Driving Force within the onward movement of the cosmos. God is not a detached Being, distant from, remote, and above the universe. His transcendence is but another term for His inexhaustability, which assures endless novelty and movement. The world of open possibilities holds therefore the probability of error. In fact, because of the world's progressive and dynamic nature, error is not only probable but almost inescapable.

Norman Pittenger makes use of Hartshorne's panentheistic doctrine: God includes the world as part of His being. He argues that God in His "consequent" aspect takes up all occurrences whether they are termed "good" or "evil." God can make the best of everything; and those happenings in the natural process which affect us in some adverse way He can use for our advantage. It is, he contends, of the nature of love to pour itself out for others; to take into itself all that is made available to us; to absorb evil and out of it distill something good.[47]

This construction has merit in the way it brings nature into close relationship with human history. Nels Ferré makes a thought-provoking statement about this important factor. Through development in nature, he contends, God has made human history possible. Nature is, in fact, the condition of human history.[48] The history of nature must not be cut off from the history of man: for even before man was created on earth, however long ago and however gradually, nature was developing the conditions of life.[49] We need, therefore, to see "how deeply intermeshed are the consequences of man's evil in nature."[50] The implication of this close association of nature and human history has important consequences for a true theology of nature; it is a fact that needs strong emphasis in these days, in view of the destruction and pollution of our natural resources and environment. But it is another question whether the general thesis of the process theology provides an adequate solution to the problem of suffering and natural evil. It is not our present purpose to consider the wider implications of process thought.[51] But process thought seems to leave the impression that evil is designated as such only when removed from the wider context of the good, or when it ceases to minister to the ongoing process of history. The idea will certainly bring little comfort to anyone involved in a specific suffering. The thesis does not provide a meaningful reason for those events in nature from which no apparent good can be distilled.

The Unnaturalness of Natural Evil

Those thinkers we have just considered put natural evil prior to moral, but there are others who, following Augustine, prefer it the other way around. For them, moral evil comes first, and natural evil is a consequence of it. Instead, then, of speaking of the naturalness of natural evil, they would speak rather of the unnaturalness of natural evil. The idea, briefly stated, is that natural evil, no less than moral, was no normal condition of nature and life in God's creation. The incoming of sin, consequent upon man's free act, did not only affect man's nature but also the order of nature in which man dwells. Accordingly, the reason for human suffering is ultimately to be found in man's "fall." The universe was somehow involved in man's rebellion and is therefore a sufferer with man on account of sin, although sin itself is the result of man's willful act of transgression.[52]

This view is claimed as the biblical and historical Christian position. And certainly the Genesis record does teach that the very ground "was cursed" as a result of man's sinning.[53] In fact, it seems that the world, as the abode of man through whom sin came, was compelled "through its laws and agencies, to subserve the purposes of man's sin; in being perverted from its true uses in service of his lusts and vices; in the suffering of the animal creation through his cruelty in the blight, famine, earthquakes, etc., to which it is subjected in consequence of his sin, and as a means to punishment of it."[54]

This doctrine is not made void by the observation that animals existed prior to man. For, it is replied that the Genesis account itself puts their creation at an earlier age than that of humans. Nor is there need to speculate about a prior corruption of the animal world by the action of some Evil Agency, since it was man's sin that introduced the vicious element that causes animals to harm man.[55] It is worthwhile noting, in this regard, that He who was perfect Man was with the wild beasts, and they were apparently subject to Him.[56]

This view certainly has the merit of recognizing the effect of the two facts fundamental to biblical faith. It brings man and nature close together, so that man's acts are seen to have cosmic consequences and reactions. Man is combination of dust and deity—he is of the ground and of God; therefore, his "fall" has results which affect both. This is the reason the Old Testament prophets often call upon the natural order to bear, as it were, witness with them for God, and against the consequences within nature of their wrongdoing. Again, this understanding of natural evil, due to the disruption of nature through man's rebellion, gives purpose to the cosmic significance of Christ's work.[57] The whole creation awaits the full effect of God's redeeming act in Christ, when a new heaven and earth of righteousness will come to be. For the Christian's future vision rests upon his saving faith. He lives in hope of the emancipation of God's universe from "the bondage of corruption" and the establishment of God's perfect order.

The relation of sin and death may be thought of as establishing a connection between sin and natural evil. Human death, the crowning evil, carries a host of attendant evils in its train, evils caused directly by man's sin. It is something in which all men are implicated; and death is, as Emil Brunner says, "for the Christian understanding an ordinance of God, but it is not an original element of the order of creation; on the contrary, it has arisen from disorder. It is a reaction of the divine anger to human rebellion."[58] Death, as far as man is concerned, was apparently no part of the purpose of God for man. But could it not be that man, by refusing to follow the dictates of his higher nature and succumbing to that which was of the earth, had to suffer already an inherent characteristic of the natural order? If so, the fact of death resulting from man's act of folly would illustrate that at least some suffering does find its ultimate origin in human sin. And could it not be that in some way the universe itself was set at odds because of man's choice to live in God's world independent of Him? This does not seem to be an improbable idea.

Relating natural evil to man's sin does not force us to conclude that any one single event of suffering is itself a direct punishment for individual transgression. We can accept the verdict of C. A. Campbell that "most of us will resolutely decline to believe, no matter who tells us, that the toddler who plays too close to the fire and is burned in agony is merely receiving just punishment for its sins."[59] But when Campbell goes on to assert that there are some "eminent theologians who apparently want to say either this or something in principle indistinguishable from it," we are not with him.[60] For in Campbell's judgment, the concept of "collective guilt" is another way of stating the conclusion about the burned toddler. Campbell refers to some chapters in H. D. Lewis's, *Morals and the New Theology*, which, he affirms, show the concept of corporate responsibility and shared guilt to be immoral and impossible. The thrust of Lewis's complaint is that responsibility and guilt cannot be transferred.[61] Each man must bear his own burden. Lewis refuses to allow that he is advocating pure "individualism" in taking this position;[62] he resents the charge of "Pelagianism."[63] Despite the high marks credited to him by Campbell, Lewis's show of success seems due to his confusion between personal and collective responsibility. Certainly, where individuals are concerned, blame and punishment follow the act: but this is not necessarily so in the case of the collectivity. That is to say, as D. E. Cooper argues, that collective responsibility cannot be reduced to individual responsibility.[64]

Reactions by some groups have consequences for nature and for the individuals. A kitchen device is altered, or the course of a river is diverted; but the firm or the council cannot be condemned as the responsible cause in the same way as an individual might. In some such cases, one cannot avoid being the cause of undeserved suffering. In fact, sometimes an individual may do evil acts which entangle the innocent in the consequences. If, for example, a husband is convicted for a crime, the other members of his family are somehow caught up in, and share in, his guilt. Although personally innocent, they suffer because of their relationship with the one condemned.

But maybe the idea of collective responsibility and shared guilt is a *suggestio falsi* (false proposition). For the first sin, in a profound sense, was humanity's sin. As such it has inevitable cosmic reactions—since man is not detached from the world. These cosmic reactions brought disorder to nature, consequences all men share. In regard to the cosmic consequences, the question of responsibility and guilt, as generally understood, is hardly meaningful, unless one wants to repudiate one's humanness and regard it as unjust to be born.

The conclusion that natural evil is a result of man's original transgression is not upset either by the counter-response that such a vast toll of evil can certainly not be due to the slip-up of the first members of the race.[65] But there is really no yardstick by which a just sum of suffering can be specified. And on the other side we find an over-abundance of benefits, yet no one is particularly eager to question the impropriety of this imbalance. "In spite of all the evidence which is claimed to support smooth and continuous change," says D. H. Doig, "it does seem nowadays that there are more and more unexplained facts indicating sudden and explosive developments, which must make us hesitate to dismiss as impossible the suggestion that a change in the destiny of the whole human race might have resulted from one individual's insight and decisions."[66] None indeed can really calculate the sum of good which has accrued to the rest of mankind from a single instance of individual insight and decision; but the issue can work the other way too. For who can rightly estimate the evil and vicious results in nature and in the race, which affect human living and destiny, that one free act of transgression can bring about? We can find no convincing reason to repudiate the doctrine that natural evil can be traced to man's rebellion against God in the world entrusted to him by God. Even so, it is comforting to remember that more good has flowed to man from the one act of Christ than human suffering has come upon the world in consequence of man's sinful deed. "But where sin was thus multiplied grace immeasurably exceeded it."[67]

A Summary

Two primary views emerge as we review the various solutions offered from the problem of evil. On the one hand, the possibility of natural evil arises out of the condition of creation, and, on the other hand, the actuality of evil is at least aggravated by the human condition of sinnerhood. In the light of this observation, two possibilities are open. One idea says that the cosmic and physical factors of natural evil were here first, and that these were later judged as evil in the light of man's sin. This is certainly not an impossible position to hold; for there is no obvious reason why earthquakes and like happenings of the natural order, should be thought of as "evil" in and of themselves. Could it be that just because man has fallen from the high position God intended him to have that he is now stupid enough to go on living near a volcano when he has learned of the tragic consequences which follow its eruption? It is a question whether such events as earthquakes would terrify unfallen man. Christ, the perfect man, could walk on the water, as we believe He did, and the boisterious billows apparently did not frighten Him.

Some, however, prefer to adopt the view that the cosmic and physical order was disrupted by sin; and, as we have attempted to show, the objections that such an idea is impossible or immoral do not hold. The facts of the situation suggest that natural evil somehow arises out of the limiting condition of the created order, as being either possible or actual from the first: at the same time, man brought the natural order into active relationship with himself by his fatal choice to live after the fashion of the world rather than in unbroken fellowship with God.

We do not, of course, pretend that this account of natural evil will convince all. For the fact of the matter is that it is often the mere spectators to whom the problem is a subject for debate. The sufferers themselves, those most involved, are usually less concerned with theoretical discussion. The onlookers prove the loudest railers against Providence. Those in the arena itself, facing the stark realities, often find suffering to be the occasion, not for philosophical speculation, but for living faith.

A Final Reflection

It may be acknowledged that Christianity has no clear-as-day answer to the question of natural evil. But it does have certain considerations which give comfort and reassurance in the hour of suffering and pain. These considerations are based upon the twin facts of the saving work of Christ and the future hope of the gospel.

The work of Christ portrays the ultimate enigma of suffering innocence. Yet, untold blessings have come from His work. God's act in Christ shows that in the bewildering tragedy of human pain and desolation God meets man. This is indeed "the place where it is demanded of men that they believe." For the trusting soul becomes aware of the "divine accompanying" of which Barth speaks. Thus, "Christianity takes the history of Jesus and urges the believer to find, in the endurance of the ultimate contradiction of human experience, that which belongs to its very substance, the assurance that in the worst that can befall his creatures, the creative word keeps company with those whom he has called his own."[68]

Rudolf Euchen rejects the idea of God as sharer in man's anguish and misery as "a decidedly wrong note."[69] But he surely overlooks the very heart of the Christian message. Only the Cross sheds light upon the road in the hour of torment and pain. In the bright noonday a man may have a satisfactory theoretical answer to the problem of suffering; but in the dark midnight of the soul his theory may lose its power to bear him up. No ready-made answer will suffice in the day of trouble. At such a time, "the speculative reply" and "the fair-weather argument," of which Arthur Balfour speaks, will prove "too abstract easily to move mankind at large" and "too frail for the support even of a philosopher in moments of extremity."[70] Such a time requires a living faith in God and His relation to man and the world that excludes unbelieving resentment against His appointed order, resentment so easily nursed at the sight of undeserved pain. Let us then admit with H. D. Lewis that we have no "exhaustively rational solution of the problem of evil, in the sense of being able to show even in principle, how all things work for good. But I believe we have sufficient independent grounds for our faith, to be able to stand the tension of this situation and even to be tempered and strengthened by it."[71]

Such faith blossoms in the light of the fact that God Himself is no unconcerned Deity. He is no remote operator of a universe to whose ills He is indifferent. Men indeed suffer: but did He not suffer on their account? Suffering does not always fall on the most guilty and deserving: but was He not the most innocent? The world sometimes seems inconvenient for us: but did not He for our sakes subject Himself to its conditions? He did even more than this: "For though God Himself did not invent suffering and death, and although it is to be reckoned to the account of sin's sentence and doom, still God from the very beginning has caught up suffering and death in His providence. He converts the very consequences of evil itself into the certain means of salvation."[72]

The historic reality of the incarnated God not only gives the man of faith light on suffering—that Christ is afflicted in all His afflictions—but also it provides new hope in the certainties of the Christian eschatology. He is confident that history has a goal, a goal in keeping with the omnipotent love of God. Human history is no revolving door, ever moving and getting nowhere. If we make the goal of history a this-world affair, then in the realization of value the meaning of value would itself vanish. Marx's view that each stage in the dialectical process is an end in itself, its own consummation, and that no stage has any intrinsic perfection, fails to consider the fundamental Christian conviction that "we without them cannot be made perfect."

The destiny of man cannot be fulfilled within history, for no stage of history is final: and in no stage can man reach his true perfection in a society of perfected beings. "The perfect state is impossible within history itself; it can," says Berdyaev, "only be realized outside its framework."[73] For as Nels Ferré contends, "The problems of history are never answered in history. . . . We can accordingly find no adequate philosophy of history since history cannot by its very nature answer its own questions . . . instead . . . there can be a theology of history . . . history seen in the light of God. . ."[74] Driven, then, beyond history, we see that the redemptive purposes of God, with its outworking of human suffering and pain, is finally realized beyond the earthly order. This gives to death a new and profounder significance. As Berdyaev explains, "To pass through death is just as necessary for personal destiny as the end of the world is for the accomplishment of its eternal destiny."[75]

This is then the Christian hope. And, surely, in the light of it, suffering, pain, and death itself receive new meaning. They are not the final facts, and experience, however tragic, must be seen against the background, or perhaps, the foreground, of the glory that is to be. But even this is not all. For while the chronological end of history is still in the future, the soteriological end is already realized. At Calvary, an end was made of suffering in the offering of the innocent One, and of sin in the atonement of the perfect One.[76] And when this is said, there is no more to be said: for there is no more to say.

Chapter 9

Moral Evil and the Constitution of Nature

The reality of sin is so plain that all attempts to explain away its presence or to lessen its actuality can be easily dismissed. For the primitive man, the presence of moral evil was not regarded as a serious matter, but he was keenly aware of the immediacy of natural evil. He could never cry, "O wretched man that I am! who shall deliver me from the body of this death?" but rather, "O wretched spirits that you are! what shall deliver me from your vicious influence?" His interests were centered upon his "goods" rather than on the "good."

Polytheism has no deep view of sin. It conceives of sin as an external force rather than an internal fact. Sin is due to the caprice of the gods, not man's open rebellion against the ultimately Holy. Naturalism, too, has no moral problem on its hands; for in all naturalistic systems the world is regarded as ethically neutral. Pantheism—although it has a religious flavor—cannot be consistent and leave room for sin in any serious sense. It may be explained (away) as ignorance or good in the making, but beyond that there is little tragic or regretful about it.

Mysticism tends to minimize the reality of sin by its failure to take seriously the breach between God and man. Man is conceived of as a chip of deity; as such man can rationally become aware of his essential divine nature. For the mystic, sin is a surface thing, the conscious absence of the divine; but man himself can remedy that. "Evil is not guilt and sin, it is not hostile will, nor is it a break in the divine order. There is nothing 'between' God and man save distance and this man can overcome."[1] Moralists lament when they fall victim to temptations which, they protest, are due to environmental pressures, but they are not likely to feel themselves sinners. For such, moral evil is not conceived of as rebellion against God but as an unfortunate lapse in consistency. It is not an act of will but a lack of will.

But if the Christian theist accepts, with F. H. Bradley, the reality of sin as a "fact too plain to be denied," he faces a problem awakened for faith by belief in God as ethical personality. The one who believes there is a God both good and omnipotent confronts the greatest difficulties of all. The simplest method of escape is to deny one or the other of these theistic predications. There are, therefore, those who want to say that while God is *relatively* good He is not *absolutely* good. They say God is involved in the historic process and is engaged with us in the ultimate struggle with evil. God is for them in the process of becoming, so that talk of His "goodness" is relative to the stage which the evolutionary on-going has reached. Others prefer to reduce the area of God's control and to see God, not as the One beyond the many, but as One among the many. God is thus conceived of as a finite Being, "one of the eaches," as William James puts it. He is powerful, to be sure, but not all-powerful. This view is thought to relieve Him of the burden of responsibility for evil.

In this chapter we will be concerned with attempts to explain moral evil as, in some manner, the necessary outworking of nature, whether of the created universe or of man's animal or psychical being.

1. Moral Evil and the Structure of Physical Nature

Certain views explain moral evil as inherent in the original constitution of the created order. The neo-Platonists and Gnostics of old told such a tale concerning the origin of sin. The view gained appeal from the Manichaeans, with whom Augustine threw in his lot for a time, "burning," as he tells us, to find an answer to the question of why evil should be. But the idea has lingered. It has reappeared throughout history as the basic premise of all pessimistic philosophies; and it acquired vehement exposition by Schopenhauer, who saw the world through the mists of his own clouded life. "From the first dawn of my existence," he confesses, "I have felt myself at discord with the world." He thoroughly detested the pleasant young widow who was his mother; while he was to her "unbearable and burdensome." Schopenhauer scorns all philosophies, especially the idealists, which allowed meaning to human existence. "The world was born in a compulsion of lust," he declared. Marriage is then the greatest evil of all, for by means of it new "lumps of evil" are let loose upon the earth. "The existence of the world," he teaches, "is itself the greatest evil of all, and underlies all other evil, and similarly the root evil of each individual is his having come into the world." His message is clear: get out of the world as quickly and quietly as possible—if need be by suicide.

When confronted by it, however, Schopenhauer was slow to practice what he preached. When an epidemic broke out in Berlin he fled to Naples, and when smallpox attacked that city he hastened on to Verona.

A more worthy idea is advanced by Leibniz in His *Monodology*. Leibniz premises that this is the best of all possible worlds, since it is the one, out of the infinite possibilities open to Him, which God chose to make. But once made it is necessarily limited, and whatever is limited is imperfect. He thus traces both physical and moral evil to what he calls "metaphysical evil"—to the limitation of being, which is inevitable to anything less than and other than God.

Even though this effort of Leibniz carries some credibility, it fails to account for the active aspect of sin. And by making imperfection an essential constituent of man as an experiencing being, it holds God to be directly the author of moral evil and thus relieves man of responsibility for his sinning. But the fact of man's sense of guilt suggests that he chose to do evil and is aware that he is responsible for his moral and immoral acts.

2. Moral Evil and False Appearance

Hegel sought to divide the responsibility for the presence of moral evil between God and man. He regarded sin, as far as man is concerned, as "good in the making"; while, as far as God is concerned, it is nonexistent. He expounds his view by declaring that man originally existed as a brute in a "park," in a state of pure naturalness without an understanding of either good or evil. When man stepped out of his natural state, the resulting experience gave him a sense of himself as a being acquiring spirit. "Man is essentially spirit," he says, "but spirit does not arise in an immediate way. It is essential for spirit to be for itself, to be free, to oppose itself to naturalness, to set itself at variance with nature and not only with nature, but with its own essence, with its own truth."[2] Hegel views the real world as a consistent, rational whole in which everything perfectly harmonizes. Evil is, therefore, appearance and disharmony—but a necessary part of the evolutionary and dialectical process. Thus, evil is "all to the good," as a state on the way to final universal order and harmony, when all will be resolved and lost in the ultimate good.

F. H. Bradley assumed the job of giving the English-speaking world the most consistent exposition of Hegel's thesis. He ends his book, *Appearance and Reality*, by declaring his allegiance to "the essential message of Hegel." The message is this: "Outside of spirit there is not, and there cannot be, any reality, and the more anything is spiritual, so much the more it is veritably real."[3] Bradley reiterates, almost to the point of weariness, the doctrine that reality is one. And it must be so, he declares, because "pluralism as real contradicts itself."[4] Thus is the Absolute an infinite block without loose ends. What about evil and error? In four chapters Bradley addresses these questions.[5] He insists that evil can have no place in the Absolute; nor can it even "appertain to the finite subject because that, with all its contents cannot fall outside the Absolute."[6] Error likewise has "no home," and "no place of existence"; it is "one kind of false appearance" and can only take its place in the Absolute by being corrected and made good.[7] "Error *is* truth, it is partial truth, that is false only because partial and left incomplete."[8]

As relationships enlarge, that which appears as error by being partial will fit in and show itself as true, just as individual musical notes can be dissolved in a fuller harmony. Evil, accordingly, only becomes a dilemma if the Absolute is conceived to be moral personality. But for Bradley it is nothing of the sort. It is "not personal, nor is it moral, nor is it beautiful or true. . . . The Absolute stands above, and not below, its internal distinctions. It does not eject them, but it includes them as elements in its fulfillment."[9] Bradley distinguishes three forms of evil: pain, failure to realize an end, and immorality. Pain is real, but only as "appearance." As such it will disappear in a higher unity, just as small pains are often swallowed up in a higher composite pleasure. This analogy assures Bradley that in the perfection of the Absolute the total sum of pain is lost by submersion in the whole. Likewise, the failure to realize an end is regarded as evil because of its partialness. The ends which we would fulfill are ends which we ourselves select, and are therefore selected more or less erroneously. "They are too partial, as we have taken them, and, if included in a larger end to which they are relative, they cease to be failures. They, in short, subserve a wider scheme, and in that they are realized. It is here with evil as was before with error."[10] Bradley deals briefly with moral evils: "The easy optimism" with which he "slides over these grave problems, and his distortion of facts into a picture nearer his heart's desire, makes one doubt whether the Absolute can provide that theoretical satisfaction for which he invented it."[11]

The truth is that, for Bradley, moral evil as such does not exist except as an inconsistency within experience, which can become lost in a higher end which is itself non-moral. Pope has caught the spirit of Bradley's doctrine is his, *Essay on Man*:

> Whatever wrong we call
> May, must be, right as relative to all.
> Discord is harmony not understood,
> All partial evil universal good.

Bradley's easy disposal of moral evil raises a question: Is it really a problem at all if it has no final reality? It is no wonder that someone suggested that his book be retitled, *The Disappearance of Reality*.[12] Looking down the index of Bradley's volume in which he professes to discuss natural and moral evil, we find, when we come to the word "Evil," we are told to "*see good.*" Here we have, in fact, the key to Bradley's thesis regarding sin. It has no status: it is appearance only.

But tell a man conscious of a wrong-doing that he is merely indulging in an appearance and that his evil will vanish into a wider good by finding its home in a non-moral Absolute, and he will think you are mocking him. Nor does the theory, for all its claims, give any certain hope of the final victory of the good. Evil on the lower level of existence, we are told, is not inconsistent with the perfection of the Absolute, which exists beyond appearance. But if this is so—if, that is, imperfection can exist in this way—what reason have we to suppose that it will ever cease to be? The type of "inverted naturalism" to which Bradley owed allegiance can have no future hope that sin will be no more when God Himself shall be all and in all.

These views of moral evil seek its origin either in the constitution of the universe or in its appearance. But other theories find its cause in man's nature, either as a survival of his animal past or as a distortion of some aspect of his psychical being.

3. Moral Evil and Man's Animal Past

A number of writers, whose ideas of the origin and significance of moral evil carry little theological interest, explain it simply as the activity of surviving animal instincts. It may be called "evil" because it hinders man in his upward climb or handicaps him in his social relationships; but more than that it cannot be. There is nothing especially tragic in man's failings, except in so far as they impede his progress. Thus, says Fiske, "we see what human progress means. It means throwing off the brute-inheritance—gradually throwing it off through ages of struggle that are by and by to make struggle needless. . . . The ape and the tiger in human nature will become extinct. Theology has much to say about original sin. This original sin is neither more nor less than the brute-inheritance which every man carries with him, and the process of evolution is an advance towards true salvation."[13]

But the difficulty these writers have failed to negotiate is the fact of "goodness." How is it that man has a sense of a good which he should attain? Along with this issue is the question of conscience and the feeling of guilt. The extensive literature which has attempted to account for man's ethical valuations on evolutionary-naturalistic premises witnesses to the inadequacy of the view.

There are, however, other statements of the thesis which have a more pronounced theological orientation.

Schleiermacher begins his exposition by rejecting the idea that man was created perfect. He then seeks to argue for the presence of sin without reference to Adam's transgression.[14] The key to his conception lies in his doctrine of the "God-consciousness." The "God-consciousness" possessed by all men is weakened by its conflict with our lower animal nature. In the conflict between "flesh" and "spirit," the former, because of its earlier start, enters the struggle with an initial advantage. The entrance of sin, according to Schleiermacher, is due to "the self-activity of the sense-life which has not yet been controlled by the spirit." Sin is indeed that which is not yet spirit. By "flesh," Schleiermacher means the animal side of man: by "spirit," the existence of the God-consciousness. Personal sin arises from the conflict between these two. "Original sin" is not hereditary but "collective"—"a thing of society." "It is in each the work of all in all the work of each." Sin is then the relic of the brute in man: it is that which is "not yet" spiritualized.

Although Schleiermacher draws heavily upon the vocabulary of Christian doctrine, his theory has little in common with the historic Church's view, beyond these borrowed terms. To say that "sin arose out of the animal nature as a collective entity" is, declares Brunner, "the very opposite" of the historic understanding of the biblical view of sin.[15]

F. R. Tennant, too, rejects the concept of sin as rebellion against God or as a fall from original righteousness. And he repudiates earlier theological views of the "Fall" and "original sin" as "accidents of history, not the outcome of the necessary development of the Faith."[16] He thereupon premises that man was natural before he was moral. As natural he had appetites and instincts: but sin did not exist where there was no law. It is, therefore, when man became conscious of law that sin entered. Although the precise point of transition cannot be marked, it is a fact that sin is not a deed such as man had never done before. It is rather, "the continuance of . . . practices—or certain natural impulses after these things had come to be regarded as conflicting with a recognized 'sanction' of ethical rank.[17] And so it is also in the case of the individual: the infant is a non-moral animal. He possesses qualities which form part of his birthright as a human being, in virtue of his animal ancestry. These non-moral qualities are the material of sin, not its cause. With the dawn of will and reason, morality becomes a possibility. In his *Concept of Sin*, Tennant deals with what he calls the "requisites of morality." He concludes that sin is a failure to completely moralize the native animal aptitudes and instincts.

Tennant fails to explain why there should be such total failure to moralize; he is obligated to do so in view of his outright denial that man is "subject from birth to an indwelling power of sin." Nor does he offer any reason for the universality of moral evil, though he rejects Schleiermacher's notion of collective sin.

One note common to all these theories is the tacit acceptance of the Gnostic concept which puts the origin of sin in the substance of the human body. But to admit this either lands the theory in some form of dualism or makes God the direct author of moral evil. And it has the further unfortunate result of sanctioning asceticism by implying that the power of sin can be lessened by weakening the appeal of the "flesh." But if this were so, it would then follow that the deterioration of the physical frame, which sets in with age, should make for less sinning: but, alas, this is not so. To explain sin as rising of necessity out of man's native constitution does not account for the reality of guilt: nor, by associating moral evil with man's organic nature, is there any explanation for those characteristic sins of human beings which have no real parallel in the animal world. We are driven, therefore, to the conclusion that the origin of moral evil must lie in something deeper than the clinging garments of man's physical descent.

4. Moral Evil as Man's Uncurbed Imagination

The theory of H. Wildon Carr, that moral evil originates in man's overlively imagination, bridges the gap between those who find it in man's physical constitution, as such, and those which seek it in some element of man's psychological make-up. Carr, dismissing the Christian doctrine as based upon "the myth of man's original state of innocence," goes on to assert that only the evolutionary theory provides the key to the existence of evil.[18] Yet we need not, he contends, be concerned with the *why* of moral evil; for that is a mystery and so stands outside "the fundamental concept of evolution."[19] Carr believes the presence of evil is due to the excercise of man's active imagination: of all creatures, man alone has the "power of detachment which enables him to shape idols of the imagination and bow down before them."[20] These projected images assume definite actuality and become embodied in theological dogma. Evil is then the dire consequences of these tyrannical ideas which spring from man's imagination, which runs beyond his reason. Man holds the "twofold division of spiritual activity," "a creative imagination and a creative reason."[21] The hope for perfecting humanity lies in giving supremacy to the creative reason. In this "rational achievement, have we not," asks Carr, "the means, if not of the salvation, at least of the amelioration of society?"[22] Of course, "man is a religious animal"; he is indeed the only animal which has emerged from the conditions of animality."[23]

Carr, however, does not make clear how and why this one animal rose to the religious level. And since he suggests that he is also a rational animal, this would not lead us to suppose that religion is, as he declares it to be, inherently irrational. Nor does he explain how man's lively imagination came to exist. Is it a necessary arrival at one stage of man's development? If so, why should man be responsible for its exercise? And if he is not responsible for its exercise, then why should it have arrived? Since no moral causes are admitted as bringing about the result, there is nothing here to account for the idea of guilt. The view that evil will decrease as education increases is not proved true by the empirical facts. To know is not to do, much less is it to be.

5. Moral Evil and Man's Repressed Instincts

An attempt to account for human moral failure in terms of psychology has been projected in turn by Freud, Adler, and Jung. In the writings of each, however, such terms as "evil," "wickedness" and "sin" are conspicuously absent from their pages. There are of course abundant references to "maladjustment," "the aggresive instinct" and so forth. For man may be frustrated, inhibited or repressed; he is not lost, rebellious, guilty. He may be classed as a rebel against society, who needs treatment, but not as a rebel against God who needs redemption.

Sin is not, then, conceived by these teachers as a positive force in man's heart. Man possesses instincts which are neutral in regard to good and evil. But since he is unable to freely express his fundamental urges because of the taboos of society, the growing individual represses them into the unconscious, and there develops, as a result, the feeling of evil and guilt. However much man, in a less sophisticated age, bottled up his native desires and virtually equates the natural with the sinful, modern man has learned that the natural is right and proper, and that inhibited instincts create a morbid sense of wrongdoing and guilt-fears. The plain recipe for living is, then, do what you wish; for that is good. Man's judgments are determined by the desire for happiness, and his conscience is "the result of instinctual renunciation."[24] Responsibility for one's actions is not to be charged to his account: we cannot help doing what comes naturally, and we should not try. The native cravings demand satisfaction; there is therefore nothing evil or sinful in itself.

The practical Epicureanism of much modern life, and the violence to which it gives vent, are their own tragic commentary upon such an understanding of human waywardness. "Where everything is uncertain," writes Joad, "and the doctrine of 'Let us eat and drink, and be merry, for tomorrow we die,' is eagerly embraced, such an attitude, whatever it may seem for a mature age, involves for the youth of the twentieth century conspicuous abandonment of those inhibitions and restraints which the nineteenth century contemptously termed its 'morals.' At the same time, the prohibitions of traditional ethics, deprived of their supernatural backing, lose their accustomed force."[25] Paradoxically, "depth" psychology fails to plumb the hidden places of man's essential being.

6. Moral Evil as the Privation of the Good

Augustine, while giving the strongest statement of evil as absence of the good, is important to our subject for his emphasis upon man's misuse of his freedom of will as the cause of human sinfulness. He recalls how before he "accepted the doctrine of the Gospel," he held the view "that sin was not a voluntary act but that some other nature, I know not what, sinned in us."[26] Such an idea, he confesses, had "flattered his pride," because it absolved him from the admission that he was himself a responsible sinner. Later, however, he came to see that "the law of sin is the force of habit, whereby the mind is drawn and held unwillingly, but deservedly in that it willingly fell into it."[27] Accepting, then, that sin came about by a free act of man, Augustine set himself to grapple with the problem of how a good will could become the cause of evil. The answer he found satisfying was that the will became corrupted in the very act of turning; "the will turning from the superior to the inferior, became bad, but because the turning is bad and perverse. No inferior thing then depraves the will, but the will depraves itself by following things inordinately."[28] And being willingly depraved, man is justly condemned. Therefore, he concludes, "this came about from the bad use of free will."[29]

We have no business, Augustine insists, to seek the cause of the vicious will. For no efficient cause can be found, for the one conclusive reason that "it is not efficient but deficient." The will became evil by falling from a higher essence to a lower. Thus, to ask for a positive cause is as meaningless as to "ask to see darkness or to hear silence." Both darkness and silence we know—not by any positive form, but by the privation of form. "Let none then seek to know that of me which I know not myself, unless he will learn not to know what he must know that he cannot know; for the things that we know by privation and not form, are rather (if you can follow me) known by not knowing, and in knowing them, are still unknown."[30] Moral evil is therefore the absence of the good. This private view of moral evil was taken up by later writers. Amaleric and David of Dinant, for example, made it central in their doctrines. The pseudo-Dionysius the Areopagite and Duns Scotus Erigena tried to give it a full Christian slant. The Areopagite, unlike Augustine, did not regard sin as rebellion against God, nor did he trace it directly to man's willful act. But he did emphasize the idea of evil as the absence of the good in the way he virtually identified "being" with goodness. He thus contends that creatures, "in so far as they are deprived of the good, neither are they good nor have being."[31]

Erigena more firmly links sin and the free act of human will. Sin, he says, originated in the irrational tendencies of the human will; it is due to the abuse of freedom. Man desired what appeared to him to be good, but he was misled by the senses; thus, the senses and the reason came into conflict; in the ensuing battle the senses conquered, and the reason became contaminated. Yet evil is not final; it appears as defect. But it is lost in the cosmic totality where it contributes to the beauty and perfection of the whole.

These views certainly emphasize important insights. They align well with a biblical theism to insist that goodness, not evil, must be ultimate. While good can exist without evil, it is difficult to see how evil can exist apart from the good. The good, so to speak, can stand alone, and its presence does not necessitate the actuality of evil; whereas the existence of evil does imply the actuality of the good. For all that, it does not seem possible to explain evil as the mere absence of something, like darkness described as the absence of light. Good and evil are not just correlates; the one does not require the other. God was "good" when there was not evil. And we can conceive of an eternally existent good Being who always chose the good. Evil is something positive; it is in essence something chosen; the result of a willed-act. Sin is a voluntary decision.

7. Moral Evil and Man's Autonomy

Kant does well to stress the place of the will in relation to sin. In the last chapter of his *Critique of Practical Reason*, he discusses the origin of evil in human nature and observes, "According to the Scriptures, evil does not begin from a fundamental propensity to it—otherwise its beginning would not spring from freedom—but from *sin* (by which is understood the transgression of the moral law as a *divine command*); while the state of man before all propensity to evil is called the state of *innocence*."[32] Sin in Adam, he maintains, followed from the "Fall"; the prior state was without sin. In us, however, it follows "from an innate depravity of our nature."[33] Kant speaks indeed of "inborn guilt" and "radical evil."

Although he does pay homage to the existence of a "Bad Principle, in Human Nature,"[34] Kant virtually rescinds this admission by declaring that "whatever may be the origin of the moral evil in man, the most unsuitable of all views that can be taken of its spread and continuance through all the members of our race and in all generations is to represent it as coming to us by *inheritance* from our first parents."[35] "Every bad action," he goes on to assert, "when we inquire into its rational origin, must be viewed as if the man had fallen into it directly from the state of innocence."[36] Whatever may have been man's previous conduct, he insists, any "evil ought to have been left undone, in whatever circumstance he may have been; for by no cause in the world can he cease to be a freely acting being."[37]

There can be no disagreement about the fact that Kant viewed moral evil as something real and radical. But his acknowledgment of an "inborn evil" drew forth the anger of Goethe, who wrote to Herder that "even Kant who throughout his long life has tried to cleanse his philosopher's cloak from various disfiguring prejudices has now deliberately allowed it to be stained with the shameful idea of radical evil in order that even Christians will be drawn to kiss the hem of his garment." Kant, nevertheless, by his insistence on man's moral autonomy, found himself unable to coordinate this reality of human personhood with the fact of universal sinfulness. And in stressing the ultimacy of the former he virtually denied the seriousness of the latter.

Julius Müller in his book, *The Christian Doctrine of Sin*, resounds Kant's constant assertion that the essence of sin is a free act of will in disobedience to the moral law. Müller, in order to escape Kant's dilemma, fell back on Origen's desperate expedient of a pre-temporal fall. He thus refused to admit that an act of disobedience by the first parents of the race involved the whole human family. No guilt, he urges, attaches to an act not freely done; and freedom itself must be unconditioned. Experience teaches us that our freedom is limited; yet we are conscious of guilt which can arise only from acts "fully and entirely" of ourselves. When, then, can we find a time when we were in such a condition? If we look back to the beginnings of our life we cannot locate such a moment, for each evil thought and act is found to be conditoned by some earlier one, until we are lost in "an unconscious twilight." Yet, it cannot be in this period that a decision so momentous, having such far-reaching consequences, was taken. We must, therefore, press beyond the portals of conscious experience to mark the point where the pure will stepped forth from the state of indecision to choose the sinful act. Beyond the bounds of this temporal life, in the region of the unconditioned and undetermined, souls had their prior existence; and here, without any predisposition to sin, the choice of evil was made. By an undetermined act of will, in full consciousness that the act was sin, every human soul took the fatal step.

Müller, however, in spite of this insistence on sin as following from every individual's free act of choice, disavows that he is a Pelagian. And in the sense that sin can be explained as an expression of unfettered human autonomy in this life his repudiation is justified. Müller does not conceive of moral evil as an act of choice in this world under the influence of example. In fact, he allows for "an abiding root of evil." Only in this way, he asserts, can sin's presence be explained. Without this "root," every act of sin would appear as "an entirely new and original fall." In each human being there must be an "innate propensity to evil"; yet this can only be the result of a "free falling away in one's own offence." The doctrine of original sin fails, he thinks, to take note of this fact. We can only be guilty for that which is actually our own. So Müller comes back to his thesis of "an extra-temporal mode of existence of created personalities" in which sin took place. Thus each person knows the awareness of sin from the first dawn of consciousness; each man finds it already confronting him and already present within him.

By pushing back the origin of moral evil further into the dimness of the unknown, Müller has only succeeded in leaving the problem to be faced at an earlier stage in God's relation to His creation. For the question persists: why should beings in this pretemporal world of the unconditioned choose to sin? In truth, Müller's thesis, when followed through, leads to some strange conclusion. In this view, what is the meaning of man's present existence? The life we now live in the flesh would seem to be conceived, as indeed Origen did conceive it, as the arena of punishment for the fatal choice made in a prior existence. If to have flesh is itself the "fall," or the punishment for it, then there is an ever-increasing number of inhabitants from that prior realm choosing to sin, for the world's population is exploding. What a vast penitentiary then the world must be!

Furthermore, the theory presupposes that because of the radical consequences following the acceptance of evil in the pre-temporal state, that act must have been the greatest sin of all. But could it be so, if all that was involved in the choice were not known? How could the first sin, which we cannot even remember having chosen to commit, bear the weight of the guilt that follows? If, on the other hand, we suppose there was ignorance of all that would result from the first act, then it was not an act of the greatest evil and should not be credited with so heavy a burden of guilt.

It is, however, the emphasis upon moral evil, as an act of free will, typical of Augustine, Kant, and Müller, which is important. For this is the idea which, we think, most parallels biblical theism. Yet, it is one, as we will see in the next chapter, which is not free from difficulties.

Chapter 10

Moral Evil and Human Freedom

Of all the proposed solutions to the problem of evil, that which credits its origin to man's free act is, according to J. L. Mackie, the "most important."[1] For here we come to the specifically Christian account of the presence of sin in the world. Christianity contends that man was not conditioned or compelled to sin. Sin, it is held, ought not to have been, and need not to have been. True, God endowed man with the gift of freedom in the first place, but by his misuse of so divine a gift humanity's sails were set on the chartless sea of moral failure and folly. This fact of freedom appears as a necessary corollary of a created moral order; it is not a freedom curbed and confined even by the divine omnipotence, but is of such a nature that man becomes the sole author of his acts. "If God controlled man directly man would not be free."[2] It is, therefore, an unconditioned freedom man possesses, for unconditioned freedom is the only true freedom. It is, as Hume says, "the power man has to do or refrain from doing any particular action according. . . as he himself wills."[3] This reality of freedom would appear to be an absolute necessary presupposition for an understanding of man's sense of guilt. Only on the hypothesis that man of his own free will fell far below what he ought to have been can we account for the fact of remorse, the awareness of responsibility, and the sense of incompleteness, which are everyday observable realities of human life.

Two Facts about Sin

Two facts, then, are stressed in the Christian view of sin. The first is that sin did not originate with God. However its presence is to be explained, it is certain that sin is eternally and essentially contrary to the divine will and nature. "What Jesus Christ, the Son of God, was grieved by and waged war with," says A. B. Bruce, "cannot have come into the world by His Father's will or with His consent."[4] The more serious one considers the existence of sin to be, the more impossible does it become to associate it with God.

The second fact upon which the Christian insists is that sin is not a necessary ingredient of human nature. It is an element foreign to man's essential being. It is, therefore, a first principle of Christian theism that sin is that which absolutely ought not to be.

Only as the possessor of freedom of choice is man seen to be man: and only as the bestower of freedom can God be known to be God. Man is specifically characterized as capable of free creativity. Other creatures do not have this distinctive. In the scale of being, from the inanimate to the animate, this reality of moral autonomy is a noticeable absentee. Any anthropology which fails to give significance to this fact and feature of human existence must inevitably fail both theoretically and practically. Man was created to have dominion over the entire realm of created realities; but requisite for the fulfillment of this high purpose would seem to be the possession of a real autonomy. This means that man appeared as a responsible being, with the ability to deal with all that is less than human and with the freedom to follow the way of the more-than-human.

On the other hand, God, by giving man this freedom, did not compromise His Godness as a result. Instead, by bestowing on man so godlike a quality, He has shown Himself to be all the more Godlike. For to create beings who could freely choose to obey Him in the warmth of a personal fellowship is so evident a display of divine power and goodness that nothing greater could be conceived of God. He did not make man in such a way that he must necessarily and unfailingly respond to Him in trust and love. Had He done so, then it would seem that man could not be seen for the distinctive human reality he is; and God could not be known as the distinctive Divine Reality He is. To force our love and to condition our trust would be to degrade both man and God, for it would make man a puppet and God a tyrant. It is indeed to expect from God that which even God could not be expected to do, since, as John Wisdom says, "It is logically impossible for God to obtain your love-unforced-by-anything-outside-you and yet force it."[5]

The Existence of Created Free Beings

The Free Will solution to the origin of moral evil is, then, based upon the conviction that a world containing autonomous beings, who could sometimes choose to do evil, is more to be desired than a world of quasi-automata, which could do nothing other than what they are compelled to do. God, so the Christian maintains, in a wisdom beyond ours, created free beings; and being free, they cannot at the same time be determined, since to do anything from necessity is not to do it freely. Thus, by creating man capable of moral good, it follows that such creatures are also capable of moral evil. And if the possibility of moral evil is there, reality cannot be prohibited without cancelling freedom. But by choosing moral evil, man chose what he was not determined to do; thus moral evil is man's fault, not his misfortune.

First man as a being created free, exercised his freedom to do what he ought not to have done; in so doing he became the sole cause of human sinfulness. The possibility of evil is inherent in the fact of human autonomy, and, as a consequence of mishandling this God-given freedom, man involved himself in the blight of sin. By his own free act man forfeited his freedom; for, "by certain free choices we may surrender freedom."[6] Man had freedom to become unfree, and he acted freely to land himself in the situation described by W. H. Auden:

> Since Adam, being free to choose
> Chose to imagine he was free
> To choose his own necessity,
> Lost in his freedom, man pursues
> The shadow of his images. . .[7]

This statement of the Free Will solution to the origin of moral evil has, particularly in recent times, endured much criticism. These attacks have been conducted mainly along two fronts, which may be characterized broadly as the anthropological and the theological.

Anthropological Criticisms of the Free Will Doctrine

The main thrust of the anthropological criticisms can be summed up in the questions put to the advocates of the Free Will thesis: could not man's freedom have been somehow determined by God?; could not man's freedom always issue in the performance of good acts?

1. Freedom Compatible with Determinism

Antony Flew raises the first of these questions when he argues that freedom and determinism are not logically exclusive. It is not, he maintains, a case of either-or but of both-and. Flew's argument comes in the context of what he regards as a "new, or at least skeptical counter-attack."[8] It amounts to the claim that there is no contradiction in affirming that Omnipotence might have made a world of wholly virtuous people who could infallibly act aright. He reiterates the thesis that such phrases as "acting freely" and "being free to choose" do not "necessarily involve unpredictable or uncaused actions." For, "not only is there no necessary conflict between acting freely and behaving predictably and/or as a result of caused causes; but furthermore that Omnipotence might have, could without contradiction be said to have, created people who would always in fact freely have chosen to do the right thing."[9]

If, then, Flew concludes, "it really is logically possible for an action to be freely chosen and yet fully determined by caused causes, then the keystone of the Free-Will Defense, that there is a contradiction in speaking of God so arranging the laws of nature that all men always as a matter of fact freely choose to do right, cannot hold."[10] The only sort of idea of God which will safeguard the divine Omnipotence and justify the ways of God to man is that of a "Great Hypnotist," whose creatures act, however unknowingly, under the direction of His absolute requirements.[11]

Yet, for all his reiterations Flew has not managed to silence the counter-question: but is it "really logically possible for an action to be both freely chosen and yet fully determined"? And especially is it so when he himself insists on using the qualifications "freely" and "fully"? For such qualifications would seem to rule out the possibility from the start. His argument shows that, as Plantigna observes, "Flew and the Free Will Defender are not using the word 'free' and 'freedom' in the same way."[12] Flew seems to have meanings *in his mind* for the words which he has not succeeded in putting *into his writings*. He has, of course, a perfect right to use a word as he pleases; but it is difficult to conduct a meaningful dialogue with anyone who keeps secret, or holds in reserve, an unusual connotation for terms used by both parties. To say that an act is both "freely chosen" and "fully determined" seems at least a bit odd. It is to surrender logic to dogmatism. And the "Great Hypnotist" concept can only be maintained by denying the Godness of God and the manness of man. For a Being of sheer arbitrary omnipotence is not God: and a puppet of mere mechanical reactions is not man.

2. Freedom to Perform Good Acts only

J. N. Mackie elaborates a more serious objection to the Free Will hypothesis.[13] Mackie poses the question: if God has made men in such a way that their choices *sometimes* prefer the good, then why did He not make them so that their choices would *always* opt for the right? He then declares that if it is not logically impossible for one man to choose good *some* of the time, then it cannot be logically impossible for him to freely choose the good on *every* occasion. God could, therefore, it is concluded, have created men free always to choose what is right. But by His failure to do so He has shown Himself to be neither omnipotent nor wholly good.

This is the sort of argument Hume, in another connection, used in his *Dialogue Concerning Natural Religion.* Hume makes the point that pleasure is more conducive to human good than pain, since it seems plainly possible to carry on the business of living without the latter. If animals, he then argues, can be free from it for an hour, might they not have been made in such a way as to enjoy a perpetual exemption from it.

Mackie is using the same sort of argument, only he substitutes free-will for pain: if man can be free from moral evil for some of the time, could he not have been so constructed as to be guaranteed against choosing moral evil all the time?

But has Mackie been successful in demolishing the Free Will solution? His contention that God could have made men so that they always opted for the good presupposes a knowledge of what was open to God to do, which we do not claim to possess. In this regard there is every reason to heed the counsel of H. D. Paton: "Those who feel entitled to speculate on the methods of creation should refrain from laying down rules for the guidance of the Almighty."[14] In making this point, however, we do not desire to muzzle criticism, nor to take away the right of any to question. "We cannot," as Pontifex says, "appeal to mystery to make sense of a contradiction. We cannot say that God is almighty and wills the good of a creature, and yet, that the creature's good is not realized, or that a man determines his own choice and yet that He is wholly determined by God, and, when challenged to explain, merely reply that it is a mystery."[15]

Undergirding Mackie's thesis, that since man can choose what is right on some occasions God should have seen to it that he would prefer to take the right road all the time, is the implication that God could have conditioned men to be free—bound to act in only one way as a moral agent. But such an assertion is surely incoherent, involving as it does a logical contradiction. For Mackie is not simply saying that God made men free, and that these autonomous beings could have always chosen the right. That would, of course, be a logically possible state of affairs. Chritians do believe in the existence of spirits created by God, some at least (granted that they were created free beings), which have in fact always chosen what is good.[16] Their doing right all the time is, however, to be attributed to the exercise of their freedom and not to their being "made" to choose only the good and the true. For a right done under duress is not done right, and what is not done right cannot be designated good.

The assertion that God made men free and that these free beings could always, or sometimes, choose right is consistent with the proposition that they could always, or sometimes, choose what is *not* right. Now the empirical evidence demonstrates that out of all these consistent possibilities men have opted for what is not right some of the time. We have, then, man's reaction to a logically possible state of affairs in his willing some of the time to do evil. There is consequently no logical inconsistency in declaring with Christian theism that God is all-powerful and all-good, and in saying, at the same time, that He created beings who used their freedom wrongly. What we cannot affirm is that since God is all-powerful and all-good, He should have made men always to do right; for that would make the concept of "freedom" incoherent. Nor, yet, can it be said that since God is all-powerful and all-good, He should not have created beings who sometimes perform evil deeds, for that is to deny Him possession of these very attributes; observable facts also contradict such an idea.

Mackie, then, has not proven his case that the theistic conception of God is at odds with the view that moral evil is the result of man's misuse of his freedom. And he certainly has not shown that the statement that God created man free, and that this being, of his own volition, chose to sin, is contradictory. T. H. Huxley used to maintain that God could have done a better job on him by making him to do right in a "clockwork" fashion. The freedom to do right, he proclaimed, is the only freedom he desired, while "the freedom to do wrong, I am ready to part with on the cheapest terms to anyone who will take it of me." Huxley apparently wished to be a sort of infallible marionette to provide an amusing pantomime for supernatural spectators—but at the cost of forfeiting his essential nature as a human being. "Freedom and clockwork," retorted James Ward to Huxley, "freedom and yet no choice, clockwork and experience, absolute routine and yet continuous progress in self-knowledge and self-control, are not these flagrant contradictions?"[17]

The verdict, therefore, which we must return on Mackie's critique of the Free Will solution is that of Marilyn McCord Adam: "The claim that the existence of an essentially omniscient and ever-lasting God is inconsistent with the voluntary character of some human actions has yet to be made out."[18]

Perfection and Choice

People sometimes ask about the apparent difficulty of understanding how a being created by God, and therefore assumed to be "perfect," should ever come to choose evil. For since there can be no bias to misconduct in such a creature, it seems impossible to account for such a fatal decision. This problem has no easy solutions. But, then, we have A. N. Whitehead's assurance that "all simplifications of religious dogma are shipwrecked upon the rock of the problem of evil."[19]

An approach, however, to an answer to the question may be made by an examination of the concept "perfect." The word conjures up in many minds the idea of a static state so complete that no further and fuller achievement is possible. But if this is how the idea is to be understood, then it is certainly hard to see how, if men were made by God in this way, that he should ever have sinned. For his willing would always be so in line with his nature that no breach between the two would be credible.

But maybe we should not conceive of man as being created by God as "perfect" in this sense, but, rather, as innocent. In this case he would be open to development and discovery. This means that man did not arrive as a full-grown being, as a perfectly polished product. He came into existence as a creature-in-innocence, with the possibility of choosing to establish himself in righteousness, or to will himself to be of the earth. This does not suggest God's creation was defective. Rather, it affirms that man, as an autonomous being, failed to take the decisive step from primitive innocence to righteousness. And by that willed act man found himself in rebellion against the purpose of His Maker.

Evil as a Pseudo-Problem

Charles Hartshorne contends that the question of evil is a "pseudo-problem."[20] The arguments of both the atheist and agnostic rest, he asserts, upon the presupposition that a God, all-powerful and wholly good, is contradicted by the empirical facts. Now a proposition contradicted by observable facts must itself be empirical: consequently, arguments against the existence of such a Being, based upon the presence of evil in the world, make the assumption that theism is not a self-evident or necessary truth. For if it were so, no empirical evidence could be produced to contradict it. Hartshorne's philosophical efforts intend to show that the case is quite otherwise.

His fundamental thesis is that God's existence *is* a necessary truth and therefore cannot be contradicted by empirical evidence. For this reason he designates the problem of evil as "pseudo-problem." He strenuously maintains that the idea that evil can be regarded as conflicting with theism is due to confused thinking. It is grounded on the supposition that God is a statically perfect Being, who has a monopoly on decision-making. Hartshorne rejects this premise and contends that "monopoly of decision-making is in principle undesirable." God cannot, he asserts, make our decisions for us, for in that case they would not be ours. To be our decisions, we must be the sole originator of them. Thus "since all creatures have some freedom, all evil can and should be viewed as involving (not necessarily or in general) wicked cases of creaturely decision."[21] By sheer coincidence, the choices of several could unite. And if that were to happen, there would indeed be the harmony as God desires. But there could be no prior guarantee of this, since God could not "force" man into such a situation; for to do that would be to deny freedom. God may, indeed He must, lay down the broad outlines in which man could operate—for there can be no game without rules—but these do not deny freedom; they, rather, provide the sphere in which freedom can operate. "Without freedom there could be nothing whether good or evil." Freedom certainly brings risk; yet it assures opportunity.[22] To be authentically human man must be free; herein is the essence of his creaturehood. "Creaturehood is precisely the status of freedom lacking the supreme qualities of divine freedom." Free beings can achieve good by harmonizing with each other. "God is needed not to put everything precisely in its place, for things put themselves into their place; but He is needed to see to it that there are appropriate places for them to put themelves into—if they are lucky and also make the right use of their freedom."[23] The world is so ordered by God that evil may occur therein. Thus, the presence of evil, with its attendant conflict and suffering, is the consequence of the existence of free beings.

Hartshorne's argument is certainly a commendable attempt to relieve God of the responsibility of human waywardness. However cogent, or otherwise, his view may be considered to be, he is surely right in his basic premise that man would not be autonomous and accountable if God took over his responsibility of decision-making. God could, to be sure, have made robots, which would undeviatingly have performed the motions for which they were conditioned. But what God cannot do is to give man freedom and then deny him the use of it.

Whether Hartshorne has been over-enthusiastic in regarding the whole issue as a "pseudo-problem" is another matter. But the point is that the Free Will Defense has not been destroyed by the arguments used against it, for when rigorously analyzed, they turn out to be pseudo-logic.

Theological Objections to the Free Will Solution

Certain objections to the Free Will solution may be designated theological, because they are based upon ideas of God presupposed by a Christian theism. One question is this: can it be that God is willing to prevent evil but is not able? If this is so, then He cannot be omnipotent. Or, maybe He is able, but is not willing. But that would be to deny that He is an all-loving God.

Yet, to maintain that He is both able and willing, and still to admit the presence of evil in the world, commits us either to reconcile these apparent contradictions or to deny the existence of an all-powerful and wholly good God. Must we then, as Hume argues, support the theistic conception by denying absolutely the misery and wickedness of man? Or, being compelled to accept the empirical facts of evil, are we confined to agnosticism, or even atheism? The problem is certainly serious for the Christian believer.

God's Omnipotence and Moral Evil

If God is in fact omnipotent, as the Christian theist holds, then could He not have prevented sin's coming and consequences?

The most usual answer to this question is to insist that the divine omnipotence is not arbitrary; omnipotence must restrict itself. By bringing into existence free beings other than Himself, God did not then proceed to interfere with their freedom of choice. "God," declares B. Webb, "has given the creature its power of free will, and nothing will alter his eternal decree to respect its free choice. Therefore, once granting it, Omnipotence cannot make it to be otherwise."[24]

This does not mean, as Mackie urges, that if men's wills are really free and God cannot control them, He cannot be believed to be omnipotent. Mackie contends that God's omnipotence is compromised once we suppose that He has made beings who can act independently of Him. It is not enough, he thinks, to affirm in rebuttal either that God has made rules by which He Himself is bound, or to say that there are things that even an omnipotent God cannot do. He therefore concludes that if we still want to hold to the idea of a God all-powerful, it is only possible by admitting that at one time prior to the creation of man, God had unlimited ability, and that now, due to the presence of other free beings besides Himself, He is no longer omnipotent.[25]

The force of Mackie's argument depends on the meaning he gives to the concept "omnipotence." It may be, as James Ward says, "a question-begging epithet," but Mackie has throughout operated with a wrong use of the term by introducing the notion of "cannot" into his discourse. There are, he reiterates, things which even God *cannot* do; beings which He *cannot* control. But clearly, a man cannot be denied his manness because he does only what belongs to his nature; and God cannot be robbed of His Godness because He only does what is Godlike and divine. This implies that the concept "omnipotence" is only relevant within its proper sphere. God is omnipotent, because He has power to translate the content of His will into reality. The only determining factor is His own will; and, of course, God's will, no more than ours, is not something which operates apart from Himself.

A god of sheer irresistible power without aim, or direction, or restraint—were such a being possible—would not command respect, much less worship. God made man free; in that, He revealed His omnipotence. He is great enough to give autonomy to man and to take the consequences of man's misuse of it. Supreme evidence of omnipotence is found in the purposeful, nonarbitrary, use of power. Human dictators can tolerate no opposition; they are not great enough for that. Only an omnipotent God can give freedom to man and take into account what he does with it. Only a sovereign

God can "take His time," can afford to say, "I can wait," for, "I know what I am doing," because "I am the I AM."

God prefers to win men out of their self-chosen imprisonment, not to destroy them as spent machines. He patiently works to draw them into fellowship with Himself, so they might fulfill their high destiny—to glorify God and enjoy Him forever. Could omnipotence ever be more graciously revealed than in such a display of Godlike restraint! The cross of Golgotha tells us God is omnipotent; He can do the incredible—stoop to the lowest depths to lift man to the highest heights.

Some philosophers of religion however, following J. S. Mill, try to reconcile God's omnipotence with the presence of sin in the world by simply denying that He is strictly all-powerful.[26] Mill declared that he could still believe in the all-goodness of God while no longer "incumbered with the necessity of admitting the omnipotence of the Creator."[27] For E. S. Brightman, belief in a finite God is alone "coherent with the facts of good-and-evil."[28] He favored, then, a form of theistic finitism, since "surd evils are not ascribed to the will of God."[29] He considered the existence of a finite God of greater religious value than that of an omnipotent Divine Being. For a God who has not all is on man's side in a way an omnipotent one cannot be. We are consequently more assured of His sympathy in our struggles; for He, too, is engaged with us in the battle for the final destruction of evil. Brightman, therefore, emphatically rejects Knudson's contention that a finite God is "inconsistent with the spirit of . . . true religion."[30] A finite God means, rather, he contends, that there can be something other than God, something which is not for man's good—or for His; something which we, together with Him, are engaged to annihilate.

Christian faith cannot, however, be content with a God who is not finally omnipotent. To drain theism of belief in an all-powerful Divine Being is to leave us with the haunting uncertainty that maybe after all He is unable to cope with the totality of affairs. A faith built on the concept of a limited God, however the term "limited" is qualified, is too precarious to enable us to meet the demands of life with the ringing certainty that, in all things, we are more than conquerors through Him that loved us. Brightman really evades the tension of the problem by eliminating the *omni* from the omnipresence and omnipotence of God. And such a God is indeed too small.

Hartshorne seeks to correct what he considers the defect in classical monopolar theism.[31] In the early church, first under the influence of Plato and then under that of Aristotle, God was understood as *actus purus* (a God of pure actuality), both simple and immune to pain. "Not the Gospels and the Old Testament but Greek philosophy was the decisive source for the Classical idea of perfection."[32] Acknowledging that this classical form of absolutist theism has the merit of preserving "something really in God," Hartshorne still regards the concept as an over-simplification of the complex nature of the Divine Being.[33] A full account of God must see that He contains both sides of the total polarities. He is, that is to say, not absolute to the exclusion of the relative; or necessary to the exclusion of being contingent. He is "supreme, yet indebted to all," and, "supreme, yet related to all."[34]

Along these lines Hartshorne develops his panentheistic doctrine, in which God is said to encompass the whole of reality, yet is not to be equated with it: if God is not to be made the sum of all, as in pantheism, certainly all is included in God.[35] This view is given sharp emphasis in an essay entitled "The Wider Context: Theism as an Integral philosophy," in which Hartshorne argues that God, if anywhere, is everywhere and, if anything, is everything.[36] For, if the last particle were allowed to be other than God, then the concept "God" would be nonsense.[37] Only this dipolar form of theism is adequate, he thinks, to meet the dilemma presented by Hume. He contrasts monopolar theism and sets out the alternatives: either mysticism, with its purely negative conception of Deity, or anthropomorphism, with its affirmation of a positive, but wholly imperfect, contingent, divine nature. For Hartshorne, no choice between such alternatives is necessary. Hartshorne claims the highest conception of God and sees Him from the perspectives of both the theistic-pantheistic and the mystic-anthropomorphic.[38]

In this context, Hartshorne discusses the problem of the relation between the divine omnipotence and the presence of evil in the world. He begins with the principle that perfection is the meeting of reality with an all-valuing process of experience; he is thus prepared to allow that all evil is experienced *by* the Perfect. But evils are, however, always contingent, and must, therefore, be related to the contingent aspect of God. Hartshorne refers to the ancient argument: why has not God, as good and powerful, constructed the world smoothly, and designed it in such a way, that evil is prevented, and the totality moves unerringly toward a wholly desirable end?

Here he stresses, once again, the dynamic nature of reality, which he has learned from A. N. Whitehead.[39] The world is not a set of things, vessels molded by the divine potter, each arranged on its appropriate shelf. All that exists, exists in relation. And, more particularly, individuals exist as active within community.[40] Indeed, the very idea of God involves that relationship. The worshipped God is He who has created. He is therefore One, not merely *able* to be Father, but One who is actually so, since qualified by this relationship.[41] Because God is love, and because love is an inter-personal relationship, it appears reasonable to identify the "divine" with some eminent meaning of "relative," rather than with any meaning of "absolute."[42] God-in-relationship cannot act in an arbitrary hard-and-fast manner. And since dipolarity is accepted, chance as well as determinism must find their unification in God. "Without the recognition of chance, no teleology!", declares Hartshorne.[43] The relationship and the reality of chance must then hold the answer to the existence of what is termed evil.[44]

God, therefore, does not stand outside the order which allows sin and evil. He is somehow caught up in their terrible reality and consequences. Hartshorne, therefore, takes special delight in stressing sufferability as a necessary ingredient of dipolar theism. "The neo-classical idea of perfection," he says, does not admit a sheer absence of suffering, either in God, or in his world.[45] He cannot conceive it possible that God can be without pathos. He therefore rejects VonHügel's studied repudiation of patripassianism (the doctrine that in the suffering of Jesus Christ, God the Father also suffered).[46] VonHügel argued for a divine sympathy that does not suffer; he goes so far, in fact, as to maintain that God is too much our Friend for us not to rejoice when He does not suffer. Hartshorne cannot see how a God who has any sympathy can be without suffering. He prefers to think that sympathetic suffering is the highest form of personality, and most of all in God. He alone must surely be the most adequate instance of vicarious suffering. Can God indeed be our Friend and not suffer? Could an unsuffering deity be one in whom we could rejoice? Hartshorne does not think so. The world is not, then, separable from suffering: and God does not separate Himself from it. On dipolar premises, suffering is a category of the Divine Being. It must, therefore, be affirmed, not only that God "contains" suffering, but that it is His very character to suffer with man on account of human evil, which even He could not experience until it came to be. The Christian idea of the Cross, together with the doctrine of the incarnation, achieves, Hartshorne contends, technical metaphysical expressions of the concept of suffering. And on this basis, he enthusiastically commends Berdyaev for his "out-and-out dipolar theology."[47]

Madden and Hare criticize Hartshorne, because he makes God a "fellow-sufferer in man's misuse of freedom." And they do not think that his "quasi-theism" has really answered the question raised by the presence of moral evil in the world.[48] Yet, Hartshorne is certainly right in underscoring that the existence of sin is not the result of God's active will; and also in making the point, which the whole Gospel attests, that He has not stood aside from the moral morass into which man has brought himself.

Two broad answers have emerged to the question of the relation of human sin to divine omnipotence. Classical theism replies that God *did not* exercise His omnipotence to make men choose the right. He has, rather, restricted its use, to allow man full freedom to act. The neo-classical theists contend that God *could not* hinder the coming about of moral evil. For God to be God, He must contain within Himself all polarities. He is consequently relative in relation to the world; He is within the process. He does not exist as an outside observer, whose omnipotence could be used to change or correct a situation, even if He desired to do so. Yet, while He could not prevent evil, He actively cooperates with man in pushing toward the goal of the final establishment of the good, on the principle, stated by Tennant, that "perfection is the destination not the original endowment of man."

The neo-classical position certainly provokes thought, especially Hartshorne's repudiation of VonHügel's idea of a divine sympathy which does not suffer. And can there not be a contingent element in God's nature, resulting from His willed relation to His created universe; a factor which prevented Him from blocking man's autonomous introduction of moral evil?

Yet, if classical theism seems to make God wear the appearance of static Fate, this neo-classical account, in which the divine nature requires the basic elements of becoming and relativity, suggests the idea of God as the ultimate Fickle. But if neither view offers a satisfactory answer to the problem of the relation between the omnipotence of God and moral evil, maybe, by extracting an acceptable ingredient from each, and seeing them in their united form, we may come up with a formula which will justify the full reality of these apparently inconsistent facts. For, if in classical theism God's omnipotence is conceived of as voluntarily restricted, and in neo-classical theism He considered to be seriously involved in sharing sin's consequences, are not these twin facts sufficient to show that God's gracious sovereignty and man's sinful responsibility are not finally contradictory?

Moral Evil and the Divine Love

The other problem which faces the Christian theist questions the ethical nature of God, in view of the presence of sin in the world. Must not God's goodness, it is asked, be discounted in light of the disturbing reality of human wickedness?

On this subject, as in so many things in divinity, we confess that we grind to a halt. Still, if we can offer no final solution here, there are, at least, some observations which will help toward taking the tension out of faith, by removing obstacles in the way of belief. Thus, if on the theoretical side one finds no clear explanation of how a God who is all-love and all-good can stand man's sin, then on the practical side, an answer to moral evil can be found in faith's response to God's redeeming act in Christ on behalf of sinners.

History testifies that the most intense believers in the love and goodness of God have not thought it necessary to deny the evil, neither in the world, nor in their own hearts. And they are sure that wherever evil is found, it does not originate with God. Some men have learned that taking responsibility for the shadowy reality of sin has actually revealed God. Not a few have testified that the sin—and the suffering—of the world, far from driving them from faith, has led them to discover a divine help and a divine hope for their challenge. If it is the love of God to shape the believing soul for Himself, perhaps He finds most effective the tools man himself has made. Keats' suggestion, to which we have referred in an earlier chpater, that the world is "a vale of soul-making," is not, after all, without its significance: and especially when we remember the suffering, because of the sin of others, of Him who was the holiest and the best. This will not, of course, satisfy the hedonistic cults. But to them, one may reply that there is no conclusive evidence to prove that the highest criterion is the maximum of pleasure. What we like best need not be the best for us.

The central conviction of the Christian message is that God in love has dealt with human sin. He has stepped into the arena of our lives and done something tremendous about man's waywardness and shame—something so tremendous that only an omnipotent God could do it, and only a God of love would. He has robbed sin of its crippling power and given assurance of its final banishment. This is the ultimate meaning of the Incarnation and the Cross. The cross of love and sacrifice vivifies a general principle of God's ordering of the universe; while He does allow evil, He is at the same time working against it, to transform it, at a cost beyond human imagination, to be the means of man's good. In this way, even the worst human tragedies become, under God, the tools of an otherwise impossible triumph.

"This is the real omnipotence of atoning love, unweariedly creating good out of evil; and it is no far off theological mystery, but, God be thanked, the very texture of human experience."[49]

To say, then, that the love of God is at variance with the evil in the world is, from one point of view, to say what is true. It is at variance; but not forever. For we are assured sin and sorrow will end, when, in God's good time, these former things have passed away.[50] God has not abolished sin—not yet; but He will. For as has been declared, "To have a theism of any kind there must be a personal being who is thought to guarantee the triumph of good."[51] Christianity has a theism; not just of any kind, but of the highest and right kind; a God sovereign in love who shall bring about the last conquest of the good.

We know some rebel against God since they cannot reconcile His existence, as a moral Being, with the terrible presence of sin in human life and experience. But they should give attention to the no-less difficult problem of goodness, and ask themselves whether the "goodness" in the name against which they revolt is of their own originating, or if it is not derived ultimately from God as the moral source and sustainer of the universe. Perhaps then they will learn the lesson of history: "humanity inevitably becomes sub-human when cut off from the supernatural; that as Chesterton expressed it, nature becomes unnatural unless redeemed by the supernatural. It is indeed possible for an atheist to be noble, selfless, devoted to his fellows, and willing to lay down his life for them; we see examples of this around us constantly. But such nobility commonly has unconfessed religious springs, deep and hidden in man's own heart, or in his family history. It is theoretically indefensible except on religious presuppositions."[52]

We need not hold that God required sin and suffering for good purposes; merely for the sake of testing and disciplining us. Yet, many religious persons have testified that the deeper awareness of the reality of either their own sin or suffering, or, in some cases, of both, rescued them from a false self-confidence and strenghtened their moral character. The experience of these people falsifies the contention that the presence of sin and suffering in the world prevents people from believing in the goodness of God. It has been, rather, quite the reverse in their case. For they have come to know and understand the goodness of God in its essential redemptive nature and action through the very awareness of their sin and through the very experience of their suffering. They have discovered God, not in isolation from the world, but as taking all the pain and poison to Himself and making them His own. This "divine magnanimity" assures believing men of no final contradiction between God's goodness and the world's sin and suffering.

Such declarations cannot be dismissed as so much pious protestation or theological jargon. They are neither. They are affirmations authenticated in the religious life of many: and philosophy must take due account of the verdict of religious experience. Human life teaches the lesson of self-sacrifice and the supreme glory of dying to live. It teaches sovereignty through suffering. It teaches the final abandonment of the hedonistic ideal. These facts are, as Pringle-Pattison says, "the open secret of the universe." We are compelled here to interpret the divine after the analogy of the human; consequently, we are led to see that the ultimate conception of God is not that of a preexistent Being satisfied in Himself. The true conception sees Him as Christian faith proclaims Him to be, a Divine Redeemer whose out-going power made a world and whose out-going love redeems it. This ultimately means for philosophy what it means already for faith: the sin and suffering of the world do not forbid us to believe in the goodness of God.

At the close of the day, we will discover that no man is barred from the kingdom of God because he is a sinner; but only because he has withheld faith in God, whose love is as great as His power. For, as Franz Kafka has observed: "We are sinful not merely because we have eaten the Tree of Knowledge but also because we have not eaten of the Tree of Life."[53] If a person allows unbelief to build up resentment against God, who shares with all and cares for each, he withdraws himself from the knowledge of God, which is eternal life.

Notes

Chapter 1

1. I.T. Ramsey, *Prospect for a Theology: Essays in Honour of H.H. Farmer*, ed. F.G. Healey, (London: Nisbet, 1966), p. 55.
2. Cf. Einstein, *Ideas and Opinions*, ed. H.H. Rowley (Oxford: Clarendon Press, 1951) pp. 46, 47.
3. T.H. Robinson, *The Old Testament and Modern Study*, p. 348.
4. Cf. *God and Personality* (London: Allen and Unwin, 1927), p. 65; Ramsey, op. cit. p. 58.
5. *The Concept of Holiness* (London: Allen and Unwin, 1961), p. 152.
6. H.H. Farmer, *The World and God*, pp. 27, 28.
7. Cf. Stuart Hampshire, *Thought and Action* (Notre Dame, Ind.: (University of Notre Dame Press, 1983), ch. i, ii.
8. *Adventure*, ed. B.H. Streeter (London: MacMillan, 1927), p. 183.
9. *The Moral Argument for Christian Theism* (London: Allen and Unwin, 1965), p. 45.
10. *Speaking of God* (London: Epworth, 1964), p. 132.
11. L. Hodgson, *For Faith and Freedom* (Oxford: Blackwell, 1957), vol. 2, p. 149.
12. *Magic and Grace* (London: SPCK, 1929), p. 115.
13. Cf. N. Smart, *Reasons and Faiths* (London: Routledge & Keegan Paul, 1958), pp. 49ff.
14. *The Christian Apprehension of God* (London: SCM, 1929), p. 119.
15. Cf. D.Z. Phillips, *The Concept of Prayer* (London: Routledge and Keegan Paul, 1965), pp. 8, 43, 72, 113.
16. See below, chapter seven.
17. Cf. S. Freud, *The Future of an Illusion*, Et. trans. W.D. Robinson-Scott (London: Hogarth Press, 1963), p. 57.
18. Cf. *Introduction to the Philosophy of Religion* (Englewood Cliffs, N.J.: Prentice-Hall, 1951, ninth ed. 1963), ch. 9; see also his, *The Person God Is*.
19. O.R. Jones *The Concept of Holiness*, p. 157.
20. Cf. Bertocci, op. cit. p. 308.
21. Webb. op. cit. p. 131.
22. *Prospect for a Theology*, p. 64.
23. W.G. Maclagan, *The Theological Frontiers of Ethics*, p. 179.
24. Ibid. p. 180.
25. Ramsey, op. cit. p. 56.

26. *Systematic Theology*, vol. 1 (Chicago: University Press, 1951-1963), p. 270.
27. *Exploration into God* (London: SCM, 1967), p. 71.
28. *Microcosmus*, (Et. 1885), p. 688.
29. *Church Dogmatics*, vol. 1, i, ed. G.W. Bromley and T.F. Torrance (Edinburgh: T & T Clarke, 1936-1968), p. 157.
30. *Systematic Theology*, vol. 1, p. 271.
31. Ibid.
32. Ibid. p. 247.
33. Ibid. p. 271.
34. D.E. Trueblood, *The Philosophy of Religion* (Rockliffe, 1957), p. 270.
35. Tillich, op. cit. p. 270.
36. *Exploration into God*, p. 32.
37. Cf. pp. 36, 41, etc.
38. Cf. "I address my prayers to God not because God is personal (I know that if He is illimitable He cannot be that), but because I myself am personal and limited. If I wear green spectacles I see everything green, although I know perfectly well that the world is not green." Tolstoy, Letters and Diary.
39. Robinson, op. cit. pp. 71ff.
40. Norman Pittenger, *God's Ways with Men*, p. 30.
41. *Prospect for Theology*, p. 65.
42. *Christian Discourse* (Oxford: OUP, 1965), p. 83.
43. *Prospect for Theology*, p. 66.
44. *Christian Discourse*, p. 88.
45. Ramsey, op. cit. p. 39.
46. Peter Winch, "Understanding a Primitive Society," (*American Philosophical Quarterly*, vol. l, 1964), Reprinted in *Religion and Understanding*, ed. D.Z. Phillips (Oxford: Blackwell, 1967), p. 13.

Chapter 2

1. There is, of course, the Illusionist view that the whole of existence is unreal. But if illusionism were to be accepted then there would be no way of showing that the illusionist thesis, that all is illusion, is not itself an illusion. Thus the illusionist can never be sure about the certainty of his basic assertion.
2. Cf. Carliss Lamont, *The Philosophy of Humanism* (London: Vision Press, 1962), ch. ii.
3. Cf. Lamont, ch. iv; Julian Huxley, *The Humanist Frame* (London: Allen and Unwin, 1961), pp. 42ff.
4. Cf. H.D. McDonald, "Theology and Culture," in, *Towards a Theology for the Future*, eds. D.F. Wells and Clark H. Pinnock (Carol Stream, Ill.: Creation House Press), pp. 255ff.
5. Eduard Thurneysen, Dostoevsky, trans. K.R. Grim, pp. 37, 38.
6. Cf. E. Brunner, *Our Faith* (London: Scribners, 1934), p. 16.
7. Cf. *The Institutes of the Christian Religion*, trans. Henry Beveridge, (London: Clarke, 1949), vol. i, ch. xiv.
8. The phrase does occur in the Vulgate translation of 2 Maccabees 7:28 where the English has "out of things that were not." The Greek is ουκεξουτων for which the Vulgate has "ex nihilo." But see Arnold Ehrhardt, *Studies Theologica*, xii, 1 pp. 68–111, and reprinted in *The Framework of the New Testament Stories*, ch. ix. Cf. *Jubilees* xii. 4 and Hebrews 11:3.
9. 2 Timaeus, 29: The idea of *creatio ex nihilo* was known to Lecretius who rejected the concept; see *De Reum Natura*, i. pp. 164–214.

10. Adv. Haer., 11, 10, 4.
11. Contra Juliaum, v. 44.
12. Cf. De Genesi, esp. *Commentary on the Six Days.*
13. De Civit. Dei, xi. 24.
14. Cf. ibid. xiv. 11.
15. The Greek of the passage which is translated quite literally by the Revised Version (1881) as "he created all things *in common.*" The Hebrew has *yahdaw,* or "together." And any one of these phrases would suit what Augustine intends. For Augustine regards the totality of all that ever could be, as having been created "at once," "in common," "together." In contrast with Aquinas, Augustine does not contemplate the possibility of a continuous act of creation.
16. Nicholas was concerned to maintain his own originality and to discount his indebtedness. In his *Apologia Doctae Ignorantiae* he states that he had not referred to Dionysius, nor to any other of the "true theologians," until after he had set down the "revelation" he had received. Yet he does make a passing reference to "the most noble Denys" in the *De Docta Ignorantiae* itself.
17. Cf. *De Visione Dei,* chs. x, xii.
18. His constant declaration that all things exist in the seeing of God has a Berkeleyan ring about it, and raises the question whether the latter bishop drew some of his inspiration for his brand of Idealism from the earlier cardinal.
19. H. Brett, *Johannes Scotus Erigena* (Cambridge: CUP, 1925), p. 178.
20. *Summa Theologia,* Q. 3, Art. 8.
21. Q. 46, Art. 2.
22. Cf. Summa Contra-Gent., ii, 4, 1.
23. Compend. Theol., 1, 68, no. 119.
24. *De hebdomadibus* (Commentary on Beothius' Essays on Axioms), 3, no. 50.
25. Cf. Monologion, chs. vi-vii.
26. A. Seth Pringle-Pattison, *The Idea of God* (New York: OUP, 1920), pp. 306, 307.
27. Ibid p. 315.
28. Cf. "Creation," in, *For Faith and Freedom,* vol. 1, pp. 143, 144.
29. *Christian Dogmatics* (Edinburgh: T & T Clarke, 1898), p. 114.
30. Ibid. p. 115.
31. Ibid p. 116.
32. *Truth and Revelation* (London: Bles, 1953), pp. 61ff.
33. *The Divine and the Human* (London: Bles, 1949), p. 7.
34. *Systematic Theology,* vol. 1, pp. 280, 281 cf. *Ultimate Concern: Dialogue with Students* (London: SCM, 1965), pp. 169, 170, 174.
35. *Systematic Theology,* p. 281.
36. Ibid.
37. J. Heywood Thomas, *Paul Tillich: An Appraisal* (London: SCM, 1963), p. 73.
38. A.H. Strong, *Systematic Theology,* 2d ed., rev. and enl. (New York: Armstrong, 1889), p. 183.
39. *Studies in Christian Philosophy,* 2d ed. (London: MacMillan, 1921), p. 211.
40. *De Principiis,* iii, v. 3.
41. *Confessions,* xi, 12.
42. Op. cit., iii, v. 3.
43. *Confessions,* xi, 14.
44. Ibid. xi, 21.
45. Cf. W. Kneale, "Time and Eternity in Theology," *Aristotelian Society Papers,* January 1961.
46. Cf. Timaeus, 37, E6–3A6.

47. Cf. *The Reith Lectures*, 1958, no. 5.
48. Cf. *The Idea of God*, ch. xvi.
49. *Christian Dogmatics*, p. 124.
50. Cf. Martensen, *Christian Dogmatics*, p. 121.
51. Cf. *The Realm of Ends*, 2d ed. (Cambridge: CUP, 1920), pp. 231ff.
52. *Studies in the Philosophy of Religion*, p. 214.
53. *Existence and Analogy* (London: Longmans Green, 1949), p. 146.
54. Gamow, *The Creation and the Universe.*
55. "The Cosmic Drama" (Pamphlet).
56. *Space and Spirit* (London: Nelson, 1947), pp. 116, 117.
57. Ibid. pp. 118, 119.
58. Milton K. Munitz, *Space, Time and Creation* (Mineola, N.Y.: Dover, 1983), p. 153.
59. *Christian Theology and Natural Science* (London: Longmans Green, 1956), pp. 138, 139.
60. Cf. *The Nature of the Universe* (Oxford: Blackwell, 1950), pp. 105ff.

Chapter 3

1. Cf. L. Gilkey, *Maker of Heaven and Earth*, (Doubleday, 1959), ch. 9; B.S. Childs, *Myth and Reality in the Old Testament*, (1960), pp. 72ff. E.L. Mascall, *Christian Theology and Natural Science*, ch. 4; A.D. Sertillanges, *L' Idée de Creation et ses retentissements en Philosophie*, (1960), pp. 6ff. see, G.W.H. Lampe, *I Believe*, (1960), p. 61.
2. "The Theology of Creation in the Old and New Testaments," in, *The Root and the Vine*, ed. Anston Fridrichsen (Et. 1955), pp. 4, 5.
3. *Church Dogmatics*, iii, 1, pp. 41ff. cf. p. 14.
4. *Credo* (London: Hodder and Stoughton, 1936), p. 13.
5. *The Heidleberg Catechism Today*, trans. Shirley C. Guthrie, Jr. (London: Epworth, 1964) p. 59.
6. *Church Dogmatics*, iii, 1, p. 44.
7. P. 13.
8. *Credo*, p. 28.
9. Cf. *Church Dogmatics*, iii, 1, pp. 3–41.
10. Cf. R. Bultmann, "Faith in God the Creator," in, *Existence and Faith; Shorter Writings of Rudolf Bultmann*, selected and translated by Schubert Ogden, (1960) (London: Hodder and Stoughton, 1961) pp. 174ff.
11. Cf. Jesus Christ and Mythology, "New Testament and Mythology," in *Kerygma and Myth: A Theological Debate*, ed. Hans Werner Bartsch, trans. H.R. Fuller (London: SPCK, 1962), c. 4, n. 62; c. 6, n. 17; c. 7, n. 11; c. 9, n. 14; c. 10, n. 36.
12. Bultmann, *Primitive Christianity and its Contemporary Setting* (London: Hudson, 1956), (Et. 1955), p. 18; *Essays Philosophical and Theological*, (1955), pp. 119ff.
13. Richard H. Overman, *Evolution and the Christian Doctrine of Creation* (Philadelphia: Westminster, 1967), p. 25.
14. *Principles of Christian Theology* (London: SCM, 1966), p. 194.
15. Ibid. p. 195.
16. Ibid. p. 197.
17. Ibid. p. 202.
18. Ibid. p. 204.
19. *The Logic of Self-Involvement* (London: SCM, 1963), pp. 247, 248.
20. Ibid. p. 244.
21. Cf. pp. 242ff.

22. *God Transcendent* (London: Nisbet, 1935), p. 230.
23. From one point of view the Occasionalism of Geulinex and Malebranche is not greatly different from Heim's view. Denying any interaction between mind and matter, they claimed that an effect in the physical world consequent upon the idea in the mind, is brought about by the direct action of God. It could almost be said that they conceive of God acting continuously to produce both natural and mental results.
24. *The Providence of God* (Grand Rapids: Eerdmans, 1952), p. 63.
25. Questions 26, 27.
26. Cf. A.N. Whitehead, *Process and Reality* (Cambridge: CUP, 1929), pp. 344, 519ff., etc.
27. Cf. p. 331.
28. J.B. Cobb, *A Christian Natural Theology: Based on the Thought of Alfred North Whitehead* (London: Lutterworth, 1966), p. 206.
29. According to Hartshorne this is Whitehead's "novel intuition" that "experience involves *becoming*, and that *what becomes* involves *repetition*, transformation into *novel immediacy*." "Whitehead's Novel Intuition," in, *Alfred North Whitehead*, ed. George L. Kline, (1963), pp. 23ff. Cf. R.H. Overman, *Evolution and the Christian Doctrine of Creation*, ch. 4; S. Ogden, *The Reality of God*, pp. 62ff.
30. "Religion and Process Philosophy," in, *Religion in Philosophical and Cultural Prospective*, ed. J. Clayton Feaver and William Horosz (New York: van Nostrand, 1967), p. 256.
31. Quoted by John Hick, *Evil and the Love of God* (London: MacMillan, 1966), p. 223.
32. *Le Milieu Divin*, (London: Collins, Fontana Books, 1957), p. 56.
33. P. 66.
34. N. Micklem, *What is the Faith* (London: Sheen & Ward, 1936), p. 79.
35. P.A. Bertocci, *Introduction to the Philosophy of Religion*, p. 450.
36. R.P.C. Hanson, *God: Creator, Saviour, Spirit* (London: SCM, 1960), p. 18.
37. Cf. E.L. Mascall, *Existence and Analogy*, p. 145.
38. *The Spirit of Medieval Philosophy* (London: Sheen & Ward, 1936), p. 91.
39. Cf. Schleiermacher, *The Christian Faith*, trans. H.R. Mackintosh and James Steward (Edingurgh: T & T Clarke, 1938) (Et. 1898), p. 153.
40. Cf. *Religion and the Scientific Outlook* (London: Allen and Unwin, 1959), p. 167.
41. "Free Will, the Creativity of God, and Order," in, *Current Philosophical Issues: Essays in Honour of Curt John Ducasse* (Springfield, Ill.: Charles Thomas, 1966), p. 229.
42. Ibid. pp. 230, 231.
43. Cf. W.A. Whitehorne, *The Six Days of Creation*, pp. 6ff. I.M. Crombie, in, *Faith and Logic*, pp. 67ff.
44. *Religion and the Scientific Outlook*, p. 166.
45. Ibid. p. 165.
46. *The Logic of Self-Involvement*, pp. 145–217.
47. Ibid. p. 251.
48. Ibid. p. 228.
49. Ibid., cf. Isa. 14:9–12; Rom. 9:19–22; see Eccl. 33:1ff., etc.,
50. Cf. pp. 230ff. cf. Gen. 1:1–9; Ps. 104:5–9; 136:6, etc.
51. Ibid. p. 251.
52. Ibid.
53. "Creation" in, *New Essays in Philosophical Theology* (London: SCM, 1955), (edition 1963), p. 179.
54. *God the Creator* (London: Hodder and Stoughton, 1937), p. 178.

55. Cf. E.L. Mascall, *Existence and Analogy*, p. 87.
56. *The Christian Doctrine of Creation and Redemption* (London: Lutterworth, 1958), ii, p. 21; cf. pp. 42ff. "It is true that a Christological exposition of the Old Testament narrative of Creation may, to some extent, fill the gap, but at the cost of using arbitrary and forced methods of exegesis." ibid, p. 7.
57. P. 8; cf. "Hence all that is taught in accordance with Scripture about the revelation of God in the works of creation, is to be understood 'Christologically.' " ibid. p. 29.
58. "The Theology of Creation in the Old and New Testaments," op. cit. p. 20. But see Brunner, "The idea that the Messianic Covenant is the basis of the Creation of the world is not yet expressed in the Old Testament." op. cit. p. 15.
59. *Church Dogmatics*, iii, 1, p. 51.
60. Ibid.
61. Ibid. p. 59.
62. Whithorne, "Christ and Creation," ed. T.H.L. Parker, in, *Essays in Christology for Karl Barth* (London: SCM, 1956), p. 128.
63. Ibid. p. 131.
64. Ibid. p.132.
65. Karl Rahner, *Theological Foundations* (London: Darton, Longman & Todd, 1963), vol. 1, p. 167.
66. Cf. *Confessions*, iii, 4.
67. John 1:3.
68. Colossians 1:16, 17 (Moffat's translation).
69. *The Justification of God* (London: Independent Press, 1916), p. 123.
70. *Summa Contra Gentes*, 2, 3.

Chapter 4

1. *The Providence of God*, p. 15.
2. "The Concept of Providence in Contemporary Theology," *The Journal of Religion*, xliii, July 1963, no. 3, p. 171.
3. Strangely the word "providence" occurs only once in the Bible (Acts 24:2) where it is used, not in reference to God, but to the forethought and work of man (see Rom. 13:14 where the same Greek word is translated "provision"). The word "provide" (from the Latin "providere") etymologically means "to see." The corresponding Greek word "pronoia" has the sense of "forethought." The two ideas concur in the concept of Providence: forethought and foresight imply a future end, a definite goal, and a plan to attain that end. Throughout the whole of Scripture such an idea of a Divine Providence is present.
4. Cf. W.L. Ysaac, "The Certitude of Providence in St. Thomas," Modern Schoolman, (1961) pp. 305ff.
5. *Institutes of the Christian Religion*, trans. H. Beveridge, vol. 1, p. 174.
6. Cf. Langdon B. Gilkey, op. cit. p. 178; H. Bavinck, *The Doctrine of God*, p. 373.
7. *The Mystery of Providence* (London: Banner of Truth, reprint, 1963), pp. 113ff.
8. Ibid. p. 151.
9. Cf. Gilkey, op. cit. p. 175; F.R. Tennant, *Philosophical Theology* (Cambridge: CUP, 1928), vol. 2, pp. 190–197.
10. Berkouwer, op. cit. p. 30.
11. "Hope and Disenchantenment," in, *A Reasoned Faith* (Oxford: OUP, 1963), pp. 24, 25.
12. Cf. "In the view of Sartre, and by Sartre's account, of Heidegger, it is the very denial of God's existence, not the search for him, that makes the inner odyssey of the self seeking philosophy's primary concern . . . there is no single concept of

humanity. Because there is no God. For the concept of *a* human nature, Sartre believes, was a by-product of the traditional idea of God the Maker; and so, when God dies, the notion of an essence dies with him." Mariorie Greene, *Dreadful Freedom*, pp. 41, 42.
13. Karl Jaspers, *Tragedy is not Enough* (London), pp. 82, 83.
14. Cf. Emmanuel Mounier, *Existential Philosophies*, p. 39.
15. Cf. S. Freud, *The Future of an Illusion*, ch. 6, see p. 58.
16. *The Modern Predicament* (London: Allen and Unwin, 1955), pp. 353–357.
17. Brunner, *The Christian Doctrine of Creation and Redemption*, ii, p. 148.
18. Cf. Roger Hazelton, *Providence—A Theme with Variations* (London: SCM, 1958), p. 52ff.
19. G. Aulén, *The Faith of the Christian Church*, 2d ed. (London: SCM, 1961), p. 172.
20. W.G. Pollard, *Chance and Providence* (London: Faber & Faber, 1959), p. 71.
21. Flavel, op. cit. p. 120.
22. P. 115.
23. Hazelton, op. cit. p. 32.
24. P. 147, Cf. "This God does not protect me, but delivers me up to the dangers of a life worthy of being called human." Alasdair MacIntyre and Paul Ricoeur, *The Religious Significance of Atheism*, p. 88.
25. Flavel, op. cit. p. 115.
26. Brunner, op. cit. p. 155.
27. W.N. Clarke, *The Christian Doctrine of God* (Edinburgh: T & T Clarke), p. 104.
28. Hazelton, op. cit. p. 35.
29. P. 42.
30. P. 157.
31. Brunner, op. cit. p. 157.
32. *Problems in the Relation of God and Man* (London: Nisbet, 1911), p. 102.
33. Hazelton, op. cit. p. 57.
34. "The Eternal Plan of Divine Providence," *Theological Studies*, March 1966, p. 27.
35. Jurgen Moltmann, *The Theology of Hope* (London: SCM, 1967), p. 30.
36. Isa. 55:11.
37. Wright, op. cit. p. 33.
38. *Existence and the Existent* (London: Mayflower, 1959), p. 122.
39. Mark Pontifex, *Freedom and Providence*, p. 68.
40. Wright, op. cit. pp. 48, 49.
41. Pp. 56, 57.
42. Gen. 1:19, 20; cf. Gen. 45:4ff.
43. Cf. George Santayana, *Introduction to Spinoza's Ethics* (London: Dent, n.d.) (Everyman's Library), p. 22.
44. Barth, *Dogmatics*, iii, 3, p. 31.
45. Brunner, op. cit. p. 152.
46. Brightman, *A Philosophy of Religion* (London: Skeffington, n.d.), pp. 139, 140.
47. Cf. Plato, *Republic*, 379c–380b.
48. Brightman, op. cit. p. 156.
49. Cf. "Evil will not be gainsaid, argued away, made out to be something other than it is. Evil is evil, a standing contradiction of any thorough-going optimistic view of the world and life." F.W. Camfield, *The Collapse of Doubt* (London: Lutterworth, 1945), p. 39.
50. E.J. Carnell, *A Philosophy of the Christian Religion* (Grand Rapids: Eerdmans, 1954), p. 303.
51. Cf. e.g. N. Berdyaev, *The Destiny of Man* (London: Bles, 1937), p. 24.

52. Brunner, op. cit. p. 133; cf. pp. 321ff.
53. P. 155.
54. Zwingli, in contrast with Brunner, allows that man's crimes are "caused, moved, and urged" by God directly, although he adds, that since man commits them he alone is responsible. Cf. *De Providentia*, ch. 2.
55. Cf. Barth, *Church Dogmatics*, ii, 1, p. 65.
56. Barth, op. cit. p. 168.
57. Ibid. p. 88.
58. Brunner, op. cit. p. 157; Cf. "For one who lives in the knowledge and certainty of the Providence of God . . . knows that he is preserved for redemption; he knows no other meaning of his existence than this, which is whole meaning and the final meaning, *the* Telos, not *a* Telos." p. 159.
59. Ibid. p. 159.
60. Cf. Barth, *The Heidleberg Catechism for Today*, trans. S.C. Guthrie, pp. 57ff.
61. Cf. Barth, *Church Dogmatics*, ii, 1, pp. 22ff., 30ff. Cf. "What could have been more obvious, one might have thought, than to equate this ruling of God with the One who according to the witness of the New Testament has a place at his right hand" (Barth is commenting on Ps. 118:16; 139:10, etc.). "Why," he then asks, "did not Calvin and others work out this insight that the hands and feet of God, like His heart, are revealed in Christ and in Him alone?" p. 35.
62. *Church Dogmatics,* ii, i. 30.
63. Cf. Barth, *Anselm: Fides Quaerens Intellectum* (London: SCM, 1960), p. 67.
64. Cf. E.L. Maxcall, "Faith and Reason: Anselm and Aquinas," *Theological Studies*, xiv, pt. 1, April 1963, pp. 67–90. "And Karl Barth has made a heroic—and in my view a heroically perverse—attempt to show that Anselm was really a Barthian before his time." p. 68.
65. *Theology in Conflict* (Edinburgh: Oliver & Boyd, 1958), p. 159.
66. *The Sense of the Presence of God,* (Oxford: OUP, 1962) p. 225.
67. Langdon B. Gilkey, op. cit. p. 185.
68. Cf. G.C. Berkouwer, op. cit. ch. 2; H. Bavink, *The Doctrine of God* (London: Banner of Truth, 1977), pp. 41–80, 373ff.
69. Cf. Berkouwer, op. cit. p. 45. Bavink, pp. 41ff.
70. Cf. Farmer, *The World and God* (London: Nisbet, 1935), p. 101.
71. J. Wendland, *Miracles and Christianity* (London: Hodder and Stoughton, new edition, 1912), pp. 164, 165.
72. Ibid. p. 165.
73. E.Y. Mullins, *The Christian Religion in its Doctrinal Expression* (Philadelphia: Judson Press, 1917), p. 269.
74. *Miracles*, pp. 208, 209.
75. Baillie, op. cit. p. 255.
76. Flavel, op. cit. p. 151.
77. Cf. H.H. Farmer, op. cit. p. 101.
78. Cf. Wendland, op. cit. p. 182; Baillie, op. cit. p. 226.
79. Cf. Langdon B. Gilkey, *Maker of Heaven and Earth*, ch. vi; Cf. ". . .from nature, or the natural man, you can only get a God who repeats on a vaster scale those anomalies of experience from which God would deliver us. We only get a natural God of preternatural scale. We cannot get a spiritual God, a God of Grace, from a natural world." P.T. Forsyth, *The Principle of Authority* (London: Independent Press, 1952), p. 358.
80. H.H. Farmer, op. cit. p. 100.
81. Cf. H.D. McDonald, "What is meant by Religious Experience?" in *Vox Evangelica*

11, (1963), pp. 58–69; See R.W. Hepburn, *Christianity and Paradox* (London: Collins, 1949), chs. 3, 4.
82. Flavel, op. cit. p. 122.
83. *Vision and Authority,* p. 223.
84. Cf. "We reflect, and prolong, even in our most vivid experiences, the vaster faith of the great Church." Forsyth, op. cit. p. 326.
85. Forsyth, op. cit. p. 178.
86. Ibid. pp. 241, 242.
87. Waldo Beach, "The Pattern of Providence," *Theology Today,* vol. xvi, no. 2, July 1959, p. 234.
88. Flavel, op. cit. p. 147.
89. Ps. 85:10.
90. Cf. H.D. McDonald, "Theology and Culture," in, *Towards a Theology for the Future,* eds. Clarke Pinnock and David F. Wells, ch. 9.
91. H. Butterfield, *Christianity and History* (London: Collins, Fontana Books, 1951), ch. 3; cf. his, *History and Human Relations,* ch. 4.
92. Shinn, *Christianity and the Problems of History,* pp. 239, 240.
93. Waldo Beach, op. cit. p. 239.
94. Flavel, op. cit. pp. 150, 151.

Chapter 5

1. David Hume (1711–1766), *Enquiry Concerning Human Understanding,* sect. x.
2. For a useful discussion of Hume's arguments the reader is referred to Ninian Smart, *Philosophers and Religious Truth* (London: SCM, 1964); ch. 2, "Miracles and David Hume"; Richard Swinburne, *The Concept of Miracle* (London: MacMillan, 1970).
3. S. Toulmin, *The Philosophy of Science* (London: Hutchinson, 1953).
4. *Scientific Explanation.*
5. Swinburne, *The Concept of Miracle,* pp. 31, 32.
6. *Miracles,* (London: Bles, 1947), p. 72.
7. "Miracles: The Scientific Approach," *Hibbert Journal,* April 1950; being a reply to Professor H. Dubs article in the same journal, April 1950.
8. Patrick Nowell-Smith, "Miracles," in *New Essays in Philosophical Theology,* eds. A. Flew and A. MacIntyre, pp. 243ff.
9. Ramsey, "Miracles: An Exercise in Logical Mapwork", in, The Miraculous and Resurrection, Theological Collections, 3 (London: SPCK, 1965), pp. 1–30.
10. Ramsey, *Religious Language* (London: SCM, 1947), p. 144.
11. Cf. Elton Hay, "Ian Ramsey—A Linguistic View of Miracles," in, *The Iliff Review,* Winter, 1971; cf. same author's, "A Contranatural View of Miracles," *The Canakian Journal of Theology,* vol. xiii, (July 1967), no. 4, pp. 279ff. Hay draws attention to the way Ramsey relates miracle to his "significant event" view of history, and he contends that, "The treatment of miracle suffers from Ramsey's ambiguous understanding of history." *Iliff Review,* p. 47.
12. Brunner, *The Christian Doctrine of Creation and Redemption,* Dogmatics, ii. pp. 160ff.
13. Ibid.
14. Barth, *Church Dogmatics,* iii, 3, p.129.
15. For an effective detailed criticism of Ramsey and Farmer, see P.J. Mitchell, "The Conception of the Miraculous and its Place in Christian Belief," an unpublished thesis for the M.Th. degree of the University of London (1962).
16. Lewis, "Miracles and Prayer," in *Our Experience of God* (London: Allen and Unwin, 1959), p. 239.

17. Ibid. p. 240.
18. Wendland, *Miracles and Christianity*, p. 3.
19. Whitehead, *Religion in the Making* (New York: MacMillan, 1926; Cambridge: CUP, 1927), pp. 155, 156.
20. *Religion and Philosophy* (London: MacMillan, 1916), p. 214.
21. Ibid.
22. Ibid. p. 210.
23. *Miracles*, ed. C.F.D. Moule (London: Moubray, 1965), pp. 41, 42.
24. Ninian Smart, *Philosophers and Religious Truth* (SCM Paperback), pp. 52, 53.
25. H.D. Lewis, *Philosophy of Religion* (London: English Universities Press, 1965), p. 305.
26. Ibid. p. 303.
27. *Miracles*, ed. C.F.D. Moule, p. 27.
28. Ibid. p. 31.
29. Woods, op. cit. p. 24; cf. Smart, op. cit. pp. 31ff.
30. E.g. Exod. 3:20; 15:11, etc.
31. E.g. Matt. 24:24; Acts 2:22, etc.
32. E.g. Matt. 11:20, 21, 23; 13:24, etc.
33. Cf. Exod. 7:11–9:11; Dan. 13:2, 3; Matt. 7:22; 2 Thess. 2:9; Rev. 13:13.
34. Swinburne, op. cit. p. 71.
35. C.S. Lewis, *Miracles*, p. 131.

Chapter 6

1. For an illustration of this see C.S. Lewis's *Surprised by Joy* (Fontana Books), p. 22.
2. *Letters and Papers from Prison* (London: SCM, 1953), p. 67.
3. C.S. Lewis, *Letters to Malcolm Chiefly on Prayer*, 2d ed. (London: Collins, Fontana Books, 1981), p. 69.
4. H.D. Lewis, *Our Experience of God*, pp. 244, 245.
5. *The Philosophy of Religion*, p. 235.
6. *The World and God*, p. 139; cf. pp. 134, 135.
7. Cf. *The Modern Predicament*, pp. 356, 357.
8. Op. cit. p. 31.
9. *Our Experience of God*, pp. 252, 253.
10. Ibid. p. 253.
11. Lewis, ibid.
12. Nels F.S. Ferré, *Making Religion Real* (London: Collins, Fontana Books, 1956), p. 56.
13. William Law, *A Serious Call to a Devout and Holy Life* (London: Collins, Fontana Books, 1968), p. 129.
14. James Hastings, *The Great Christian Doctrines*, ed. J. Hastings (Edinburgh: T & T Clarke, 1915), p. 247.
15. Ferré, op. cit. p. 52.
16. Ibid. p. 62.
17. *Letters to Malcolm*, p. 38.
18. H.H. Farmer, *The World and God*, pp. 142, 143.
19. A.J. Worlledge, *Prayer* (London: Longmans Green, 1902), p. 20.
20. Ferré, op. cit. p. 61.
21. Farmer, op. cit. p. 139.
22. H.C. Witherington, *Psychology of Religion*, p. 117.
23. A.J. Worlledge, op. cit. p. 67.
24. Farmer, op. cit. p. 138.

25. H.D. McDonald, *I and He* (London: Epworth, 1966), ch. 3.
26. H.D. Lewis, op. cit. p. 254.
27. Op. cit. p. 157.28.
28. C.S. Lewis, *Letters to Malcolm*, p. 69.

Chapter 7

1. D.Z. Phillips, *The Concept of Prayer*, p. 31.
2. Phillips, op. cit. p. 43.
3. *Letters to Malcolm*, pp. 33, 34.
4. Phillips, op. cit. p. 120, italics in text.
5. Cf. *Religion and the Scientific Outlook*, ch. 17.
6. Cf. Drya Krishna, "Religious Experience, Language and Truth," in, *Religious Experience and Truth*, ed. Sydney Hook (New York: New York University Press, 1961; London: Oliver and Boyd, 1967), p. 240.
7. W.A. Christian, *Meaning and Truth in Religion* (Princeton University Press, 1964), p. 79.
8. *Philosophy of Religion*, pp. 102, 103.
9. C.S. Lewis, *Undeceptions* (London: Bles, 1971), p. 79.
10. Hab. 1:2 (RSV).
11. H.D. Lewis, *Our Experience of God*, p. 253.
12. *First Chapters in Religious Philosophy*, p. 252.
13. Ps. 66:18.

Chapter 8

1. Cf. *God and Evil* (London: Faber and Faber, 1964).
2. See his *God and Philosophy* (London: Hutchinson, 1966).
3. *Spiritual Counsels and Letters of Baron Friedrich von Hügel*, ed. Douglas V. Steere (London: Darton, Longman & Todd, 1964), pp. 67–68.
4. Joad, op. cit. p. 110.
5. R.L. Patterson, *Introduction to the Philosophy of Religion* (New York: Holt, 1958), p. 178.
6. William Temple, *Nature, Man and God* (London: MacMillan, 1934), p. 356.
7. Cf. Ezekiel 18.
8. Cf. *Philosophical Theology* vol. 2, ch. 7.
9. *Philosophy of Religion* (New York: van Nostrand, 1965), p. 129.
10. Cf. Maritain, *God and the Permission of Evil* (Milwaukee: Bruce Publishing Co., 1966), ch. 2.
11. *Evil and the Love of God*, p. 284.
12. Ibid. p. 291.
13. J. Hick, "The Problem of Evil in the First and Last Things," *Journal of Theology*, New Series, vol. xix, pt. 2 (Oct. 1968) p. 598.
14. Cf. *Evil and the Love of God*, pp. 68, 69.
15. *Borderlands of Theology* (London: Lutterworth, 1968), p. 48.
16. John Hick, op. cit. p. 371.
17. *The Uniqueness of Man* (London: Chato and Windus, 1943), pp. 292, 293.
18. *On Selfhood and Godhood* (London: Allen and Unwin, 1957, pp. 285ff.
19. Ibid. p. 305.
20. Ibid. p. 303.
21. Ibid. pp. 305, 306.
22. *The Destiny of Man*, p. 24. Cf. Campbell, op. cit. p. 292.
23. *The Destiny of Man*, p. 43.

24. Ibid. pp. 29, 30.
25. Ibid. pp. 24, 25.
26. Cf. p. 35.
27. Berdyaev, *The Divine and the Human*, p. 83.
28. Fielding Clarke, *Introduction to Berdyaev* (London: Bles, 1950), p. 77.
29. Cf. H.D. Lewis, "God and Mystery," in, *Prospect for Metaphysics* (London: Allen and Unwin, 1961), ed. I. Ramsey, ch. xii.
30. Cf. Dom Pontifex, *Freedom and Providence*, p. 49.
31. Cf. Berdyaev, *The Meaning of History* (London: Bles, 1936), pp. 47, 48.
32. Cf. *The Divine and the Human*, p. 84.
33. "The Question of Evil," in, *Prospect for Metaphysics*, ed I. Ramsey, p. 125.
34. Ibid. p. 122.
35. Ibid. p. 136.
36. Ibid. pp. 136, 137.
37. Cf. "The Question of Evil Re-examined," *Theology*, vol. lxix, no. 557, pp. 484ff.
38. Ibid. p. 489.
39. *The Problem of Pain* (London: Centuary Press, 1940), p. 77.
40. Ibid. p. 21.
41. Ibid. p. 16.
42. *The Philosophy of Religion* (Edinburgh: T & T Clarke, 1914, reprint 1948), p. 540.
43. Ibid. p. 540.
44. Ibid. p. 541.
45. Ibid. p. 541.
46. Ibid. p. 520.
47. *Process Thought and Christian Faith* (London: Nisbet, 1968), p. 33; cf. pp. 31ff.
48. Cf. his chapter "Nature and the Problem of Evil," in his, *Reason and Religion*, pp. 236–280; see p. 238.
49. Ibid. p. 236.
50. Ibid. p. 247.
51. Cf. Langdon B. Gilkey, "A Theology of Process," *Interpretation*, vol. xxi, no. 4, October 1967, pp. 447ff. H.D. McDonald, "Monopolar Theism and the Ontological Argument," *The Harvard Theological Review*, vol. 58, no. 4, October 1965, pp. 387–416.
52. Cf. "Destruction in nature also has meaning in terms of the consequences that follow the sinful or irresponsible use of freedom." Ferré, op. cit. p. 246.
53. Cf. Genesis 3:17; 5:2. See Rom. 8:18ff., and see the comment by R.J. Knowling in the *Expositors Greek Testament* on the passage.
54. James Orr, *The Christian View of God and the World* (Edinburgh: T & T Clarke, 1893), p. 195.
55. Cf. C.S. Lewis, *The Problem of Pain*, pp. 121ff. H.L. Martensen, *Studies in the Life and Teaching of Jacob Boehme*, rev. ed. (London: Hodder and Stoughton, 1885; London: Rockliffe, 1949), pp. 135ff.
56. Mark 1:13.
57. Colossians 1–3.
58. *Eternal Hope* (Et.) (London: Lutterworth, 1954), p. 103.
59. *On Selfhood and Godhood*, p. 24.
60. Ibid. p. 25.
61. Cf. *Morals and the New Theology* (London: Gollancz, 1947), chs. v-vii.
62. Ibid. pp. 76ff.
63. Ibid. p. 138.
64. Cf. "Collective Responsibility," *Philosophy*, vol. xliii, no. 165, July, 1968; see J.

Comperz "Individual, Social, and Collective Responsibility," *International Journal of Ethics*, vol. xlix, pp. 329ff.

65. We are not intending here to argue for the implication of the Genesis story that the whole human family descended from an original pair, although the account has, in this particular, according to E.L. Macsall (Christian Theology and Natural Science ch. 7) sound scientific justification. It should not be rejected in the *a priori* manner of some modern writers.
66. Doig, op. cit. p. 491.
67. Romans 5:20.
68. Donald Mackinnon, *Borderlands of Theology*, p. 93.
69. *Truth of Religion* 2d ed. (London: Williams Norgate, 1913), p. 433.
70. *The Foundation of Belief*, 8th ed. (London: Longmans, 1901), p. 354.
71. H.D. Lewis, in, *We Believe in God*, ed. Rubert E. Davies (London: Allen and Unwin, 1968), pp. 141, 142.
72. E. Schillebeeckx, "The Death of a Christian," in, *The Layman in the Church and Other Essays*, p. 82.
73. N. Berdyaev, *The Meaning of History*, p. 197.
74. Ferré, op. cit. pp. 272–274.
75. Berdyaev, *The Divine and the Human*, p. 96.
76. Cf. E. Rust, *Towards a Theological Understanding of History* (New York: OUP, 1963), chs. 8, 9.

Chapter 9

1. *The Mediator*, (Et.) (London: Lutterworth, 1934), p. 126.
2. *Lectures on The Philosophy of Religion*, vol. i, (Et.) (London: Kegan Paul, Trench, Trubner, 1895), p. 268.
3. Bradley, *Appearance and Reality*, 7th ed. (London: Allen and Unwin, 1920), p. 552.
4. Ibid. p. 51.
5. Cf. ibid. chs. xvi, cvii, xxv, xxvii.
6. Ibid. p. 186.
7. Ibid. p. 187; cf. p. 192.
8. Ibid. p. 192.
9. Ibid. p. 553.
10. Ibid. p. 200.
11. R. Metz, *A Hundred Years of British Philosophy* (London: Allen and Unwin, 1950), p. 343.
12. Cf. A.W. Benn, *History of English Rationalism in the 19th Century* (London: Longmans, 1906), vol. ii, p. 421.
13. *Man's Destiny*, p. 103.
14. Cf. *The Christian Faith*, (Et.), pp. 217–314.
15. *The Mediator*, (Et.), p. 133.
16. *The Origin and Propagation of Sin* (Cambridge: CUP, 1902), p. 153.
17. Ibid.
18. *The Changing Background of Religion and Ethics* (London: MacMillan, n.d.), p. 147.
19. Ibid. pp. 205, 206.
20. Ibid. p. 206.
21. Ibid. p. 222.
22. Ibid. p. 210.
23. Ibid. p. 208.

24. S. Freud, *Civilization and its Discontents* (London: Hogarth Press, 1963), pp. 114, 143.
25. C.E.M. Joad, *Guide to Modern Thought* (London: Pan Books), p. 274.
26. Cf. *Confessions*, bk. v. ch. 10.
27. Bk. viii. ch. 5.
28. Cf. *The City of God*, bk. xii, ch. 6.
29. Bk. xii, ch. 14.
30. Bk. ch. 7.
31. *The Divine Names*, iv. 20.
32. *Critique of Practical Reason*, 6th ed., trans. T.K. Abbott (London: Longmans, 1948), p. 349.
33. Cf. ibid. pp. 339ff.
34. Ibid. pp. 325ff.; cf. Robert Mackintosh, *Christianity and Sin* (London: Duckworth, 1913), pp. 119ff.
35. *Critique of Practical Reason*, p. 347.
36. Ibid. p. 348.
37. Ibid. These quotations come from the First Part of the Philosophical Theory of Religion, added with the Theory of Ethics, to the Critique.

Chapter 10

1. "Evil and Omnipotence," *Mind*, p. 64, no. 254, April 1955. Reprinted in *Problems and Perspectives in the Philosophy of Religion*, eds. George I. Mavrodes and Stuart C. Hackett (Boston: Allyn and Bacon, 1967), pp. 28ff.
2. Nels F.S. Ferré, *Reason in Religion*, p. 239.
3. *Essay Concerning the Human Understanding*, bk. ii, ch. xxi, sect. 15.
4. A.B. Bruce, *Apologetic or Christianity Defensively Stated*, 3rd ed. (Edinburgh: T & T Clarke, 1892), p. 61.
5. Article, "Gods," in *Proceedings of the Aristotelian Society*, 1944; reprinted in *Essays on Logic and Language* (1951), ed. A. Flew.
6. Ferré, op. cit. p. 241.
7. *For the Time Being; A Christmas Oratorio.*
8. "Divine Omnipotence and Human Freedom," in, *New Essays in Philosophical Theology*, eds. A. Flew and A. MacIntyre, p. 149.
9. Ibid. p. 152.
10. Ibid. p. 153.
11. Ibid. p. 168.
12. A. Plantigna, "The Free Will Defence," in, *Philosophy in America*, ed. Max Black, reprinted in, *Problems and Perspectives in the Philosophy of Religion*, eds. George I. Mavrodes and Stuart C. Hackett, pp. 293ff.
13. "Evil and Omnipotence," *Mind*, lxiv, no. 54, April 1955.
14. *The Modern Predicament*, p. 336.
15. *Freedom and Providence*, p. 94.
16. Cf. "He made both angels and men possessed of free will for the practice of righteousness. . . . He knew that it was good that they should have free will . . . free will being kept intact." Justin Martyr, *Dialogues*, p. 213.
17. *The Realm of Ends*, p. 370.
18. "Is the Existence of God a 'Hard Fact'?" *The Philosophical Review*, October 1967, p. 503.
19. *Religion in the Making*, p. 77.
20. Cf. "A New Look at the Problem of Evil," in, *Current Philosophical Issues: Essays in Honor of Curt John Ducasse*, pp. 201ff.

21. Op. cit. p. 205.
22. Cf. "By whatever name direct control is not freedom. But by providing man with the opportunity of making real choices and taking the consequences, God has given man the chance to learn for himself what kind of freedom he most deeply craves. Man's choices are real and he can and often does choose against his own real good. Choices would not be real unless they were risky." Ferré, op. cit. p. 23.
23. Hartshorne, op. cit. p. 210.
24. Cf. "God and Mystery," *Downside Review*, no. 75.
25. Mackie, op. cit., ad. loc.
26. Cf. e.g. R.P. Perry, *The Approach to Philosophy*, (1905), pp. 361ff. E.H. Reeman, *Do We Need a New Idea of God?* (1907); see C.C.J. Webb, *God and Personality*, 1919, pp. 134ff.
27. *Three Essays in Religion*, 1874, p. 186.
28. Cf. Brightman, *Philosophy of Religion*, chs. 8–10; also his *Problem of God*, (1930); *The Finding of God*, (1931); *Personality and Religion* (1934); "A Temporalist View of God," *Journal of Religion*, 12 (1932), pp. 545ff. For a criticism of Brightman's view see R.D. Baker, *The Concept of a Limited God*, (1934); E.W. Layman, *Meaning and Truth of Religion*, (1938); Andrew Banning, "Professor Brightman's Theory of a Limited God," *The Harvard Theological Review*, 27 (1934), pp. 145ff.
29. Brightman, op. cit. p. 337.
30. A.C. Knudson, *The Doctrine of God* (Abingdon: 1930), p. 28.
31. Cf. *Philosophers Speak of God*, eds. Charles Hartshorne and William Reece; Schubert M. Ogden, "Bultmann's Demythologizing and Hartshorne's Dipolar Theism," in, *Process and Divinity*, ed. William Reece and Eugine Freeman (1964), pp. 493ff.
32. Hartshorne, *Logic of Perfection and Other Essays in Neo-Classical Metaphysics*, 1962, p. 34. Cf. N. Berdyaev, "The static conception of God as *actus purus* having no potentialty and completely self-sufficient is a philosophical, Aristotelian, and not a Biblical conception." *The Destiny of Man*, p. 37.
33. *Philosophers Speak of God*, p. 76.
34. Cf. Hartshorne, *The Divine Relativity* (Princeton University Press, 1948)), ch. 1.
35. Cf. *The Logic of Perfection*, p. 42; also his article, "Panentheism," *Encyclopaedia of Religion*, ed. V. Ferm, 1945.
36. *The Logic of Perfection*, ch. 2.
37. Ibid. p. 126.
38. Cf. *Philosophers Speak of God*, 5, 434; see Hartshorne, "The Structure of Givenness," *The Philosophical Forum*, 18 (1960–1961), "God as the sole fully conscious being will always and without qualification contain each item of reality which he experiences or knows as but a constituent of his total reality," p. 34.
39. Cf. *The Logic of Perfection*, ch. vii. *Man's Vision of God*, ch. ii: see his contributions to, *Philosophical Essays in Memory of Edmund Husserl* (1940); "On some Criticisms of Whitehead's Philosophy," *The Philosophical Review*, 44 (1935), 323; "Is Whitehead's God the God of Religion?" *Ethics*, 53 (1942–1943), 219.
40. *The Logic of Perfection*, p. 313.
41. Ibid. p. 270.
42. Ibid. p. 268.
43. Ibid. p. 214.
44. Cf. H.D. McDonald, "Monopolar Theism and the Ontological Argument," *The Harvard Theological Review*, 38, no. 4, October (1965), pp. 388–416.
45. *The Logic of Perfection*, p. 44.
46. Cf. F. vonHügel, *Essays and Addresses on the Philosophy of Religion*, 2d ed. (London: Dent, 1926), pp. 197ff.

47. Cf. *Philosophers Speak of God*, pp. 152ff. *The Logic of Perfection*, p. 44; Charles Hartshorne, "Whitehead and Berdyaev: Is there Tragedy in God?" *Journal of Religion*, 37, (1957), pp. 71–84.
48. Edward Madden and Peter H. Hare, "Evil and Unlimited Power," *The Review of Metaphysics*, 20, no. 2, December, 1966, Cf. the same, "On the Difficulty of Evading the Problem of Evil," *Philosophy and Phenomological Research*, 28, no. 1, September, 1967.
49. A. Seth Pringle-Pattison, *The Idea of God*, p. 417.
50. Cf. Revelation, ch. xxi.
51. E.H. Madden and P.H. Hare, op. cit. p. 283.
52. Basil Willey, *Christianity Past and Present* (Cambridge: CUP), pp. 80, 81.
53. *Aphorisms—The Great Wall of China*, 79, p. 279.